Water law

Water law

A practical guide to the Water Act 1989

MASONS IN ASSOCIATION WITH
THE CENTRE FOR
ENVIRONMENTAL LAW,
UNIVERSITY OF SOUTHAMPTON

Woodhead-Faulkner
NEW YORK   LONDON   TORONTO   SYDNEY   TOKYO   SINGAPORE

 Published by Woodhead-Faulkner Limited,
Simon & Schuster International Group,
Fitzwilliam House, 32 Trumpington Street,
Cambridge CB2 1QY, England

First published 1990

British Library Cataloguing in Publication Data

Water law: a practical guide to the Water Act 1989.
1. Great Britain. Water supply industries. Law
I. Masons. *Firm*   II. University of Southampton. *Centre for
Environmental Law*
344.1046338476281

ISBN 0-85941-670-4

Designed by Geoff Green
Typeset by Hands Fotoset, Leicester
Printed in Great Britain by BPCC Wheatons Ltd, Exeter

Contents

Preface   ix
Introduction: historical background to the
   Water Act 1989   xi
Table of cases   xiii
Table of statutes   xv
Table of statutory instruments   xxii

1 Institutional framework   1
  1.1 Water and sewerage undertakers   1
  1.2 Statutory water companies   3
  1.3 National Rivers Authority   3
  1.4 Director General of Water Services   6
  1.5 Department of the Environment   7
  1.6 Ministry of Agriculture, Fisheries and Food   8
  1.7 Local authorities   8
      Notes   9

2 Water and sewerage undertakers   11
  2.1 Initial transfers   11
  2.2 Making and conditions of appointment   12
  2.3 Modification of appointment conditions   31
  2.4 Functions of the Director General of Water Services 32
  2.5 Enforcement   34
  2.6 Special administration orders   40
  2.7 Ownership and finances   41
  2.8 Statutory water companies   42
  2.9 Provision and acquisition of information   44
  2.10 'Functions' of undertakers   45
      Notes   45

3 Water supply   52
   3.1   General duties of water undertakers   53
   3.2   Enforcement of duties   59
   3.3   Ownership of and responsibility for
         water supply pipes   60
   3.4   Powers to disconnnect service pipes and
         cut off supplies   62
   3.5   Powers to prevent misuse, etc., of water   63
   3.6   Offences in relation to water supply   63
   3.7   Rights and powers of work   64
   3.8   Water resources   77
   3.9   Drought   80
   3.10 Charging   84
   3.11 Consumer protection   89
         Notes   93

4 Sewerage services   105
   4.1   General duties of sewerage undertakers   105
   4.2   Trade effluent functions   110
   4.3   Rights and powers of works, etc.   111
   4.4   Consumer protection   111
         Notes   111

5 Water quality   113
   5.1   Measurement and standards of water quality   113
   5.2   Classifications of water and water quality objectives 115
   5.3   Role of European Community law   116
   5.4   Water supply quality   118
   5.5   Discharges by sewerage undertakers   133
   5.6   Discharges to water by industry   140
   5.7   Discharges from agricultural activities   173
   5.8   Discharges of radioactive matter   175
   5.9   Discharges of trade effluent into sewers   176
   5.10 Precautions against pollution   185
         Notes   192

6 Land, conservation and recreation   207
   6.1   General duties   207
   6.2   Code of Practice on Conservation, Access and
         Recreation   210
   6.3   Disposals of land   215

6.4 Planning requirements 217
6.5 Flood defence/drainage 217
6.6 Salmon and freshwater fisheries 218
6.7 Navigation, conservancy and harbour authority
functions 218
Notes 219

Index 221

Preface

This book, which takes as its subject the new regime of water resources in England and Wales, in itself represents a new departure. It is the result of collaboration between a major firm of commercial solicitors, Masons, with a developing practice in environmental law, and a research institute in the law faculty of Southampton University, which is distinguished by its long association with the development and teaching of that branch of law.

Hitherto, not enough attention has been paid to the role of water as the life-blood of industry and commerce. Water supply and quality are now a matter of everyday concern to industrial managers. Management is concerned, not only by the security and cost of supply, but also increasingly by the need for assured water quality (for process requirements) and the prevention of pollution, especially at a time when such intense public interest in the subject is evident. Now that water pollution fines have topped £1 million, no industrial manager can afford to be lackadaisical about water quality and the impact which, for example, his own waste-management operations may have on it.

Water issues may now also play a part in investment decisions. Not only is the privatised water industry itself an appealing target for acquisitions, but the impact of water and waste management on the profitability of almost every manufacturing enterprise make it now a perfectly legitimate area for investors to address.

Collaboration between commercial practitioners and a university law faculty active in this field is no accident, for the management and conservation of the environment is a discipline in which lawyers, no less than other specialists, are learning that many of the principles by which they are accustomed to direct their affairs are uncertain guides, as unparalleled and unprecedented demands are laid upon them. It is this new urgency and commitment in industry and commerce which is the distinctive feature of environmental affairs in the 1990s, and it has produced a state of affairs in which much of the creative development in the law over the next few years will take place, not so much in the law professor's study or even in the chambers of Lords Justices of Appeal, but in the offices of solicitors throughout the country.

The sheer speed of change and development of the subject, however, and the enormous volume of legal material which it generates, both within the jurisdiction and beyond, are such that most industrialists, or even the most active and alert practitioner, must doubt their ability, amid all other concerns, to keep abreast of what is happening, far less to be able to predict what may come to pass, especially as so much of the future shape of the national law is fashioned in an international or transnational forum.

This book, on a topic which in itself combines fundamental matters of natural resources law with questions of everyday importance to enormous numbers of people, corporations and public bodies, presents an ideal subject for what would perhaps have been regarded, not so very long ago, as a curious symbiosis between practitioner and academic lawyer. If environmental conservation depends on changing attitudes, then perhaps one can now make a case for saying that lawyers, perhaps not always thought of as the embodiment of progressive thinking, have at least made a start.

We should like gratefully to acknowledge the invaluable contribution of Mark Christensen, a New Zealand solicitor, who undertook the preparation of the text.

David Jones
Partner, Masons Solicitors

Malcolm Forster
Director, Centre for Environmental Law, University of Southampton

Introduction: historical background to the Water Act 1989

Prior to the coming into force of the Water Act 1989 on 1 September 1989, the structure of the water industry was that established by the Water Act 1973. This Act came about as a result of recommendations by the Central Advisory Water Committee in 1971 on ways to improve the organisation of functions relating to water management, water supply, sewerage, sewage disposal and prevention of pollution then exercised by river authorities, public water undertakings and sewerage and sewage disposal authorities. The Water Act 1973 was designed to enable a comprehensive water management plan to be formulated for each river basin, to be put into effect by a smaller number of regional water authorities, thus avoiding the conflicts of interest that were generated by the divisions of responsibility between the various authorities. From 1 April 1974, responsibilities for the provision of water supplies, sewerage services and the protection of water resources were transferred from a large number of diverse public authorities to ten regional water authorities. This combined role of having both utility and regulatory functions gave rise to a potential conflict of interest, in that the water authorities were in the position of being both a major discharger to water and the pollution control authority. To rectify this potential for conflict of interest, the Water Act 1973 provided that new outlets and discharge by water authorities were subject to control and consent by the Secretary of State.

In 1974 the Control of Pollution Act brought about a range of reforms in the law relating to water pollution, although the rationale behind the legislation remained consistent with that of earlier legislation. This was the existence of a licensing system where controls over discharge to water were exercised through discharge consents, and the legality of such discharge could be determined by the extent of its compliance with conditions attached to the consents.

In February 1986 the Government announced its intention to privatise the water industry. The White Paper *Privatisation of the Water Authorities in England and Wales* (Cmnd. 9734, February 1986) proposed to maintain the system of so-called integrated river basin management of the water cycle as the responsibility of public limited companies (with the exception of land drainage), but within a clear framework of national regulatory environmental policy (see *The Water Environment: The next steps* (DoE WO Consultation Paper, April 1986)).

A major weakness of the integrated river basin management system, however, remains the conflict of interest where a body is at the same time charged with monitoring and maintaining water quality and is also given effluent treatment and disposal responsibilities.

As the consultation process progressed it became clear that the idea of keeping the authorities intact was both politically unacceptable to almost all interests and susceptible to challenge in the European Court of Justice as being inconsistent with European Community legislation on water pollution. Accordingly, in July 1987 the Department of the Environment issued a discussion paper, *The National Rivers Authority: The Government's proposals for a public regulatory body in a privatised water industry*, which announced the intention of transferring the main regulatory and water management functions of water authorities to this body, while leaving the utility roles of water supply and sewerage services to be carried out by the private sector.

In 1988, the Public Utility Transfers and Water Charges Act paved the way for the changes by conferring powers on water authorities to transfer property and functions to new bodies and to reorganise themselves internally into standard regulatory and utility divisions.

The Water Act 1989 obtained the Royal Assent on 6 July 1989 and most provisions were brought into effect by 1 September 1989. The water industry was publicly floated in November 1989. The price of shares was announced on 22 November, and the share offer closed on 6 December. The public flotation of the water industry was the second most popular privatisation, with the shares being oversubscribed by some six times.

Table of cases

Alphacell Limited v. *Woodward* [1972] 2 A11 ER 475 *143, 144, 198*

Clark v. *Epsom Rural District Council* [1929] 1 Ch. 287 *59, 95*

EC Commission v. *Kingdom of Netherlands* 96/81 [1982] ECR 1791 *117, 193*
Edwards v. *National Coal Board* [1949] 1 KB 704 *153, 200*

Hoffman-la Roche & Co. v. *Secretary of State for Trade and Industry* [1975] AC 295 *39, 50*
Hutton v. *Esher Urban District Council* [1974] Ch. 167 (CA) *106, 111*

Impress (Worcester) Ltd v. *Rees* [1971] 2 A11 ER 357 *144, 198*

John Young & Co. v. *Bankier Distillery Co.* [1891–4] A11 E. Rep. 439 *113, 192*

McColl v. *Strathclyde Regional Council* [1984] JPL 350 *119, 193*
McLeod v. *Buchanan* [1940] 2 A11 ER 179 *143, 198*
Molkerei-Zentrale Westfalen/Lippe GmbH v. *Hauptzoellamt* 28/76 [1968] ECR 143 *117, 193*

Pasmore v. *Ostwaldtwistle Urban District Council* [1988] AC 387 *37, 50*
Price v. *Cromack* [1975] 2 A11 ER 113 *144, 144–5, 198*

R. v. *Secretary of State for the Environment ex p. Rose Theatre Trust Co.* (1989) *37–8, 50*

R. v. *Wessex Water Authority, ex p. Cutts* (1988) *37, 50*
R. v. *West Metropolitan Stipendiary Magistrate ex parte Klahn* [1979] 1 WLR 933 *152, 200*
Robinson v. *Workington Corporation* [1897] 1 Ch. 619 *59, 95–6*
Rush & Tompkins Ltd v. *West Kent Sewerage Board* (1963) 14 P & CR 469 *68*

Severn Trent River Authority v. *Express Food Group Ltd* (1989) 153 JP 126 *147, 199*
Smeaton v. *Ilford Corporation* [1954] Ch. 450 *105, 111*
Southern Water Authority v. *Pegram* (1989) *144, 198*

Thames Water Authority v. *Blue and White Launderettes Ltd* [1980] 1 WLR 700 *204*
Trent River Authority v. *Drabble & Sons Ltd* [1970] 1 A11 ER 22 *201*

Wales v. *Thames Water Authority* (1987) *139–40, 151, 198, 200*
West Mersey Urban District Council v. *Fraser* [1950] 2 KB 119 *56, 94*
Wheat v. *Lacon & Co. Ltd* [1966] A11 ER 582 (HL) *204*
William Leech (Midland) v. *Severn Trent Water Authority* [1980] JPL 753 *107, 112*
Wrothwell Ltd v. *Yorkshire Water Authority* [1984] Crim. L.R. 43 *143–4, 198*

Table of statutes

Acquisition of Land Act
    1981 *64, 97, 99*
Agriculture Act 1986
    s.18 *212, 215, 219*
Airports Act 1986 *66*

Building Act 1984
    s.18 *110, 112*

Coast Protection Act 1949 *8*
Companies Act 1985 *20, 40, 43, 47*
Compulsory Purchase Act
    1965 *64, 97*
Control of Pollution Act 1974
    general references *134, 138, 139, 147, 152, 170, 174*
    s.5 *200*
    s.30 *200*
    s.34 *154, 200–1*
    s.43 *184*
    s.45 *179, 204*
    s.108 *190, 206*
    sch.4 *190, 206*
Control of Pollution Act 1989
    s.31 *198*
Countryside Act 1968
    s.22 *206*

European Communities Act 1957
    s.2 *193*
European Community Directives
    general references *116–18, 119, 193*
    asbestos 87/217 *170, 202–3, 204*
    bathing water 76/160 *117, 135–7, 197*
    'black list' 88/347 *165, 204*
    conservation of wild birds
        EED/79/409 *212, 219*
    dangerous substances 76/464
        137, 163–7, 202
    daughter directives *165*
    dangerous substances 86/280
        165, 202
    drinking water 80/778 *193, 194*
    freshwater fish 78/659 *137, 168–9, 202*
    groundwater 80/68 *138, 168, 202*
    municipal waste (draft) *138*
    shellfish 79/923 *137, 169, 202*
    surface water quality 75/440
        123, 193, 194–5

Fair Trading Act 1973 *32, 33, 49*

Fire Services Act 1947 *36, 85, 103*

Food and Environment
   Protection Act 1985 *152, 200*

Gas Act 1986 *66*

General Rate Act 1967 *103*

Highways Act 1980
   general references *97, 132*
   s.100 *153*

Insolvency Act 1986 *40, 41*

Land Compensation Act 1961
   64, 68, 97, 98

Land Compensation Act 1973
   64, 97

Land Drainage Act 1976 *5, 98, 217, 218, 220*

Local Government Act 1972
   s.181 *172, 203*

Local Government Finance Act
   1988 *16, 103, 217*

Magistrates' Court Act 1980
   s.40 *190, 205*
   s.127 *151, 200*

Mines and Quarries Act 1954
   s.180 *153, 200*

National Parks and Access to the
   Countryside Act 1949 *99, 209, 216, 220*

Powers of the Criminal Courts
   Act 1973
   s.35 *190, 205*

Public Health Act 1875
   s.68 *154, 200*

Public Health Act 1936
   general reference *85*
   s.17 *106, 109, 111, 112*
   s.18 *106, 109, 111*
   s.19 *106, 111*
   s.20 *204*
   s.27 *110, 112*
   s.34 *109, 112*
   s.36 *109, 112*
   s.287 *76, 100*
   s.343 *105–6, 111*

Public Health Act 1961
   general reference *203*
   s.59 *179, 204, 205*
   s.60 *179, 184, 204*
   s.61 *178, 204*
   s.68 *184, 205*

Public Health (Drainage of Trade
   Premises) Act 1937
   general references *176, 184*
   s.1 *176, 204*
   s.2 *176, 178, 204*
   s.3 *178, 182, 204*
   s.7 *36, 102, 179, 182*
   s.7A *184, 205*
   s.9 *184, 205*
   s.10 *76, 100*
   s.14 *111, 176, 204*
   s.59 *177–8, 204*

Public Utilities Street Works Act
   1950
   general reference *100*
   s.1 *97*
   s.39 *102*

Public Utility Transfers and
   Water Charges Act 1988
   19, 86

Radioactive Substances Act 1960
   175

Rivers (Prevention of Pollution)
    Act 1951
    general reference *153*
    s.2 *143, 198–9*
Rivers (Prevention of Pollution)
    Act 1961
    general reference *201*
    s.10 *150, 199*
    s.12 *203*

Salmon and Freshwater Fisheries
    Act 1975
    general reference *218*
    s.4 *154, 200, 202*

Telecommunications Act 1984
    sch.2 *66, 98*
Town and Country Planning Act
    1971 *2, 217, 220*
Transport Act 1968
    s.113 *73, 99*

Water Act 1945
    general references *52, 96*
    s.11 *206*
    s.17 *35*
    s.18 *190, 206*
    s.21 *131, 196*
Water Act 1973
    general references *52, 107*
    s.2 *206*
    s.9 *206*
    s.20 *35*
    sch.6 *200*
    sch.7 *206*
Water Act 1989
    general references *52, 151,
        154, 178, 190, 197, 206*
    s.1 *3, 9*
    s.2 *4, 6, 9*
    s.3 *4, 9*

s.4 *11–12, 41, 45, 50*
s.6 *91, 104*
s.7 *6, 9, 16, 19, 24, 30, 31, 37,
    46, 47, 48, 49, 69, 89, 90,
    91, 98, 103, 104*
s.8 *5, 9, 35, 37, 49, 207–8,
    210, 219*
s.9 *5, 9, 35, 208–10, 219*
s.10 *43, 51, 210–11, 219*
s.11 *12, 19, 30, 41, 45, 48, 50*
s.12 *12, 19, 30, 31, 40, 45, 48,
    50*
s.13 *19, 26, 31, 47*
s.14 *13, 19, 29, 45–6, 176,
    204*
s.15 *12, 17, 19, 29, 31, 45, 46,
    48*
s.16 *12, 17, 19, 31, 45, 46, 48*
s.17 *12, 19, 32, 45, 49*
s.18 *12, 17, 19, 32, 45, 46, 49*
s.19 *12, 19, 32, 45, 49, 78,
    101*
s.20 *6, 9, 19, 24, 32, 34, 35,
    36, 36–7, 37, 38, 39, 40,
    47, 49, 50, 58, 59, 78, 95,
    101, 105, 129, 196, 210,
    219*
s.21 *6, 9, 19, 36, 38–9, 50*
s.22 *6, 9, 19, 37–8, 39, 50,
    59–60, 96, 129, 196*
s.23 *6, 9, 19, 26, 38, 40, 41,
    47, 50, 79, 101*
s.24 *19, 40, 41, 50, 79, 101*
s.25 *19, 40, 50*
s.26 *6, 9, 19, 23, 29, 32, 34,
    49, 93, 104*
s.27 *19, 91, 92, 104*
s.28 *6, 9, 19, 32, 33, 49*
s.29 *19, 33, 49*
s.30 *19, 33, 49*
s.31 *6, 9, 19, 33–4, 39, 49, 50*

Water Act 1989 *continued*

s.32 *19, 29, 34, 35, 39, 44, 49,
      50, 51*

s.33 *6, 9, 19, 29, 39, 45, 49,
      50, 51*

s.34 *6, 9, 19, 29, 34, 49, 93,
      104*

s.35 *6, 9, 19, 34, 49, 93, 104,
      149, 199*

s.36 *19, 80, 101*

s.37 *36, 53, 59, 94, 95*

s.38 *24, 25, 47, 90, 103*

s.39 *20, 46, 53, 94*

s.40 *53, 54, 59, 68, 94, 95,
      98*

s.41 *54, 90, 94, 103*

s.42 *55, 56, 59, 61, 94, 95, 96*

s.43 *55–6, 90, 94, 103*

s.44 *55, 94*

s.45 *56, 57, 59, 80, 94, 95, 96,
      101*

s.46 *19, 20, 46, 57, 60, 62, 85,
      88, 95, 96, 102, 103*

s.47 *35, 58, 59, 60, 95, 96*

s.48 *36, 58, 59, 95*

s.49 *56, 62–3, 79, 93, 94, 96,
      97, 101, 104*

s.50 *61, 62, 87, 88, 96,
      103*

s.51 *35, 56, 57, 58, 59, 94, 95,
      96*

s.52 *35, 38, 50, 118, 121, 128,
      129, 130, 193, 194, 195,
      196*

s.53 *118*

s.54 *131, 196*

s.55 *35, 126, 129, 195, 196*

s.56 *8, 10, 125, 126, 195*

s.57 *8, 10, 61, 96, 126–7, 194,
      195–6*

s.58 *127, 194, 196*

s.59 *77, 100, 128, 194, 196*

s.60 *7, 10, 77, 80, 100, 101,
      130, 196*

s.61 *64, 97, 131, 196*

s.62 *64, 77, 97, 100, 131, 132,
      196, 197*

s.63 *56, 57, 60, 63, 94, 95, 96,
      97, 131–2, 196–7*

s.64 *76, 100, 122, 132, 194,
      197*

s.65 *119*

s.66 *62, 63, 96, 97, 126, 131,
      195, 196*

s.67 *36, 105, 111*

s.68 *24, 25, 47, 90, 103, 105,
      111*

s.71 *68, 98, 103, 106–7, 108,
      111–12*

s.72 *90, 103, 107–8, 112*

s.73 *8, 10, 110, 112*

s.74 *180, 204*

s.75 *19, 84, 102*

s.76 *19, 57, 84, 102, 179,
      204*

s.77 *88, 96, 103*

s.78 *87, 103*

s.79 *17, 46, 85, 103*

s.80 *86, 103*

s.81 *85, 103*

s.82 *86, 103*

s.83 *41, 42, 50*

s.84 *42, 51*

s.85 *42, 50, 51*

s.86 *42, 50, 51*

ss.87–93 *42, 51*

s.95 *42, 51*

s.97 *42, 51*

ss.98–100 *43, 51*

s.102 *43, 51*

s.103 *142, 198*

s.104 *7, 9, 116, 192, 199*

Water Act 1989 *continued*
s.105 7, 9, 115, 116, 142, 157,
       164, 170, 172, 192–3,
       198, 201, 202, 203
s.106 4, 9, 149, 157, 164, 199,
       201, 202
s.107 138, 141–2, 143, 145,
       146, 147, 148, 150–1,
       151, 159, 174, 188, 197,
       198, 199, 201, 203, 205
s.108 99, 152–4, 161, 200,
       202
s.109 147–8, 151, 161, 171,
       198, 199, 202, 203
s.110 141, 174, 188, 198, 203
s.111 185, 205
s.112 186, 187, 205
s.113 154, 200
s.114 73, 99, 153, 189, 192,
       205, 206
s.115 189, 205
s.116 174, 203
s.117 149, 170, 171, 184, 199
s.118 6, 9, 172, 203
s.119 35, 79, 101, 172, 203
s.120 172, 203
s.121 151, 200
s.122 154, 200
s.123 175, 203
s.124 133, 141, 142, 146, 197,
       198, 199
s.125 53, 77, 94, 101
s.126 11, 35, 45, 78, 101
s.129 80, 101
s.130 35, 79, 101
s.131 81–2, 101, 102
s.132 35, 82–3, 102
s.133 81, 83, 101, 102
s.135 83, 102
s.136 206, 217, 218, 220
s.137 206, 217, 220

s.138 206, 218
s.139 206, 218, 220
s.140 206, 218, 220
s.141 190, 205, 206, 218, 220
s.143 5, 9
s.144 5, 9
s.145 6, 9, 163, 199, 202
s.146 172
s.147 76, 100, 163, 189, 199,
       202, 205
s.148 149, 171, 199, 203
s.149 5, 9, 150, 199
s.150 4, 5, 9, 61, 96, 150, 199
s.151 45, 51, 64, 97
s.152 5, 9, 27, 45, 51, 216–17,
       220
s.153 60, 61, 96
s.154 97, 98, 191, 206
s.155 45, 51, 71, 99, 200, 210,
       219
s.156 75–6, 100, 101
s.157 35, 210, 219
s.158 72, 73, 99, 190, 206
s.159 73, 99
s.160 66, 67, 98
s.161 36, 74, 90, 100, 103
s.162 35, 36, 68–9, 90, 91, 92,
       98, 103, 104, 128, 196
s.163 217, 220
s.164 128, 196
s.165 35, 59, 95
s.166 35, 109, 112
s.167 74–5, 100
s.170 7, 9–10, 35, 39, 49, 50
s.171 7, 10
s.172 132–3
s.173 3, 9
s.174 29, 39, 44, 50, 51, 173,
       203
s.175 44, 51, 154, 201
s.176 44, 51

Water Act 1989 *continued*
s.178 *76, 77, 83, 88, 100, 101,*
      102, 103, 128, 132, 163,
      189, 196, 197, 202, 205
s.179 *77, 83, 100, 101, 102*
s.180 *77, 101*
s.185 *8, 10, 45, 51*
s.186 *206*
s.188 *26, 45, 47, 51*
s.189 *25, 44, 47, 51, 54, 55,*
      57, 59, 60, 61, 66–7, 94,
      95, 96, 97, 98, 99, 106,
      111, 118, 146, 172, 193,
      196, 199, 200, 203, 219
s.225 *205*
sch.1 *4, 9*
sch.2 *11, 45, 106, 111*
sch.3 *6, 9*
sch.4 *29, 48, 91*
sch.5 *26, 41, 47, 50, 106, 111*
sch.6 *41, 50*
sch.7 *186, 205*
sch.8
   general reference *105*
   para.3 *19, 36, 46, 85,*
      179, 204, 205
sch.9 *7, 10, 35, 182–3, 184,*
      204–5
sch.10
   para.1 *76, 87, 100, 103*
   para.2 *88, 103*
   para.3 *89, 103*
   para.4 *89, 103*
   para.5 *88, 103*
sch.11 *187–8, 205*
sch.12
   general references *154, 200*
   para.1 *155, 156, 171, 201,*
      203
   para.2 *156, 157, 160, 161,*
      201, 202

paras 3–4 *158, 201*
paras 5–6 *159–60, 201*
para.7 *160, 201*
para.8 *161, 202*
para.9 *162, 202*
sch.13 *79, 99, 101*
sch.14 *82, 83–4, 102*
sch.15 *217, 220*
sch.16 *217–18*
sch.17 *218*
sch.18 *97*
sch.19
   general references *78, 96*
   para.1 *65, 95, 96, 97, 109,*
      112
   para.2 *60, 65–6, 96, 97,*
      103, 191, 206
   para.3 *66, 97, 98, 103,*
      191, 206
   para.4 *67–8, 98*
   para.6 *68, 98*
   para.7 *69, 98*
   para.8 *69–70, 98*
   para.9 *70–1, 99*
   para.10 *76, 100*
sch.20 *35, 72, 99*
sch.21 *64, 73–4, 77, 97, 99,*
      100
sch.24 *191–2, 206*
sch.25 *36, 99*
sch.26
   para.5 *94*
   para.11 *96*
   para.16 *19, 46*
   para.19 *35*
   para.41 *35*
   para.57 *191, 206*
Water Resources Act 1963
   general references *4, 9, 72, 79,*
      98, 99, 102
   s.2 *78, 101*

Water Resources Act 1963
  continued
  s.19 *78, 101*
  s.22 *101*
  s.65 *80, 101*
  s.67 *80, 101*
  s.69 *80, 101*
  s.79 *73, 99, 190, 206*
  s.81 *80, 101*

s.135 *79, 101*
sch.7 *78, 101*
Wildlife and Countryside Act
  1981
  general references *209, 212,
    219*
  s.28 *216, 220*
  s.39 *216, 220*

Table of statutory instruments

Companies Act 1985 (Modifications for Statutory Water Companies) Regulations 1989 *51*

Control of Industrial Major Accident Hazards (CIMAH) Regulations *140, 189, 198*

Control of Pollution (Consents for Discharges) (Notices) Regulations 1984 *155, 201*

Control of Pollution (Consents for Discharges, etc.) (Secretary of State Functions) Regulations 1989 *158–9, 161, 201, 202*

Control of Pollution (Discharges by the National Rivers Authority) Regulations 1989 *162, 202*

Control of Pollution (Radioactive Waste) Regulations 1976 *175, 203*

Control of Pollution (Radioactive Waste) Regulations 1984 *175, 204*

Control of Pollution (Registers) Regulations 1989 *150, 170–1, 199, 203*

Control of Pollution (Silage Slurry and Agricultural Fuel Oil) Regulations 1990 (draft) *205*

Controlled Waters (Lakes and Ponds) Order 1989 *198*

Director General of Water Services' Register (Inspection and Charges) Regulations 1989 *49*

Environmental Assessment (Afforestation) Regulations 1988 *203*

National Rivers Authority (Levies) Regulation 1990 *9, 220*

Nitrate Sensitive Areas (Designation) Order 1990 *205*

Rivers (Prevention of Pollution) Act 1951 (Continuation of Byelaws) Order 1989 *153, 200*

xxii

Surface Waters (Classification) Regulations 1989 *116, 123, 192, 195*

Trade Effluents (Prescribed Processes and Substances) Regulations 1989 *35, 110, 112, 176, 180–2, 188, 204, 205*

Water Appointment (Monopolies and Mergers Commission) Regulations 1989 *31, 48*
Water Re-organisation (Pensions, etc.) (Designated Persons) Order 1989 *3, 9*
Water Re-organisation (Pensions, etc.) Regulations 1989 *3, 9*
Water Re-organisation (Successor Companies) (Transfer of Loans) Order 1989 *42, 51*
Water and Sewerage (Conservation, Access and Recreation) (Code of Practice) Order 1989 *210, 219*
Water and Sewerage (Works) (Advance Payments) Regulations 1989 *68, 98*
Water Supply and Sewerage Services (Customer Service Standards) Regulations 1989 *24, 47, 92–3, 104, 105, 111*
Water Supply (Water Quality) Regulations 1989
  general references *35, 119, 193, 198*
  reg.2 *122, 194*
  reg.3 *119–20, 193, 194*
  reg.4 *120, 121, 194*
  reg.5 *120, 121, 194*
  regs 6–8 *121, 194*
  regs 11–13 *122, 194*
  regs 17–21 *122, 194*
  reg.22 *123, 194*
  reg.24 *118, 123, 193, 195*
  reg.25 *123, 125, 195*
  reg.26 *124, 195*
  reg.27 *123, 195*
  regs 28–9 *124, 195*
  regs 30–1 *125, 195*
  reg.33 *125, 195*
  sch.2 *119, 120, 121, 122, 193, 194*
  sch.3 *122, 194*
  sch.4 *125, 195*
  sch.5 *125, 195*

CHAPTER 1

Institutional framework

1.1   Water and sewerage undertakers

The ten successor companies to the water authorities hold instruments
of appointment as water and sewerage undertakers made by the
Secretaries of State for the Environment and for Wales.

These companies are able to concentrate on the provision of water
supply and sewage disposal services and to diversify into other
activities, by means of additional subsidiary companies, if they wish.
They are not subject to public sector borrowing regulations, but are
free to borrow money in the private capital markets and may compete
in the wider provision of commercial services, both in the United
Kingdom and abroad. The companies are subject to corporation tax
and are eligible for capital allowances.

The water and sewerage undertakers face the normal corporate
choice of whether to finance particular activities by borrowing, by
increases of equity, from profits or from cash flows. How they decide to
finance will affect their costs. In the past, water authorities were
required by annual orders to earn a rate of return on their assets.
Following privatisation, water and sewerage undertakers substituted
for these capital finance costs the costs of remuneration, equity and
debt in a corporation structure.

Every water undertaker is under a general duty to develop and
maintain a water supply system within its area, including a duty to
maintain, improve and extend the undertaker's water mains and other
pipes.[1]

Every water undertaker is also bound by certain other obligations
such as those to comply with a request to provide a main to supply
water sufficient for domestic purposes, to provide a supply of water for
non-domestic purposes including fire-fighting and for other public

purposes, and to maintain constant supply and adequate pressure in all pipes used for supplying water for domestic purposes and to fire hydrants.[2]

Water undertakers are required to supply only water which is wholesome as defined in regulations made under the Act when they supply water to any premises for domestic purposes.[3] It is a criminal offence to supply water which is unfit for human consumption.

Every sewerage undertaker is under a general duty to provide and maintain a system of sewers and sewage disposal within its area and, inter alia, to provide public sewers to be used for the drainage of premises used for domestic purposes.[4] They may enter into agreements whereby local authorities perform certain sewerage functions on their behalf,[5] though sewerage undertakers are responsible for the control of discharges of trade effluent to sewers.[6]

It is for water and sewerage undertakers to fix charges for the services they provide in the course of carrying out their functions, either by an individual agreement with a customer or under a charges scheme, and to demand and recover these charges. However, water undertakers may not charge for the availability of water or for water taken for fire-fighting purposes, and sewerage undertakers may not charge highway authorities for the drainage of their roads.[7]

In order to carry out their functions, water and sewerage undertakers are given compulsory purchase and works powers. They may lay pipes and carry out related works, and those pipes will be tested in the undertaker which laid or constructed them. Undertakers are empowered to carry out works to prevent pollution and to deal with foul water, to discharge water into underground strata or inland water, and to enter any premises to carry out surveys or tests to determine whether land should be acquired, or works carried out in connection with their functions.[8]

Undertakers must obtain general planning permission for any of their works controlled under the Town and Country Planning Act 1971.

In carrying out their functions, undertakers are bound to further conservation and the enhancement of natural beauty, and to provide for the recreational use of their lands and water. They must also keep in mind the desirability of safeguarding public freedom of access to their land, protected historic buildings and archaeological remains. A code of practice issued in July 1989 gives guidance on the conservation, access and recreation duties of undertakers.[9]

They are able to dispose of their land and interests in that land only with the consent of the Secretary of State, or in accordance with a general authorisation given by him or her. Where the land is in a National Park, the Broads, an area of outstanding natural beauty or a Site of Special Scientific Interest, the Act enables the Secretary of State to impose special conditions on disposal. For example, management agreements or covenants may be used to protect the land, or it may be required to be offered for sale first to a conservation body.[10] Provision has been made for the transfer of liability for the payment of pensions from water authorities to the National Rivers Authority (NRA) and undertakers.[11]

1.2 Statutory water companies

The twenty-nine statutory water companies, most of which date from the nineteenth century, are restricted to abstracting, purifying and supplying water on behalf of the water authority in whose areas they are situated.

Under the Act, the statutory links between the former water authorities and the companies have been severed and the companies have powers to operate as water undertakers in their own right.

If a company decides to convert to PLC status it can also become a sewerage undertaker either by agreement with the current undertaker or on sites where there is no testing service. A procedure is provided whereby companies can convert to PLC status and the former restrictions on the companies' finances and on the methods by which they can offer shares are relaxed. All water suppliers are now regulated by price control rather than dividend capping.[12]

1.3 National Rivers Authority

The National Rivers Authority (NRA) was established as a corporate body, independent from the Government,[13] with the resources to inspect, the right to direct and the legal powers to compel business, industry, agriculture and others to act in the most responsible fashion toward water and water resources. At its inception it employed around 6,500 people; it operates through ten regions based on the river catchment areas of England and Wales.

The NRA's board, which consists of between eight and fifteen members, two of whom are appointed by the Minister of Agriculture, Fisheries and Food ('the Minister of Agriculture'), while the rest are appointed by the Secretary of State for the Environment,[14] oversees and directs NRA policy across the regions. The origination, procedure and finances of the NRA are provided for in Schedule 1 to the Act.

It is intended to be largely self-financing, recovering much of its costs for flood defence works from local authorities[15] and through charges for water abstraction licences[16] and discharge consents.[17]

The NRA may borrow from the Government with the consent of Treasury and other such sources as agreed to by the Secretary of State or the Minister with the consent of the Treasury.[18] Any deficit in the recovery of its costs may be met by Government grant.[19]

The NRA is required to forward an annual report of its activities and audited accounts during the past financial year to the Minister of Agriculture and the Secretary of State, and is answerable to Parliament through the latter. The Secretary of State is to publish the annual reports in such manner as he or she considers appropriate.[20]

Each region is served by a regional rivers advisory committee whose function it is to consider and advise on the manner in which the NRA carries out its functions in that area.[21] A special advisory committee has been established to advise the NRA with regard to its functions in Wales.[22]

It is the NRA's task to ensure compliance with objectives as to rivers, lakes, estuaries, coastal waters and water stored naturally beneath the ground.[23] It is authorised to monitor and regulate materials flowing into all types of water. All discharges require a discharge consent from the NRA, each consent being subject to constant scrutiny by regular sampling and laboratory analysis to ensure compliance with set standards.[24]

In order to monitor the well-being of waters, the NRA is to conduct five-yearly quality surveys to examine the chemical quality and biological indices of the rivers of England and Wales.[25] This will allow the NRA to establish the effectiveness of pollution control measures and to determine the ability of receiving waters to accept waste discharges. These and other functions are supervised in each of the NRA's co-regions by an Environment Quality Manager, to whom all pollution control officers and sampling personnel report.

As regards water resources, the NRA has functions relating to the measurement of river flows, ground water levels, rainfall and evaporation, and the licensing of abstractions by users.[26] It also lays down minimum requirements for river flows, particularly in view of the uses to which they are put. Such uses can include navigation, fishing and recreational activities, in addition to social, amenity and conservation uses. The NRA can require water users to develop their facilities: for

NATIONAL RIVERS AUTHORITY   5

example, by building enlarged reservoirs or readjusting the balance between abstraction and use. The function of water resource management is financed by charges levied on holders of abstraction licences.

The NRA maintains over 1,000 kilometres of sea defences and many thousands of kilometres of river embankments.[27] Before implementing projects for the maintenance, improvement or development of its flood defences, the NRA engages in consultation with affected and interested people, and carries on a capital works programme to reconstruct obsolete defences. In addition, the NRA undertakes a programme of main river maintenance and river improvement – it removes weeds, dredges silt banks, tests and operates flood-excluding structures such as gates, sluices and pumping stations – and is responsible for forecasting flood risk. The NRA discharges these responsibilities through Regional Flood Defence Committees. Existing internal drainage districts and internal drainage boards established under the Land Drainage Act 1976 continue to exercise their functions under that Act.

The NRA is required to maintain, improve and develop salmon, trout, freshwater and eel fisheries. They are to be regulated and financed by a system of licences and the NRA is assisted in these functions by Regional Fisheries Advisory Committees.

In specified areas, the NRA will have certain navigation, conservancy and harbour authority functions.

In exercising all of its functions, the NRA is under the same duty as water and sewerage undertakers to further conservation and the enhancement of natural beauty, and to promote conservation, amenity and recreation on inland waters and lands associated with them.[28]

The NRA is given compulsory purchase and works powers,[29] while the Secretary of State's consent is required for the disposal of compulsorily acquired land.[30] The NRA also has to account for its activities by providing any information required by the Secretary of State or the Minister of Agriculture, Fisheries and Food,[31] and by preparing an annual report and statement of accounts.[32] It is required generally to carry out research and related activities in respect of its various functions, and to collate and publish information from which assessments can be made of the actual and prospective demand for water, and of actual and prospective water resources, in England and Wales.[33] It may, with the consent of the Secretary of State, provide advice and assistance to persons outside the United Kingdom,[34] and is given general powers to do anything, which in its opinion, is calculated to facilitate, or is conducive or incidental to, the carrying out of its various functions.[35]

In carrying out any of its functions, the NRA must have particular regard to the duties imposed on any undertaker which appears to it to be or likely to be affected by the exercise of power in question.[36] It must give all such advice and assistance as requested by the Secretary of State and the Minister of Agriculture as appears to it to be appropriate to facilitate the carrying out of their functions.[37]

1.4   Director General of Water Services

The Act makes provision for the appointment, by the Secretary of State, of a Director General of Water Services.[38] His or her main duties are to protect customers' interests in respect of the quality of service and levels of charges, to facilitate competition between utility companies, and to ensure that they carry out their functions efficiently and economically.[39] He or she is required to keep under review the activities connected with the functions of water and sewerage undertakers, to collect information about the undertakers and the way in which they carry out their functions, and to advise and assist the Secretary of State and the Director General of Fair Trading.[40]

Ten independent customer service committees have been established to investigate customer complaints and to approach the companies and the Director on matters which affect customer interests.[41] Both the Director and the Secretary of State have powers to refer various matters to the Monopolies and Mergers Commission.

In addition, the Director is empowered to monitor each undertaker's compliance with the Instrument of Appointment, including the codes of practice relating to customer services, practice and procedure on disconnection and pipe leakage and the disposal of land.

The Director has powers to enforce compliance with the conditions of an undertaker's appointment and with certain other statutory requirements, and in extreme circumstances may institute proceedings leading to the appointment of a special administrator to carry out the functions of the undertaker until they have been transferred to another company.[42]

The Director is required to publish information and advice for the benefit of customers[43] and to make an annual report to the Secretary of State to be laid before Parliament.[44] He or she maintains a public register containing details of companies' appointments as water and sewerage undertakers,[45] and possesses powers to obtain information,[46] which may be published, subject to consideration of confidentiality.[47]

1.5   Department of the Environment

The Secretary of State for the Environment is responsible to Parliament for the activities of the Director General of Water Services and the National Rivers Authority. He or she may enforce the conditions of appointment of undertakers and their duties with regard to the supply of water and the provision of sewerage services, and is empowered to classify waters according to their quality and to set water quality objectives in respect of those classifications.[48]

Together with the Secretary of State for Wales, he or she is responsible for monitoring compliance with, and implementation of, European Community (EC) directives on water quality.[49]

If it appears to the Secretary of State requisite or expedient to do so in the interests of national security or for the purpose of mitigating the effects of any civil emergency, he or she may, after consultation with the NRA or an undertaker, give to that body directions requiring it to do, or not to do, specified things. A civil emergency is a natural disaster or other emergency which is or may be likely to so disrupt water supplies or sewerage services or involve such destruction of or damage to life or property as seriously and adversely to affect the inhabitants of an area.[50] The NRA or an undertaker must comply with any such direction, despite any other duty imposed on them, and an undertaker's during in this respect is enforceable by the Secretary of State.[51] It is an offence to disclose anything done by virtue of a direction where the Secretary of State has given notification that a disclosure is against the interests of national security.[52]

The Secretary of State or the Minister of Agriculture may, by regulations, provide for the implementation of European Community obligations, or any international agreement in relation to water supply, the control of pollution and fisheries.[53]

HM Inspectorate of Pollution is responsible for the regulation of the discharge of particularly noxious substances to the aquatic environment. It also issues discharge consents to the NRA,[54] provides technical auditing of sampling and monitoring procedures and technical advice to undertakers on water quality problems. The Drinking Water Inspectorate has particular responsibility for monitoring compliance with the standards set by the Secretary of State in water quality regulations made under the Act. The inspectorate possesses certain powers to obtain information and to enter premises in connection with its functions.[55]

Where the Secretary of State and the Minister of Agriculture are given powers under the Act to make regulations, they are given supplementary powers to include provisions with respect to enforcement, determination of disputes, prosecution of offences of making of false statements, etc., and other consequential or supplemental matters.[56]

1.6   Ministry of Agriculture, Fisheries and Food

General responsibility for pollution control lies with the Department of the Environment, but other departments, including Trade and Industry, Energy and Agriculture, have a close interest because of the environmental impacts of the industries with which they deal.[57]

In 1986 a reorganisation of the Ministry of Agriculture, Fisheries and Food took place which resulted in the creation of the Land and Environmental Affairs Group to take the lead on a range of policies relating to the interface between agriculture and the environment. Since then a further restructuring within that Group has taken place, with the Conservation Policy Division having responsibility for general countryside conservation issues and the overview of Environmentally Sensitive Areas. The Environmental Protection Division of the Group has functions in relation to agricultural pollution. Both divisions report to a single Under-Secretary. The Ministry has played a major role in the development of codes of good agricultural practice which give advice to farmers on the prevention and diminution of agricultural pollution.[58]

1.7   Local authorities

Local authorities have a general duty to monitor the wholesomeness and sufficiency of water supplies in their areas, and to take matters up with the water undertaker if a public supply is unwholesome or insufficient.[59] They may also require measures to be taken to improve the quality and sufficiency of private supplies.[60]

In relation to sewerage functions, a local authority may enter into an agreement with a sewerage undertaker to perform certain sewerage functions on the undertaker's behalf.[61]

Local authorities continue to exercise their previous coastal protection functions under the Coast Protection Act 1949.

Notes

1. See below, Chapter 3.
2. See below, sections 3.1.4–3.1.7.
3. See below, section 5.4.
4. See below, section 4.1.
5. *ibid.*
6. See below, section 4.2.
7. See below, sections 2.2.1–2.2.4.
8. See below, Chapter 3.
9. See below, Chapter 6.
10. See below, sections 6.1 and 6.3.
11. S.173; Water Re-organisation (Pensions, etc.) Regulations 1989 S.I.1989/1161; Water Re-organisation (Pensions, etc.) (Designated Persons) Order 1989, S.I.1989/1155.
12. See below, section 2.8.
13. S.1.
14. S.1(2).
15. Sch.1, para.16, and see National Rivers Authority (Levies) Regulations 1990, S.I. No. 118.
16. Under the Water Resources Act 1963; see below, section 3.8.
17. See below, sections 5.5–5.9.
18. Sch.1, paras. 18 and 19.
19. Sch.1, para.17.
20. S.150, Sch.1, para.21.
21. S.2.
22. S.3.
23. S.106.
24. See below, section 5.6.3.5.
25. The DoE has undertaken one such study in 1985, and the NRA is expected to carry out its first survey in 1990.
26. See below, sections 3.8 and 3.9.
27. See below, section 6.6.
28. Ss.8 and 9; see below, Chapter 6.
29. See below, section 3.7.
30. S.152.
31. S.149.
32. S.150.
33. S.143.
34. S.144.
35. S.145.
36. S.7(6).
37. S.118(1).
38. S.2, Sch.3, referred to in the Act as 'the Director'.
39. Ss.7 and 28.
40. S.26.
41. See below, section 2.2.6.
42. Ss.20–23.
43. S.34.
44. S.35.
45. S.31.
46. S.33.
47. S.34.
48. Ss.104 and 105; see below, section 5.2.
49. See below, section 5.6.3.6.
50. S.170.
51. S.170(3).

52. S.170(5).
53. S.171.
54. See below, section 5.6.3.4.
55. S.60, Sch.9, para.7.
56. S.185.
57. See 'Observations by the Government on the Third Report of the House of Commons Environment Committee in Session: 1986–87' (22 June 1988), paras. 3.29–3.32.
58. See below, section 5.7.
59. S.56.
60. S.57.
61. S.73.

CHAPTER 2

Water and sewerage undertakers

2.1   Initial transfers

Prior to the transfer date of 1 September 1989, the ten water authorities were required to prepare a scheme for approval by the Secretary of State, for the division of all their property, rights and liabilities between their successor company[1] and the NRA.[2]

In approving any scheme or approving it with modifications, the Secretary of State was required to have regard to the need to ensure that any such division allocated property, rights and liabilities in such proportions as were appropriate in the context of the different functions which are carried out by the companies and the NRA. The Secretary of State was also required to ensure that the division provided sufficiently for matters relating to water resources management schemes entered into between the NRA and water undertakers.[3]

The schemes provided for the transfer of property (situated in the United Kingdom or elsewhere), rights and liabilities (whether current or future), the creation of new rights and liabilities, or their transfer, whether or not they were otherwise capable of being transferred or assigned by the water authority.[4] They were able to contain supplemental, consequential and transitional provision for the purposes of, or in connection with, the division or any other provision made by the scheme.[5]

On the transfer date, the NRA received from the water authorities property and assets to the value of approximately £444 million, the remainder being transferred to nominated successor companies.

Following the entry into force of these schemes, the water authorities remain in existence until such time as they are dissolved by the Secretary of State.[6] However, they consist only of a chairman appointed by the Secretary of State and any members if so appointed and their duties relate only to ensuring that the transfer of all property, rights and liabilities, particularly foreign assets or liabilities, is fully effected.[7]

2.2   Making and conditions of appointment

Under Chapter I of Part II of the Water Act, the Secretary of State, or the Director with the consent of the Secretary of State, is authorised to appoint companies as water and sewerage undertakers for any area of England and Wales.[8]

Without prejudice to each company's conditions of appointment, an appointment by the Secretary of State has the following effect:[9]

1.   To require the company to perform any duty imposed by or under any enactment on an undertaker of the relevant description.
2.   To authorise the company to carry out the functions and exercise the powers conferred by or under any enactment on an undertaker of that description.
3.   To require enactments and subordinate legislation authorising, requiring or referring to anything to be done in relation to an undertaker of the relevant description to be construed as referring to or requiring that thing to be done in relation to that company.

Appointments were made by an instrument in writing containing the appointments and describing the area for which they were made. In respect of the appointments of the ten water and sewerage undertakers, each instrument contained that company's appointment as a sewerage undertaker for a specified area and an appointment as a water undertaker for specified parts of that area.[10] The Secretary of State was required to appoint the nominated successor companies as water and sewerage undertakers covering the areas of their predecessor authorities and the existing statutory water companies as water undertakers in the area they served.[11]

In certain circumstances the Secretary of State, or the Director with the consent of the Secretary of State, may terminate an appointment or vary the area to which it relates[12] or make a modification of the appointment conditions.[13]

The Secretary of State, or the Director in accordance with a general authorisation given by the Secretary of State, is empowered to set conditions of appointment (whether or not relating to the supply of water, the provision of sewerage services or the performance of any power or duty imposed or conferred on undertakers) as appear to him or her to be requisite or expedient having regard to the duties imposed on the Secretary of State by Part I of the Act.[14]

The Secretary of State may make regulations on the procedure to be followed with respect to the reference of any matter to the Monopolies Commission in pursuance of a provision contained in an appointment.[15] Where any matter falls to be determined by the Monopolies Commission, in pursuance of a provision contained in an appointment, the Director must, if required by the company holding that appointment, refer the matter to the Commission, and the Commission must determine it in accordance with Part I of the Act and any regulations made.[16]

The instruments of appointment of water and sewerage undertakers came into force on 1 September 1989. A Compendium of the Instruments of Appointment for the water and sewerage undertakers, and for water undertakers only, has been published and contains the common text of the Instrument of Appointment followed by Annexes listing the variations specific to each company and maps illustrating the areas of appointment.[17]

An Appendix to Schedule 1 of the Compendium contains a list of premises and installations outside the boundaries of the Water Supply Area but deemed to comprise part of that Area, and, conversely, premises inside the boundaries, but deemed not to comprise part of that Water Supply Area.[18]

Schedule 2 of the Compendium contains a list of the conditions of each appointment.[19]

2.2.1   CHARGES[20]

The purposes of this condition are as follows:[21]

1. To limit increases in standard charges made by the appointee for the supply of water, the provision of sewerage services and the reception, treatment and disposal of trade effluent. The sum of percentage increases from one year to another in charges for each of five basket items, each weighted according to revenue, must not exceed the percentage change in the Retail Price Index plus a numerical adjustment factor K, where K may be positive, negative, or zero.

2. To enable a review of the appointed business to be carried out at five- or ten-yearly intervals so that the Director can determine whether the adjustment factor should be changed.

3. To enable the appointee to refer to the Director at five-yearly intervals the question whether the adjustment factor should be changed, or whether an interim adjustment should be made because of certain circumstances.

4. To enable the Director to change the adjustment factor in the light of certain circumstances.

5. To enable the appointee to require the Director to refer certain matters to the Monopolies Commission, and to require the appointee to give information to the Director to enable him or her to make determinations.

Part II of the condition on charges sets out the charges limit, rules for dealing with changes in circumstances, and procedures for verification of compliance with the charges.

The charges currently made by undertakers are divided between two main sectors. The first, principally domestic customers with un-measured supplies, are commonly charged on the basis of the rateable value of the property served, subject to a standing or minimum charge related to the diameter of the supply pipe. The second, principally industrial and commercial customers, are charged on the basis of measured consumption, subject to a standing or minimum charge and, in some cases, a rateable value based charge. An annual charges limit is to be calculated on the basis of adjustment factors (K) which are specified in each undertaker's conditions of appointment. The actual charges limit is calculated annually by adding this specified adjustment factor to the previous year's Retail Price Index. The charges limit in turn represents the maximum allowable Weighted Average Charges Increase.

The definition of 'Weighted Average Charges Increase' sets out algebraically the rules for calculating the increases in charges from one year to the next. The formula applies to charges for five defined 'basket items' of service:

1. Unmeasured water supply.
2. Unmeasured sewerage services.
3. Measured water supply.
4. Measured sewerage services.
5. Reception, treatment and disposal of trade effluent.

The limit set by the formula applies to the sum of the increases in each of these five elements, and applies annually to the tariff increases proposed by undertakers as the basis for billing. Shortly before the beginning of the financial year in which the tariffs are to apply, each intended percentage increase is multiplied by the proportion of total revenue from charges included in the basket that it represented in the previous year's accounts of each company. This multiplication is known as 'weighting' and the result is the 'weighted increase' in the charge. The sum of the weighted increases in any year must not be more than the charges limit. For example, if the charges limit formula (RPI+ K) for the following year is 4 per cent, then if it is proposed to increase one of the basket items by say 5 per cent, the other tariffs taken together must rise by less than the 4 per cent allowed increase. If the item which is to be increased by 5 per cent represents one half of all revenue, and all other increases (except for one which represents one quarter of the total revenue) were to be at 4 per cent, then that item representing one quarter of revenue may only rise by a maximum of 2 per cent to offset the 5 per cent increase.[22] In this way, different increases for different services are permitted, so long as they do not in total exceed the charges limit. Where the Weighted Average Charges Increase is less than the charges limit for any one year, undertakers may carry forward any unused freedom to increase charges in the two subsequent charging years, after which any unused allowable increase is lost.[23]

The proportion of total revenue represented by each basket item and, consequently, the revenue weights, are to be calculated from audited data of each undertaker, and to be presented to the Director General each January in respect of charges increases for the following financial year beginning 1 April.[24] If revenue weights have been changing rapidly it is open to an undertaker or the Director to claim that data from accounts is out of date, and to agree that alternative weights should be used. The permitted charges increase fixed each January for the forthcoming financial year will be related to the immediately preceding December to December increase in the published Retail Price Index figures.

The Director may modify the condition relating to charges to take account of charges in the basis of calculation of the Retail Price Index. He or she is able to obtain information from undertakers about any changes which affect the basket of charges relevant to the charges formula calculations.[25] The values of K for a period of ten years beginning on 1 April 1990 have been set in each undertaker's Instrument of Appointment.

The Director may undertake a review of the charges limit at five-yearly intervals, by serving a 'review notice' on the undertaker on or before 1 January, fifteen months before the modified charges limit would take effect. Serving a review notice requires the undertaker to provide the information required by the Director to enable him or her to carry out a review and to determine whether the adjustment factor should be changed for the next ten years. The undertaker is required to furnish to the Director all information he or she reasonably requires by 31 March following the service of the review notice.[26] In undertaking a review the Director must have regard to his or her general duties under Part I of the Act.[27]

Where no review notice is served by the Director, a periodic review is to take place automatically after a period of ten years. The undertaker must provide the specified information to the Director by 1 April and further information as necessary thereafter during the review year.[28]

Five-yearly reviews may also be initiated by the undertaker. Such a review is effected by serving a notice on the Director during the first two weeks in January, where the Director has not him- or herself given notice of a review prior to 1 January, fifteen months before the new charges limit would take effect.[29]

Provision is also made for a review of the business, where the Secretary of State has given notice that the appointment may be terminated within ten years.[30]

The Director may make changes to the adjustment factor K to take account of all the changes that will occur in the rates paid by undertakers from 1 April 1990 as a consequence of the introduction of the new rating system created by the Local Government Finance Act 1988. These changes will affect the basis on which the rateable values of water and sewerage undertakers' assets are determined, and they will introduce a national business rate. The introduction of these measures will be subject to provisional arrangements. At the time of the initial determination of adjustment factors, the full effect on undertakers was not known, so the Director is empowered to make such changes to K as will compensate for the amount by which rates are materially higher or lower than rates allowed for in determining those adjustment factors.[31]

The Instrument of Appointment also provides for the 'cost pass through' of additional burdens resulting from new legal requirements imposed on an undertaker.[32] 'Legal requirements' are defined[33] as including legislation and subordinate legislation of the United Kingdom and the European Communities, consents and authorities granted by the Secretary of State, the NRA or other competent bodies, enforcement orders made under Section 20,[34] interpretations of law by the courts, and obligations resulting from agreements between an undertaker and any enforcement authority about the obligations under any such legal requirement. The purpose of this provision is to enable an interim adjustment to the charges limit to be made in order to keep the undertaker in the same financial position as it would have been if the new obligation had not been applied until the next periodic review of the limit.

The power only applies to obligations not in effect on 1 September 1989 or at the last periodic review, unless any statutory requirements were notified at that time as not have been taken fully into account.

The Director may also make changes to the adjustment factor where he or she determines that other circumstances have had a substantial adverse affect on the business of the undertaker and would not have been avoided by prudent management action. The Director may make an interim adjustment to the charges limit pending a periodic review, to enable the undertaker to cope with the effect of a serious unforeseen event (e.g. a major disaster), the costs of which could threaten its ability to fulfil its obligations without an increase in charges.[35]

An undertaker must provide all information it believes is necessary to enable the Director to make an interim determination and any further information required by the Director as soon as is reasonable practicable.[36]

In the case of any disputes about interim determinations, or where the Director has not made a determination within one year in the case of periodic reviews or three months in the case of an interim determination, the undertaker may within one month require the Director to refer the matter to the Monopolies Commission.[37]

Determination by the Director on periodic or interim reviews and by the Monopolies Commission following a reference to it are to be given effect by modifying the condition on charges by the necessary change to the adjustment factor.[38]

2.2.2   INFRASTRUCTURE CHARGES[39]

Infrastructure charges relate to the fixing of a charge for the initial connection to a water supply or to a public sewer of premises which have never at any previous time been connected to a water supply for domestic purposes or a sewer used for drainage for domestic purposes.[40]

Where an undertaker makes a water connection, it must as soon as reasonably practicable inform the sewerage undertaker which provides services to those premises of that fact, and the number of water connections made.[41]

Each undertaker must ensure that the amount of any infrastructure charges made in any charging year after 1 April 1990, does not exceed the Infrastructure Charges limits less any amount paid or agreed to be paid to the undertaker in respect of works which have been allowed for in determining the Infrastructure Charges limits from time to time.[42]

The Infrastructure Charges limits are set for the initial year beginning on 1 April 1990 in the Instruments of Appointment. In respect of any charging year beginning on or after 1 April 1991 the limits are the Initial Specified limited increased or decreased according to changes in the Retail Price Index published in November of the prior year using November 1989 as a base.[43]

Periodic reviews and determinations may be made by the Director at five- or ten-yearly intervals in such manner as they are made for other charges.[44]

The undertaker must furnish to the Director all information it believes is necessary for him to make a determination and such other information as the Director may reasonably require.[45]

In cases of dispute or where the Director fails within one year to make a determination, provision is made for reference to be made to the Monopolies Commission.[46] Modification of the condition on infrastructure charges may be made following a determination by either the Director or the Commission.[47]

2.2.3   CHARGES SCHEMES[48]

Section 76 provides for water and sewerage undertakers to fix their charges for any services provided in the course of carrying out their functions in charges schemes.[49] This condition requires undertakers to have charges schemes in force in all respects by 1 April 1990, which:

(a) fix the charges to be paid for supplies of water for domestic purposes and for the drainage for domestic purposes of premises except where such charges are determined by an agreement with a customer;
(b) fix the charges to be paid for initial connections to a water supply for domestic purposes or to a sewer used for the drainage of domestic premises.[50]

With respect to initial connections, every scheme must provide that the charges may be paid in full within a reasonable period specified by the undertaker, or, at the option of the customer, by means of instalments over a period of 12 years.[51]

In relation to non-domestic water supplies, which are not covered by this condition, section 46 provides that the Director may determine charges in the absence of agreement, except where there is a charges scheme setting out the charge for the case in question. In relation to charges fixed under trade effluent consents,[52] the Director similarly may not determine payment of charges in cases for which charges have been set out in a charges scheme.

In respect of other charges fixed under section 75,[53] there is no provision in the Act for the Director to determine charges for services in individual cases. This condition is intended to ensure that undertakers publish standard tariffs for the provision of their statutory services, but does not prevent the fixing of charges by agreement under section 76, and where there are such agreements the condition provides for an exception to the requirement to have a charges scheme.[54]

Copies of charges schemes must be made available for inspection at the offices of the undertaker, and a copy must be provided free of charge to any person requesting it.[55]

2.2.4 PROHIBITION ON UNDUE DISCRIMINATION AND UNDUE PREFERENCE AND INFORMATION ON CHARGES[56]

The Secretary of State and the Director are required to exercise their powers under Chapter I of Part II of the Act (Appointment and Regulation of Water and Sewerage Undertakers, ss.11–36) so as to ensure that the interest of the customers or potential customers are protected as respects the fixing of charges and, in particular, that no undue preference is shown, and that there is no undue discrimination, in the fixing of those charges.[57] This condition accordingly makes provision with respect to charges at standard rates and charges fixed in individual cases by agreement.

The undertaker must provide the Director with such information as he or she may reasonably require to satisfy him- or herself that the undertaker is complying with this condition.[58]

The condition is stated not to apply in the following cases:[59]

1. Metering trials made by water authorities under the Public Utility Transfers and Water Charges Act 1988 and which continue in force after the transfer date.[60]
2. Terms or conditions determined in respect of a supply of water for

non-domestic purposes[61] and conditions imposed in respect of an appeal or determination by the Secretary of State on trade effluent.[62]

3. Infrastructure Charges which do not exceed the specified limit.[63]
4. Terms and conditions in respect of a supply of water in bulk between undertakers.[64]

2.2.5   ACCOUNTS AND ACCOUNTING INFORMATION[65]

Any company appointed as a water or sewerage undertaker may engage in other business apart from the supply of water and the provision of sewerage services. This condition specifies requirements for separate accounts and certain other accounting information which must be prepared by the undertaker, so that the finances of the appointed business (the 'core services') and the relevant relationship between the financial affairs of the appointed business and any other business of the undertaker or associated company[66] will be disclosed to the Director in his or her capacity as economic regulator.

An undertaker must provide accounting statements relating to the statutory appointed business (the provision of water supply and sewerage services), to its other businesses, and a combined statement of all business of the undertaker including the appointed business. The statement must so far as practicable have the same content as annual accounts prepared under the Companies Act 1985 to enable comparison. The statements required are a profit and loss account and a balance sheet, with sufficient detail to reconcile net assets at the beginning and end of the period in question and showing costs, revenues, assets and liabilities. Principal accounting policy statements must include segmental information on the appointed business, showing an analysis of operating costs, turnover and tangible fixed assets.[67]

Paragraph 6 of Condition F requires disclosure of information about transactions between the appointed business and other business of the undertaker and companies in the undertaker's group. The transactions covered by this condition are listed in an appendix to the condition. Such disclosure allows the extent of any cross-subsidy to or from the appointed business to be determined and taken into account by the Director in exercising his or her powers, particularly that of setting the charges limit in condition B. Disclosure is also required of details of the basis of apportionment or allocation of assets, revenues, costs and liabilities amongst associated companies.[68]

An undertaker must obtain the prior written authorisation, not to be unreasonably withheld or delayed, of the Director before changing the basis of specified allocations and apportionments, in order that comparisons may be made between accounts from year to year.[69] An auditor's report must be obtained on the accounting statements required by this condition and must be provided together with the statements no later than six months after the end of each financial year. The accounting statements must be published[70] with the undertaker's annual accounts, and copies made available upon request to customers.[71]

The Director is given power to issue guidelines with respect to accounting statements,[72] and an undertaker may within one month of the issuing of such guidelines require the Director to refer to the Monopolies Commission the question whether the guidelines are appropriate and reasonable.[73]

2.2.6   CODE OF PRACTICE FOR CUSTOMERS AND RELATIONS WITH THE CUSTOMER SERVICE COMMITTEE[74]

Subject to approval by the Director, each undertaker must have in effect a code of practice for customers providing information about its services, domestic customers' tariffs, payment of bills and complaint procedures, testing of meters, liability for metered charges, offences concerning tampering with meters, enquiries and emergencies, and the functions of customer service committees.[75] The code must be reviewed at least every three years and in carrying out any review the undertaker must consult the Director and the customer service committee.[76] A copy of the code and any revision of it, must be sent to the customer service committee, drawn to the attention of domestic customers, made available for inspection at the offices of the undertaker, provided free of charge on request, and those parts relating to information about metering included with every metered bill.[77]

The undertaker must also have in effect a procedure for dealing with complaints from customers, which is to include particulars of training of staff in the handling of complaints.[78] Special means of identification must be carried out by the undertaker's staff when visiting customers' premises.[79] The undertaker must meet the customer service committee upon request, and must be represented by a director of the company at such meetings at least once a year.[80]

2.2.7   CODE OF PRACTICE AND PROCEDURE IN DISCONNECTION[81]

Subject to approval by the Director, each undertaker must have in effect a code of practice on disconnection of water supplies for non-payment of bills. The code is intended to give guidance to domestic customers who have difficulty in paying their bills and to describe the procedure adopted by the undertaker, in accordance with the conditions specified in paragraph 7, which the undertaker will follow before it disconnects a supply of water to any domestic premises.[82]

The code is to be reviewed at least once every three years and in carrying out a review the undertaker must consult the Director and the customer service committee.[83] Copies of the code and any revision of it must be sent to the customer service committee, drawn to the attention of domestic customers with their bills, made available for inspection and provided free of charge upon request to any person.[84] The undertaker must provide the customer service committee every six months with the number of domestic premises in respect of which the supply of water has been disconnected for non-payment of charges.[85]

2.2.8   CODE OF PRACTICE AND PROCEDURE ON LEAKAGE[86]

Subject to approval by the Director each undertaker must have in effect a code of practice (in accordance with paragraph 8) concerning liability for charges of domestic customers occupying metered premises where there is an unidentified leak of the supply pipe for which they are responsible.[87] The code must be reviewed at least once every three years, following a process of consultation with the Director and the customer service committee, drawn to the attention of metered domestic customers with their bills, made available for inspection and provided free upon request.[88]

2.2.9   LEVELS OF SERVICE INFORMATION AND SERVICE TARGETS[89]

The Director of Water Services is under a duty to ensure that the interests of customers are protected as regards the quality of service provided by an undertaker. This condition establishes a framework for the Director to monitor the levels and quality of service provided, and for certain aspects of service, for undertakers to set service targets.

Each undertaker must report annually to the Director on the levels of service they have achieved on the following indicators:[90]

1. Water availability.
2. Mains water pressure.
3. Supply interruptions.
4. Hosepipe restrictions.
5. Flooding from sewers.
6. Response times to billing enquiries.
7. Response times to written complaints.
8. Replies to planning application consultations.

Generally, the levels of service indicators are the percentage of customers receiving service at or above a common specified reference standard. For example, water pressure can be measured in terms of metres of 'head' at the customer's stop tap. The reference standard in this case is set at a pressure of ten metres head to be maintained. The level of service can then be measured as the percentage of customers with pressure at or above the reference standard.

The Director may vary the information to be provided annually if he or she is satisfied that the information is inadequate to enable him or her properly to keep the quality of the services under review, subject to prior consultation with the undertaker. In so doing he or she must have regard to his or her duties under section 26 of the Act.[91]

The information provided annually to the Director must be accompanied by a report specifying the methods used to monitor, assess and report information on levels of service, and a statement explaining the reasons why and the extent to which any service falls below any specified reference standard.[92] Service falling below the reference standard is not of itself a breach of the conditions of appointment.

An undertaker is required to provide the Director with details of its intentions about the quality of its services in the form of service targets for achievement by a date or over a period of time, in respect of water supply pressure, constancy of supply and foul flooding from sewers. Where the Director considers it requisite or expedient for the purpose of enabling him or her properly to keep the quality of services under review, he or she may require the undertaker to notify him or her of its intentions in respect of other services.[93] These targets set bench marks for the expected level of service to be achieved and for the levels of investment in the maintenance and improvement of infrastructure and assets which are required as a consequence. Generally, service targets state the intended level of service year by year over a five-year period and give forward targets for performance to be actioned at the end of ten and fifteen years. The costs of meeting these service targets have been and are to be taken into account by the Director in setting and reviewing charges limits in the regular periodic reviews of charges.[94]

The undertaker must monitor and assess the quality of services in relation to the service targets[95] and submit an annual report to the Director.[96] The report must include all the information which the undertaker considers necessary to provide proper explanation of the report and the quality of services as compared with any relevant service target. It must also include a statement of the methods used by the undertaker to keep the quality of services under review and the steps taken to monitor and assess the quality of service.

In any service target report the undertaker may revise any services target, changing either the absolute value of the target or the time for achieving it, and may specify different targets for different areas.

The Secretary of State and the Director General are under various obligations with respect to the regulation of water supply and sewerage services.[97] Generally, the Director will try to reach agreement with an undertaker about action to secure improvements in the quality of service where he or she considers such improvements to be necessary. However, the Act provides that the Director may propose to the Secretary of State regulations defining or imposing service obligations on a specific company or undertakers generally.[98] These are binding on the undertaker and, if not complied with, are enforceable by the Secretary of State or the Director.[99] These provisions are in addition to any right an individual customer may have to bring a civil action against an undertaker for failing to comply with a statutory obligation.

Where the Director believes that a company should be required to meet specific targets for some aspect of quality of its service, should take particular steps in order to provide an appropriate level of service, or should have a different target from a target proposed or previously set by the company, then, in the absence of agreement, he or she may recommend that the Secretary of State make appropriate regulations. The Director must take into account the costs of complying with the service obligations imposed on the company as part of his general duty to ensure that companies can finance the performance of their functions.[100] The Director is required to give reasons for concluding that an undertaker's existing performance or service target is unsatisfactory or inadequate. Before making any regulations, the Secretary of State must consider any representation made by the undertaker about the Director's proposals, and about any proposed change to them.[101] Regulations may apply to an aspect of service quality across the whole of a company's area, or be restricted to certain parts of it.

The annual levels of service information and service target reports must be accompanied by a certificate signed by the undertaker's auditors supporting the adequacy of the methods used to ascertain the information provided and confirming whether those methods were the same as those notified to the Director by the undertaker.[102] The undertaker must cooperate fully with the Director in any investigation and allow him or her access to records, equipment or premises.[103]

This condition also requires that customers be informed of the existence of annual information provided on levels of service and reports (but not the accompanying information), and that copies of this be made available for inspection or sent to persons requesting them.[104]

2.2.10 'RING FENCING', DISPOSALS OF LAND AND CHANGES OF USE OF LAND[105]

This condition is intended to ensure the following:

1. That the assets needed to provide water and sewerage services would be available to a special administrator appointed under section 23[106] and a successor appointee in the event of the insolvency of, or major default by, the undertaker.[107]
2. That the best price is received from disposals of land so as to secure benefits to customers through the application of the proceeds of such disposals to reduce charges.

The undertaker is required to make a formal declaration, published with its audited accounts each year, as to whether it was meeting the first requirement at the end of that financial year.[108] It must ensure that the terms on which relevant rights and assets are provided to it by a group company are sufficient for the purpose of complying with the condition.[109]

With respect to disposals of land the condition applies to 'protected land' which is defined[110] as being any land, or any interest in or right over land, which:

(a) was transferred to the company under an initial transfer scheme[111] or if the company is a statutory water company, is or was held by

that company at any time during the financial year beginning 1
April 1989;

(b) is or has at any time on or after 1 September 1989 been held by the
company for purposes connected with its functions as a water or
sewerage undertaker;[112] or

(c) has been transferred to the company in accordance with a scheme
operating on the termination of an appointment.[113]

'Disposal' includes the creation of an interest or right, and a disposal
effected by means of the surrender or other termination of any such
interest or right.

At least ten working days before entering into an obligation
(whether conditional or unconditional) relating to the disposal of land,
the undertaker is required to furnish to the Director a Disposal
Certificate[114] which:

(a) identifies the protected land in question;

(b) describes the interest in or right over the land to be disposed of;

(c) sets out the terms of the proposed disposal;

(d) describes the consideration to be received or expected to be
received and its timing;

(e) sets out details of any other disposals related to, or connected or
interdependent with the proposal, or if none, a statement to that
effect;

(f) confirms that the protected land is, or will no longer be required for
the carrying out of the core services and will not be so required in
the forseeable future;

(g) confirms that the proposed disposal is an arm's length transaction,
that the consideration certified is the total value to be received or
derived, that the consideration is the best price[115] that could
reasonably be obtained[116] and that the undertaker or an associated
company will cease to have any interest[117] whatsoever in the land
following the proposed disposal.

The Director may request that the undertaker prior to disposal provide
him or her with such further information as he or she may reasonably
require.[118]

In situations where the requirements of (f) and (g) cannot be fully
certified, the company may still obtain prior written consent from the
Director for the disposal, such consent not to be unreasonably
withheld or delayed.[119] These provisions are expressed not to apply:

(a) to any disposal which consists of the creation of any interest in or right over protected land which the company has an unconditional right to terminate without penalty at any time and from time to time by not more than thirty months' notice, or which expires or otherwise ceases in accordance with its terms within thirty months of the date of its creation; or

(b) to any disposal made in accordance with any provision referred to in section 152(5)(a) to the relevant person referred to in that section.[120]

Where a disposal of protected land is proposed to be made by way of auction or formal tender, the company, in addition to providing a Certificate of Disposal containing the above information, must set out the reserve price (if any) and confirm that the auction will be conducted on the basis that no bid will be accepted by an associated company or a nominee of an associated company.[121]

Where the proposed disposal is to be made to an associated company, the undertaker must, not later than a date prior to entering into an obligation as specified by the Director, furnish to him or her a Disposal Certificate, a certificate by a valuer stating that the consideration is the best price likely to be obtained from an unconnected third party, and a statement of the amount of consideration to be received or expected to be received. Alternatively, the Director may give his or her prior written consent to the proposed disposal, such consent not be unreasonably withheld or delayed.[122]

Where an undertaker changes the use of any protected land to a use which consists of it being held or used for some purpose other than for purposes connected with the carrying out of its core services it is required to inform the Director within twenty-eight days of any such change.[123] It must furnish to the Director a Disposal Certificate identifying the protected land, describing the change of use of the land and any consideration received and confirming that the land is no longer required for carrying out its core services and will not be so required in the forseeable future. It must also furnish to the Director a certificate from a valuer as to the best price which in his or her opinion is obtainable from a disposal of the land in question. Unless the Director otherwise consents, or the undertaker otherwise disposes of the land, it must within twelve months from the date of the valuer's certificate transfer the land in question to an associated company for the price certified by the valuer.[124]

2.2.11 UNDERGROUND ASSET MANAGEMENT PLANS[125]

This condition relates to the underground asset network of water and sewerage undertakers. It requires them to adopt a system of long-term planning in respect of those assets in order to protect the interests of present and future customers by maintaining, and where necessary improving, the quality of service.

Each undertaker is required to prepare and submit a plan to the Director showing estimates of required expenditure over a period of a minimum of fifteen years commencing on 1 April 1990 (or fifteen years following a periodic review of the charges limit) in order to maintain and develop its asset networks. In doing so it must take into account the expenditure necessary to enable it to carry out its functions (including service targets) economically and efficiently, for the purpose of ensuring that it will have at all times available to it for use all infrastructures as is necessary to fulfil its obligations, and that the capacity of the systems of water supply and of public sewers is sufficient for demand. The plan must be kept under review and a revised plan must be submitted to the Director from time to time and in any event by the date of each periodic review.[126]

The undertaker must establish, maintain, and keep under review systems and procedures for collecting information on underground assets, and for reviewing the plan both for providing the required long-term expenditure estimates and providing information to the Director in respect of periodic or interim reviews of charges limits.[127]

If required by the Director, an independent 'assessor' may be appointed to report on any revision of the underground asset management plan or of the systems and procedures.[128]

At the same time as it delivers accounting statements in respect of the financial year under condition F, the undertaker must provide to the Director a statement of expenditure made or incurred during the year, together with details of any differences between that expenditure and the expenditure which it intended to make or incur during that financial year.[129] It is difficult in accounting terms to assess depreciation on underground assets. Instead of adopting either the historic cost or the current cost accounting convention, the water industry favours a compromise solution known as infrastructure accounting. This assumes that all existing assets are to be maintained in perpetuity. Any money spent maintaining the system is charged against profits as current expenditure. Investment in the extension or improvement of infrastructure is counted as capital expenditure and is capitalised in the balance sheet. Depreciation is not charged, as it is assumed that the system is to be maintained indefinitely.

2.2.12 PROVISION OF INFORMATION TO THE DIRECTOR[130]

This condition sets out the requirements for undertakers to provide information to the Director to enable him or her to carry out his or her functions. The duty to provide information to the Secretary of State is imposed by section 32 of the Act. An undertaker is required to provide any information the Director reasonably requires in the form, at the times and with such supplementary explanation as he or she specifies.[131]

Sections 15 (modifications of conditions of appointment by agreement), 26 (the Director's duty to keep matters under review and to collect information) and 34 (Directors' powers to publish information and advice), are functions of the Director for which he or she may not require information under this condition, although the undertaker is required on request by the Director to comment on information or advice to be published. However, the Director is not prevented from using or disclosing information obtained under the conditions of appointment, subject to the general restrictions upon disclosure in section 174. Section 33 sets out the powers of the Director and the Secretary of State to obtain information for enforcement purposes, but this condition does not extend to obtaining information for such purposes. The undertaker is not required to provide information which it would be entitled to refuse to provide in the High Court on grounds of legal professional privilege.[132]

2.2.13 FEES[133]

Section 14(1)(c) of the Act provides that the conditions of appointment may require the appointee to render payments to the Secretary of State. This condition provides for payments to be made to cover the costs of regulatory measures. The payments required are an initial payment specified in the conditions of appointment, annual payments on 1 April to cover the estimated costs of references to the Monopolies Commission and a fair proportion of the costs estimated by the Director as likely to be incurred in the forthcoming year by him or her carrying out his or her regulatory functions,[134] including payments made in relation to the costs of customer service committees.[135] They also include annual payments on 1 January to cover regulatory costs in the current year, to the extent that those costs exceed the Director's estimate at the preceding 1 April.[136] Where the Director apportions costs, he or she must disclose the method in writing to the undertaker.[137]

A specific cash limit on the sum of the first renewal fee and special fee payable is provided in the Instrument of Appointment. In addition, this condition provides for the limit on the sum of the renewal fee and special fee payable in subsequent years to be increased in line with the Retail Price Index, except that a higher limit of 0.3 per cent of the turnover of the appointed business will apply during a year in which the Director will be conducting a periodic review prior to resetting the charges limit.[138] At the time of either a periodic or interim review the Director may refer to the Secretary of State the question whether the limit on the sum of the renewal fee and special fee in respect of any year starting on or after 1 April 2000 should be changed.[139]

2.2.14 CIRCUMSTANCES IN WHICH A REPLACEMENT APPOINTMENT MAY NOT BE MADE[140]

Appointments continue in effect unless a replacement appointment is made, either in relation to the appointment of a company for any area or the variation of an area for which a company holds an appointment.[141] Such an appointment or variation may only be made where the existing appointee consents, and the appointment or variation relates only to parts of an area none of the premises in which is served by the existing appointee.[142] The Director, in exercising his or her powers to make a replacement appointment or variation (termed 'inset appointments') pursuant to a general authorisation, must take into account, in particular, his duty to facilitate effective competition between persons holding appointments.[143] However, the Director must also have regard to any arrangements made or expenditure incurred by the existing appointee for the purpose of connecting up any premises not served by the existing undertaker,[144] made in the circumstances set out in the conditions of the Instrument of Appointment of the existing appointee.[145] Condition O provides that a replacement appointment may only be made with at least ten years' written notice, and not within twenty-five years of the initial appointment.

The Secretary of State and the Director are under a duty, in making a replacement or variation order and in determining what provision is to be made with respect to the fixing by the new appointee of charges and other amounts, to ensure, so far as this is consistent with their other duties, that the interests of the members and creditors of the existing appointee are not unfairly prejudiced as respects the terms on which the new appointee could accept transfers of property rights and liabilities from the existing appointee.[146] This is a specific reference to the possibility that new appointees offering lower service charges and squeezing down the consideration for transferred property, would unfairly prejudice existing appointees.

The procedure for making a replacement appointment is specified in section 13 and Schedule 5 which provide for transitional arrangements for the period between existing and replacement appointees and for the approval by the Director or Secretary of State of a scheme for the transfer of property, rights and liabilities.

2.3   Modification of appointment conditions[147]

Upon an agreement with an undertaker, the Director may modify any of that undertaker's conditions of appointment.[148] Before making such a modification, the Director is required to publish[149] a notice and serve a copy on the company and on the Secretary of State, stating that he or she proposes to make the modification and setting out its effect, the reasons why he or she proposes to make it, and specifying a period of at least twenty-eight days in which representations or objections may be made.[150] In certain circumstances the Secretary of State may within that time period direct that the Director may not make such modifications as are specified in the Director's notice.[151]

The Director may make a reference to the Monopolies Commission requiring the Commission to investigate and report on whether any matters which relate to the carrying out of any function of the company operate, or may be expected to operate, against the public interest, and if so, whether the effects adverse to the public interest could be remedied or prevented by modifications of the conditions of the company's appointment.[152] As soon as practicable after making such a reference, the Director must serve a copy of the reference on the company in question and publish particulars of the reference in such manner as he or she considers appropriate for the purpose of bringing it to the attention of persons likely to be affected.[153] In determining whether a referred matter operates against the public interest, the Commission is required to have regard to the considerations that are covered by the duties of the Director and Secretary of State under Part I of the Act.[154] The Commission is to make a report to the Director including definite conclusions on the questions comprised in the reference and if relevant, what modifications to the conditions are necessary to remedy or prevent any adverse effects.[155] Upon receipt of the report, the Director must send a copy to the company in question and the Secretary of State, and unless the Secretary of State so directs for reasons of public or commercial interest, must publish a copy of the report.[156]

Subject to certain rights of notification and objection,[157] the Director is required to make such modifications of the conditions of the appointment as appear to him requisite for the purpose of remedying or preventing the adverse effects specified in the report.[158] The Director may not make any modifications to conditions which relate to termination and variation or to the disposal of protected land.[159]

Water and sewerage undertakers are also subject to the general legislation concerning monopolies and competition. The Secretary of State may make modifications to appointment conditions using powers conferred on the Secretary of State by the Fair Trading Act 1973 or the Competition Act 1980.[160]

2.4   Functions of the Director General of Water Services

The Director is under a duty to keep under review the activities of water or sewerage undertakers and to collect information with respect to the carrying out of the functions of appointed companies, and about the companies themselves.[161] The Director is further required to advise and assist the Secretary of State and the Director General of Fair Trading with respect to the functions of water and sewerage undertakers.[162]

The Secretary of State may give directions to the Director indicating considerations to which the Director should have particular regard either in determining the order of priority in which matters are to be brought under review pursuant to section 26 or in determining whether to exercise any of his or her powers under Part II of the Act.[163] It does not enable him or her to issue directions with regard to any of the Director's other obligations, such as those relating to competition (section 28) or the power to make a final enforcement order under section 20(1).[164]

When requested by the Director General of Fair Trading to do so, the Director General of Water Services is to exercise certain functions under Part III of the Fair Trading Act 1973 so far as relating to courses of conduct which are or may be detrimental to the interests of consumers of water and sewerage undertakers' services, whether those interests are economic or in respect of health, safety or other matters.[165] The functions under the Fair Trading Act 1973 include a duty to use his or her best endeavours to obtain from the undertaker concerned a written assurance that it will refrain from the practice in question, with the power to obtain an enforcement order through the courts if that assurance is broken.

The Director is given powers to require undertakers to provide him or her with sufficient information to establish whether a monopoly exists[166] and, together with the Director General of Fair Trading, to make references to the Monopolies and Mergers Commission.[167] The Director may also make preliminary investigations of possible anti-competitive practices and make reference to the Monopolies Commission with respect to competition matters. He or she may require assurances to be made by undertakers so that such references are not necessary.[168] Before exercising any of those powers, each Director must consult the other and resolution of any disputes between them may be determined by the Secretary of State.[169]

The Secretary of State is required to refer to the Monopolies Commission mergers between undertakers each with assets exceeding £30 million.[170] Where a reference is made[171] the provisions of the Fair Trading Act 1973 are to apply.[172] The Commission is required to consider a merger against criteria which reflect the need not to prejudice the ability of the Director to compare the efficiency of a sufficient number of appointed undertakers who are independently owned or contracted.[173]

The Director is required to maintain a register which, subject to any direction given by the Secretary of State on questions of public interest must contain the following:[174]

1. Every appointment, every termination or transfer of any such appointment, every variation of an appointee's area, and every modification of the conditions of any such appointment.
2. Every direction, consent or determination given under such appointment by the Secretary of State, the Monopolies Commission, or the Director him- or herself.
3. Every provisional or final order made under section 20, every revocation of such an order and every notice made and undertaking given under that section.[175]
4. Every special administration order and every discharge of such an order.

The contents of the register are to be made available on such terms as are specified by the Secretary of State by statutory instrument.[176]

Every undertaker is under a duty to provide such information as the Secretary of State may reasonably require relating to, or connected with, any proposals relating to the carrying out of its functions, or material to the carrying out by the Secretary of State of any of his or her functions under the Act.[177] A requirement is to be contained in a direction which may describe the information to be furnished in a specified manner, on a particular occasion, in particular circumstances or from time to time, and may be given to a particular company or to some or all companies.[178] This duty is enforceable under section 20 by the Secretary of State.[179]

The Secretary of State may arrange for the publication of such information relating to any matter connected with the carrying out of undertakers' functions as appears to him to be in the public interest to publish.[180] The Director may arrange for publication of such information and advice as appear to him or her to be expedient to give to any customer or potential customer.[181] In arranging for such matter to be published, the Director and the Secretary of State must have regard to the need for excluding, so far as that is practicable, any information that would or might seriously and prejudicially affect the interests of any individual or body.[182]

At the end of each calendar year, the Director is required to make a report to the Secretary of State, to be laid before Parliament and published in such a manner as the Secretary of State considers appropriate.[183] The report is to contain a statement of the Directors' activities during that year, the Monopolies Commission's activities so far as relating to references by him or her, a general survey of developments in respect of matters falling within the scope of his or her functions, and any directions given by the Secretary of State[184] indicating considerations to which the Director should have particular regard in reviewing the activities of water and sewerage undertakers.[185]

The Director may also prepare and publish other reports relating to his various functions which could include matters relating to complaints referred to him or her by customer service committees.[186] However, in doing so, the Director should have regard to the need for excluding any information that would or might seriously and prejudicially affect the interests of any individual or body.[187]

2.5   Enforcement

Where the Secretary of State or the Director is satisfied that any company holding an appointment is contravening any condition of its appointment or any statutory requirement enforceable under section 20, or that that company has contravened any such condition or requirement and is likely to do so again, they are required to make a final order, making such provision as is requisite for the purpose of securing compliance with the condition or requirement in question.[188] Certain duties are enforceable by the Secretary of State alone, others by the Director acting alone, and some by either the Secretary or the Director. Those enforceable by the Secretary of State are as follows:

Section 8	(general environment and recreational duties)
Section 9	(environmental duties with respect to sites of special interest)
Section 32	(duty to furnish information)
Section 47	(supply of water for fire-fighting)
Section 51	(constancy and sufficiency of water supplies)
Section 52	(quality and sufficiency of water supplies)
Section 55	(provision of alternative means of supply)
Section 119	(exchange of information on pollution incidents)
Section 126	(water resources management schemes)
Section 130	(provision of information on water flows)
Section 132	(emergency drought orders)
Section 157	(recreational facilities at reservoirs)
Section 162(6)	(code of practice regarding laying of pipes on private land)
Section 165	(maps of water mains and underground works)
Section 166	(sewer maps)
Section 170	(directions in the interest of national security)
Schedule 9	(controls on certain types of trade effluent discharged into sewers)
Schedule 10, para. 4	(meter readings)
Schedule 20, para. 5	(publication of notices concerning compulsory purchase)
Schedule 26, para. 19	(byelaws preventing waste of water etc.,) (transitional in respect of s.17 Water Act 1945)
Schedule 26, para. 41	(recreational facilities at reservoirs) (transitional in respect of s.20(5) Water Act 1973)

Duties under the Water Supply (Water Quality Regulations 1989)
Duties under the Trade Effluents (Prescribed Processes and Substances) Regulations 1989.

Those enforceable by the Director General of Water Services are as follows:

Section 20(1)(a)   (conditions of appointment of undertakers)
Section 48   (supply of water for certain public purposes)
Section 161   (duty to move pipes in certain cases)
Section 162(3)   (provision of information following complaints about the exercise of powers to lay pipes on private land)
Schedule 8   (availability to public of trade effluent consent
para. 3   records under s.7A Public Health (Drainage of Trade Premises) Act 1937
Schedule 25   (duties and agreement in relation to water supplies
para. 9   for fire services under s.14 Fire Services Act 1947).

The duties enforceable by either the Secretary of State or the Director are as follows:

Section 37   (general duty to maintain water supply system)
Section 67   (general duty to maintain system of public sewers)

Instead of taking steps to make a final order, the Secretary of State or the Director may instead make a provisional order. In determining whether a provisional rather than a final order should be made, they must have regard, in particular, to the extent to which any person is likely to sustain loss or damage in consequence of anything which, in contravention of any condition or requirement, is likely to be done, or omitted to be done, before a final order may be made.[189] A provisional order may be confirmed, with or without modifications where they are satisfied that the company is contravening or has contravened and is likely to do so again, any condition or requirement, and the provision made by the order is necessary for the purpose of securing compliance with that condition or requirement.[190] In this way, a provisional order may be used in situations of serious contravention where loss or damage is likely to occur before the procedures for making a final order are complete. It takes immediate effect for a maximum of three months[191] unless confirmed under the specified procedures. By contrast, final orders do not take effect until the procedural requirements have been followed.

Although the requirement in section 20(1) to take steps towards making a final order is a positive duty of the Secretary of State or the Director, they may exercise a discretion not to do so in three situations.[192] Firstly, where the contravention or apprehended contravention is of a trivial nature. Secondly, where the company in question has given, and is complying with, an undertaking to secure compliance with the condition or duty in respect of which an order may be made. This is an important provision which allows the Secretary of State or Director to agree a compliance programme with an undertaker rather than instigating enforcement procedures. A failure to comply with an undertaking will, however, activate the enforcement procedures in the absence of either of the other two exceptions. The third exception is where the duties imposed on the Secretary of State or the Director by Part I of the Act preclude the making or confirmation of the order. In considering whether to make a provisional or final order, the Secretary of State must also take into account these general duties, which include a requirement to secure that the undertakers' functions are properly carried out and that they are properly able to finance the carrying out of their functions.[193] They are also required to take into account their various environmental and recreational duties.[194] This exception allows the Secretary of State and Director a discretion not to make an enforcement order where they consider these other duties to be paramount.

Copies of any undertakings accepted by the Secretary of State must be given to the Director and made available for public inspection in the Director's register. A copy of the notice must also be published in such manner as the Secretary of State or the Director considers appropriate to bring it to the attention of persons likely to be affected by it.[195]

Where any act or omission constitutes a contravention of a condition of appointment or of a statutory requirement enforceable under section 20, no other remedies are available in respect of that act or omission unless express provision is made.[196] This is consistent with general case law, where courts have been slow to intervene where the statute itself provides a remedy or method of enforcement,[197] although it would not necessarily prevent a civil action being sought for breach of a statutory duty. Undertakers have a right to challenge the making of an order on the grounds that the Secretary of State or Director had no powers in that situation to make an order (ultra vires) or that there was a failure to comply with the procedural requirements.[198] Whether third parties could challenge a decision not to make an order is open to question, particularly with respect to the more general duties such as those relating to environmental and recreational matters. Not all persons are given the right to apply for a judicial review by the courts. As a recent judgment has indicated:[199]

The court would look at the matter to which the application related and the statute under which the decision was taken and decide whether that statute gave that individual expressly or impliedly a greater right than any other citizen to have that decision taken lawfully. We all expected our decision makers to act lawfully. We were not all given the rights to apply for judicial review.

The obligation to comply with a final or provisional order is, however, a duty owed to any person who may be affected by a contravention of the order. Any breach of this duty which causes a person to sustain loss or damage is actionable at the suit of that person.[200] In any such proceedings brought against any company[201] it is a defence for the company to show that it took all reasonable steps and exercised all due diligence to avoid contravening the order.[202]

In addition to any right for a person to bring an action, the Director or the Secretary of State, as the enforcement authority, may institute civil proceedings for an injunction or other appropriate relief for either a contravention or apprehended contravention, or with respect to the contravention or a provisional order before it is confirmed.[203] Extreme default, contraventions or likely contraventions of final orders or confirmed provisional orders constitute one ground for applying to the High Court for a special administration order.[204]

The procedural requirements before making a final order or confirming a provisional order are set out in section 21. Notice must be given stating that an order is proposed and what the effect of the order will be. It must specify a period of at least twenty-eight days within which representations or objections may be made[205] and the Director or Secretary of State is then required to consider such representations or objections.

The notice is to be published in such manner as the Secretary of State or the Director considers appropriate to bring it to the attention of persons likely to be affected, and a copy must be sent to the company in question.[206] It must also be made available for public inspection by placing it on the Director's register.[207] Further notice and opportunity for representations must be given where it is proposed to make modifications to any order, unless the company in question agrees to the modifications.[208]

As soon as practicable after making a final order or confirming a provisional order, the Secretary of State or the Director must serve a copy on the company in question and publish a copy of it, in order to bring it to the attention of persons likely to be affected by it.[209] Similar requirements of notice and rights to make representations and objections apply where it is proposed to revoke an order.[210] Once made or confirmed, all enforcement orders must be made available for public inspection in the Director's Register.[211] The requirements of this section may be dispensed with where the Secretary of State so directs in the interests of national security.[212]

If any company to which an order made under section 20 relates is aggrieved by the order, it may, within forty-two days of the date of service on if of a copy of the order, apply to the High Court, but only on the grounds that the making or confirmation of the order was not within the powers conferred by section 20, or that the requirements of section 21 have not been complied with.[213] Where the High Court is satisfied that the making or confirmation of the order was not within those powers or that the interests of the company have been substantially prejudiced by a failure to comply with those requirements, it may quash the order or any provision of the order.[214] An application to a court does not affect the operation of a provisional order because it will already have taken effect before confirmation. It also appears that a final order remains valid until held otherwise by a court.[215] On the question of whether an order was within the powers conferred by section 20, it is obviously more difficult to challenge the validity of a provisional order. In the former case the court need only be satisfied that the Secretary of State or Director made such provision 'as appeared to him' requisite for the purposes of securing compliance with the condition or requirement in question.[216] In the case of a final or confirmed order, the court can apply a more objective test, in that an order must make 'such provision as is requisite' for securing compliance with the condition or requirement.[217] The validity of any order may not be questioned in any legal proceedings except as provided under this section.[218]

The Secretary of State or the Director may, for enforcement purposes, by notice require any person to provide him or her with specified information or to furnish specified documents,[219] unless those documents or that information could not be required or produced in civil proceedings in the High Court.[220] It is an offence intentionally to alter, suppress or destroy any document, or to fail, without reasonable excuse, to do anything required by such a notice.[221] In addition, the High Court may make an order requiring any default to be made good.[222] Further powers are given to the Secretary of State to require undertakers to furnish information with respect to their functions and those of the Secretary of State,[223] and the Instrument of Appointment of each undertaker also contains provision for the supply of information to the Director.[224]

2.6   Special administration orders

In certain circumstances the Secretary of State, or, with his consent, the Director, may petition the High Court for a special administration order in respect of a particular company.[225] This is the ultimate sanction against an undertaker which is unable to carry out its functions or to comply with its obligations under the Act, and enables the transfer of a sufficient part of the undertaking as a going concern to a replacement appointee to enable it to carry on the statutory functions.[226] During the period for which the order is in force, the affairs, business and property of the company are managed by a special administrator appointed by the Court in such a way as to achieve the purposes of the order and in such a manner that the respective interests of the members and creditors of the company are protected.[227] The government may offer financial assistance in the form of grants or loans to a company while an order is in force.[228] A petition for an administration order may be made in the following circumstances:[229]

1.   There has been, is or likely to be such serious default on the part of the company in relation to the general duties of water supply or the provision of sewerage services as to make it inappropriate for the company to continue to hold its appointment.[230]
2.   There has been, or is likely to be such a serious contravention of any order made under section 20, as to make it inappropriate for the company to continue to hold its appointment.
3.   The company is unable to pay its debts within the meaning of the Insolvency Act 1986.
4.   The Secretary of State has certified that it would be appropriate for him or her to petition for the winding up of the company under the Companies Act 1985 but for the restrictions on winding up in section 24.
5.   The company is unable or unwilling adequately to participate in arrangements relating to the termination or variation of an appointment certified necessary by the Secretary of State or Director.[231]
6.   Where an application has been made for the winding up of an undertaker, a court may make a special administration order, in circumstances where it would have granted winding up but for the restriction in section 24.[232]

Where a company holds an appointment as a water or sewerage undertaker, it may not be wound up voluntarily, no administration order may be made under Part II of the Insolvency Act 1986, and no person may enforce any security over the company's property except where that person has served fourteen days' notice of his or her intention to do so on the Secretary of State and the Director.[233] This latter requirement gives the Secretary of State opportunity to apply for an administration order.

The Act modifies the provisions of the Insolvency Act 1986 to apply to administration orders and substitutes those procedures for winding up procedures under Part II of that Act. It provides for transitional measures including schemes for the transfer of property rights and liabilities.[234]

2.7   Ownership and finances

All the property, rights and liabilities of the ten water authorities, except those which were transferred to the NRA, were transferred to nominated successor companies[235] which were appointed water undertakers and sewerage undertakers for their areas.[236] In cases of serious default or insolvency they will be subject to a special administration order regime,[237] but, as such a regime should not apply to activities not directly carried out in furtherance of water and sewerage duties, a corporate structure has been established.[238] Initially, the structure consisted of the appointed successor company for each water authority and a holding company which was put in place over it. The holding company is able to set up other companies, enterprise subsidiaries, within its group structure and transfer the appropriate assets to them by intra-group transfers. A condition[239] of each successor company's Instrument of Appointment ensures that it will always retain the assets it needs to provide its core services.

This corporate structure reflects the policy that the core activities of the provision of water supply and sewerage services be regulated under the Act, while also allowing the companies to engage in other commercial activities if they wish. Only the successor companies are regulated by the Act and the conditions in their Instruments of Appointment as undertakers, while the holding companies and any other subsidiaries fall outside the regulatory scope of the Act. On the public flotatation in late 1989 shares were only issued in the nominated holding companies.

Chapter V of the Act contains provisions relating to the procedures and financial arrangements for the flotation of the water authorities. Prior to flotation, provision was made for the capital structure to be adjusted by the issue of shares and debentures and the write-off of debt.[240] Provision was also made for Government financial assistance to be given to the group companies prior to flotation, the transfer of liability for the principal of National Loans Fund debt from the successor company to its nominated holding company,[241] and the issue of debentures by a successor company to its nominated holding company.[242] The National Loans Fund debt could then be written off.[243]

The Government may invest in securities of the nominated holding companies,[244] but, as with previous privatisations, the Government is prevented from buying back shares above a certain limit (the target investment limit) as fixed by the Secretary of State.[245] The initial order must be made within six months of flotation and the limit must not exceed 0.5 per cent of the proportion of ordinary voting rights held by the Government at that time. Subsequent orders must contain limits less than that amount, making re-nationalisation of the water industry by a future Government not possible without the passing of primary legislation.

Other provisions put the companies on fair terms with each other and with other companies in terms of accounting provisions and tax,[246] enable composite listing of particulars of holding companies so that they were able to be offered for sale separately without needless repetition of common particulars,[247] provide the Government with powers to determine the capital structure for flotation,[248] and provide a temporary limit on borrowing for each group of companies prior to flotation.[249]

2.8   Statutory water companies

The Act provides for the continuation of the twenty-nine statutory water companies, established by Private Acts of Parliament in the nineteenth century, as water undertakers for their areas of supply. The original Acts, local Acts and statutory orders have in the past subjected statutory water companies to strict financial controls on their powers to borrow money, raise capital and pay dividends and interest to shareholders. These controls were designed to restrain shareholders from abusing their monopoly position.

General powers are given to statutory water companies appointed as water undertakers for any area to do anything (whether in their area of appointment or not) which, in the opinion of the company is calculated to facilitate, or is conducive or incidental to, the carrying out of its water supply functions.[250]

Previous limits on the amount of capital that may be raised or borrowed by a statutory water company, and the limits on the dividends payable on shares or stock in the company, may be modified (or removed) to such an extent as is approved by a special resolution of the company.[251] A special resolution is defined as passed by a majority of at least three-quarters of the members of the company who vote (in person or by proxy) at a meeting of which at least twenty-one days' notice, specifying the intention to propose the resolution, has been duly given.[252] Where there is a division of shares or stock of a company into different classes, any modification or removal of a limit must be approved by at least three-quarters, in nominal value, of the members of the company holding shares or stock of that class.[253] In relation to any such modification the holders of at least 15 per cent of issued shares or stock of any class of the company may apply to the High Court to have the modification cancelled on the grounds of unfair prejudice.[254]

The former restrictions on the payment of interest on sums borrowed, the maintenance of reserve and contingency funds, the application of profits and the methods by which shares may be issued, have been removed.[255]

Subject to the approval by order of the Secretary of State, a statutory water company may by special resolution, in accordance with the provisions of the Companies Act 1985, convert to a public limited company.[256] Where a special resolution has been passed converting a statutory water company to PLC status, an application for the resolution to be cancelled may be made to the High Court within twenty-one days:[257]

(a) by the holders of at least 15 per cent, in nominal value, of the company's issued share capital or issued stock; or
(b) if the resolution varies the rights attached to any class of shares or stock, by the holders of at least 15 per cent of the issued shares or stock of that class; or
(c) if the resolution includes a modification of the company's objects, by the holders of at least 15 per cent of such of the company's debentures as entitle the holders to object to such a modification.

The High Court is given wide powers to deal with an application, although, in contrast to section 98, it is given no guidance on how those powers should be exercised.

2.9   Provision and acquisition of information

There is a general restriction on the disclosure of information[258] which has been obtained by virtue of any of the provisions of the Water Act and which relates to the affairs of any individual or to any particular business. Such information may not be disclosed during the lifetime of that individual, or so long as that business continues to be carried on, without the consent of that individual or the person for the time being carrying on that business.[259]

Exceptions are made for the disclosure of information made to enable the carrying out of the functions of the Secretary of State, the Minister of Agriculture, the NRA, the Director General of Water Services, the Monopolies Commission, and local authorities. Also included are obligations (but not powers) imposed on water and sewerage undertakers and certain duties imposed on the Director. Further exceptions relate to the disclosure of information pursuant to obligations under other legislation, principally with respect to the functions of public bodies, in pursuance of a European Community obligation and for the purposes of civil and criminal proceedings.[260]

A person who discloses information in contravention of this section is guilty of an offence, and liable on summary conviction to a fine not exceeding the statutory maximum and on conviction or indictment to imprisonment for a maximum of two years, an unlimited fine, or both.[261]

Any person who, in furnishing any information or making any application, knowingly or recklessly makes a statement which is false in a material particular, is guilty of an offence and liable on summary conviction to a fine not exceeding the statutory maximum[262] and on conviction or indictment to an unlimited fine.[263]

Where, on a notice given to any person to provide supplementary information in respect of any application or notice under any enactment, and that information is required within a specified period, the failure to provide the information does not of itself invalidate the application or notice made by that person, but the person who has required the supplementary information is entitled to delay taking any action until a reasonable time after the required information is provided.[264]

Undertakers are under a duty to furnish such information to the Secretary of State relating to the carrying out of his or her functions or the functions of undertakers as he or she may require.[265] The conditions of the Instruments of Appointment also contain a number of requirements for undertakers to provide information to the Director.[266] The Secretary of State and the Director are also given wide powers to obtain documents and information for enforcement purposes from any person.[267]

2.10   'Functions' of undertakers

A crucial distinction must be made between the functional and non-functional activities of undertakers operating in the private sector, since most of the duties and powers under the Act only relate to their functional activities.[268] Section 188 extends and defines the meaning of 'functions' as it applies to both the NRA and undertakers under the Water Act and all other enactments.[269] It includes the NRA and undertakers acting jointly or as agents for one another in acquiring land and carrying out works,[270] and undertaking activities such as research, provision of houses, buildings and recreational facilities for employees, and the provision of both supplies of water.[271] The functions of these bodies shall be taken to include protection against pollution of underground and surface waters, reservoirs and underground strata used for abstraction.[272] The purpose of this provision is obscure. It may be that it is intended to impose additional duties on the NRA and undertakers, but in the Act there is no specific method of enforcement. Similarly, if it is intended to confer powers to take such action given the general nature of the provision, it cannot take precedence over the specific provisions in the Act on this subject.

Notes

1. As nominated by the Secretary of State prior to the transfer date, s.4(2).
2. Sch.2, para.1.
3. Under s.126; see below, section 3.8.
4. Sch.2, para.2.
5. Para.3.
6. When he or she is satisfied that nothing further remains to be done by the water authority under any scheme, s.4(5).
7. S.4(4), Sch.2, para.4.
8. S.11(1).
9. S11(2).
10. S.11(3). The areas not included were those areas for which a statutory water company was appointed as a water undertaker.
11. S.11(4).
12. S.11(6) and (7), s.12; see below, section 2.2.14.
13. Ss.15–19; see below, section 2.3.
14. S.14(1).
15. S.14(7).
16. S.14(6).

17. All the conditions included in an instrument have effect, irrespective of their subject matter, as conditions of appointments both as a water undertaker and a sewerage undertaker, s.14(8).
18. The list is contained in the Instrument of Appointment of each undertaker and is available for inspection at the Office of Water Services, Birmingham.
19. See, generally, 'Model instrument of appointment of the water and sewerage undertakers: explanatory notes', DoE and Welsh Office, 1988; 'Water restructuring and privatisation policy: utility company regulation for core services', DoE, 3.3.88.
20. See below, sections 5.6.3.3, 3.10.
21. Compendium Condition B, Part I, para.1.
22. DoE, 3.3.88, para.19.
23. Compendium of Conditions, paras. 4.4 and 4.5.
24. Or such other timetable as the Director General may agree, Compendium Condition B, para.6.
25. Compendium Condition B, para.5.
26. Condition B, para.8.
27. S.7.
28. Para.9.
29. Para.10.
30. Paras. 11 and 12; Condition N; see below, section 2.2.13.
31. Condition B, Part IV.
32. *ibid.*
33. Para.13.2.
34. See below, section 2.5.
35. Para.14.3.
36. Condition B, Part VI.
37. Para.16. The Director's powers to refer a matter to the Monopolies Commission are given in s.16 of the Act, see below, section 2.4.
38. Para.17; ss.15 and 18; see below, section 2.3.
39. Condition C.
40. S.79(2).
41. Condition C, para.2.7.
42. Or, if greater, any amount paid or agreed to be paid to the water authority or the appointee prior to 1 April 1990 in respect of the relevant connection or connections.
43. Para.2.
44. Para.3; see above, section 2.2.1.
45. Paras.3.3 and 3.4.
46. Para.4.
47. Para.5; ss.15 and 18.
48. Condition D.
49. See below, section 3.10.
50. Para.2.1.
51. Para.4.
52. Sch.8, para.3(4).
53. See below, section 3.10.
54. Para.6.
55. Para.5.
56. Condition E.
57. S.7(3)(a).
58. Paras. 4 and 5.
59. Para.6.
60. By virtue of Sch.26, para.16, as if the scheme were made under s.76; see below, section 3.10.2.
61. Under s.46; see below, section 3.1.5.
62. See below, section 5.9.
63. See above, section 2.2.2.
64. Under s.39.

65. Condition F.
66. Meaning any subsidiary or holding company of the undertaker, any subsidiary of any holding company (other than the undertaker itself), and any related company within the meaning of Sch.4, para.92, to the Companies Act 1985, Condition A, para.3.
67. Para.5.
68. Para.6.
69. Para.7.
70. With the exception of intra-group transactions, the basis of allocations and apportionments and certain other internal information.
71. Para.9.
72. Paras. 5.3, 7.3 and 8.1.
73. Para.10.
74. Condition G.
75. Para.1.
76. Para.2.5.
77. Para.6.
78. Para.7.
79. Para.8.
80. Paras. 9–11.
81. Condition H.
82. Para.1.
83. Paras. 2–5.
84. Para.6.
85. Para.8.
86. Condition I.
87. Para.2.
88. Para.7.
89. Condition J; see, generally, 'Water restructuring and privatisation policy: utility company levels of service for core services', DoE, November 1988.
90. See table A.
91. Para.1.2.
92. Para.2.
93. Para.3.
94. See above, section 2.2.1.
95. Para.4.
96. Para.5.
97. S.7.
98. Ss. 38 and 68. Certain service obligations have been imposed by the Water Supply and Sewerage Services (Customer Service Standards) Regulations 1989, see below, section 3.11.3.
99. Under s.20; see above, section 2.5.
100. S.7(2)(b).
101. Ss. 38 and 68.
102. Para.7.
103. Paras. 8 and 9.
104. Para.13.
105. Condition K.
106. See below, section 2.6.
107. Para.3.
108. Para.3.2.
109. Para.3.3.
110. S.189(1).
111. See above, section 2.1.
112. As defined in s.188.
113. Ss. 13 and 23, Sch.5; see below, section 2.6.
114. Which must be signed by all the directors or approved by a duly convened meeting of the board of directors and signed by a director or the secretary confirming that it has

been so approved and having attached to it a certified copy of an extract of the minutes of the relevant meeting containing the resolution to approve the certificate, para.2.1.

115. For the purpose of calculating 'best price', see para.2.2.

116. The undertaker may alternatively furnish a report by a valuer appointed by it stating that in his or her opinion the consideration is the best price that could reasonably be obtained for the protected land in question.

117. 'Interest' includes an entitlement to a share of profits or participation in assets, rights or benefits but excludes any interest which consists solely of an entitlement to receive instalments of consideration, para.4.4.

118. para.4.3.

119. Para.4.6.

120. See below, section 6.3.

121. Para.5.

122. Para.6.

123. The commencement of material works to implement a proposed change of use is deemed to be a change of use.

124. Para.7.

125. Condition L.

126. Para.2.

127. Para.3.

128. Para.4.

129. Para.5.3.

130. Condition M.

131. Paras. 1 and 2.

132. Paras. 3–5.

133. Condition N.

134. Termed 'the renewal fee'.

135. Under Sch.4; see below, section 3.11.2.

136. Termed 'the special fee'.

137. Para.1.

138. Under Condition B.

139. Para.3.

140. Condition O.

141. S.11(6).

142. 'Existing appointee' is defined in s.12(5).

143. S.7(3)(e).

144. S.12(3).

145. S.12(2)(c).

146. S.12(4).

147. This relates to modifications of the conditions of an appointment only and not to modifications of an area of an appointee or charges of the appointee itself; see above, section 2.2.

148. S.15.

149. He or she must publish it in such manner as he or she considers appropriate for the purpose of bringing it to the attention of persons likely to be affected by the making of the modification, s.15(3)(a).

150. S.15(2) and (3).

151. S.15(4) and (5). But only where modification relates to conditions concerning modification or termination of an appointment, the disposal of protected land (see below, section 6.3) or where he or she considers a reference should first be made to the Monopolies Commission.

152. S.16(1). The Water Appointment (Monopolies and Mergers Commission) Regulations 1989, S.I. 1989 No.1162, regulate the procedure of the Commission on such references. They provide for such matters as the time limit for the Commission to report on references, the service of copies and publication of references, and the power of the Commission to require the attendance of witnesses and the production of documents.

153. S.16(4).

154. S.7.
155. S.17(1).
156. S.17(4).
157. S.18(3) and (4).
158. S.18(1). Although he or she need not make the precise modifications recommended by the Commission.
159. S.18(5); see above, section 2.2.10, and below, section 6.3.
160. S.19.
161. S.26. He or she may also obtain information from undertakers and others in connection with his or her enforcement powers under s.33. The conditions of appointment also require undertakers to provide the Director with information to enable him or her to carry out his or her duties; see above, section 2.2.
162. S.26(4).
163. S.26(3).
164. See below, section 2.5.
165. S.28(1).
166. S.28(2)(a).
167. S.28(2)(b).
168. S.28(3).
169. S.28(4) and (6).
170. S.29. Or such other sum as specified in 64(1)(6) of the Fair Trading Act 1973. The £30 million figure may be altered by regulations made by the Secretary of State, in respect of both the amount of or the criteria for valuation of assets, s.28(10).
171. It must be made within six months of the date of the merger, s.30(5).
172. S.30(1).
173. S.30(3). This concept has been termed 'comparative competition' and is seen as a pressure towards corporate efficiency.
174. S.31(2).
175. See below, section 2.5.
176. S.31(4)–(6). The Director General of Water Services' Register (Inspection and Charges) Regulations 1989, S.I. 1989 No.1154, provide that the register shall be open for inspection without charge between 9.30 a.m. and 1 p.m. and 2 p.m. and 4.30 p.m. on weekdays, and that the fee payable for a certified extract or copy is £1 for any number of pages up to and including ten and ten pence for each additional page.
177. S.32(1).
178. S.32(4).
179. S.32(5); see below, section 2.5. Further requirements on undertakers to supply information to the Director are contained in the Instrument of Appointment of each undertaker; see above, section 2.2.
180. S.34(1).
181. S.34(2).
182. S.34(3).
183. S.35.
184. Under s.26(3).
185. S.35(1) and (2).
186. See below, section 3.11.2.
187. S.35(4)–(6).
188. S.20(1) and (2).
189. S.20(3).
190. S.20(4).
191. S.20(9).
192. S.20(5).
193. S.7.
194. S.8; see below, section 6.1.
195. S.20(6). Except where the Secretary of State directs that this requirement should not apply in the interests of national security under s. 170.
196. S.20(10).

197. *Pasmore* v. *Oswaldtwistle Urban District Council* [1988], A.C. 387; *R* v. *Wessex Water Authority, ex p. Cutts* (D.C., 18 March 1988, unreported).
198. S.22(1).
199. *R* v. *Secretary of State for the Environment ex p. Rose Theatre Trust Co., The Independent,* 18 July 1989.
200. S.22(4) and (5).
201. Except proceedings in relation to the duty to supply only wholesome water under s.52(1)(a); see below, section 5.4.
202. S.22(6).
203. S.20(7).
204. Under s.23; see below, section 2.6.
205. S.21(1).
206. S.21(2).
207. S.31(2)(c).
208. S.21(3) and (4).
209. S.21(5).
210. S.21(6)–(8).
211. S.31(2)(c).
212. S.21(9); see s.170.
213. S.22(1).
214. S.22(2).
215. See *Hoffman-la Roche & Co.* v. *Secretary of State for Trade and Industry* [1975], A.C. 295.
216. S.20(2).
217. S.20(1), s.20(4)(b).
218. S.22(3).
219. S.33(2).
220. S.33(3); the general instructions under s.174.
221. S33(4) and (5).
222. S.33(6).
223. S.32.
224. See above, section 2.2.12.
225. S.23(1).
226. S.23(3); see also above, section 2.2.10.
227. S.23(2). A special administrator may pay creditors that existed before an administration order is made, and new creditors arising during the currency of the order, but a conflict of interest may arise, as the administrator is required to ensure the carrying out of the statutory functions of the undertaker. It is a fundamental policy of the Act that there is no disruption of water supply or the provision of sewerage services. In the event of any conflict, priority must be given to the carrying out of the undertaker's statutory functions rather than protecting the interests of members and creditors, and if at all possible assets should be sold as a going concern rather than being split piecemeal.
228. S.25.
229. S.23(4).
230. A petition for an administration order is an alternative to enforcing these duties by way of enforcement order under s.20.
231. S.12(2)(c); see below, section 2.2.14.
232. S.24(2).
233. S.24(1).
234. S.23(5)–(9), Schs. 5 and 6.
235. S.4; see above, section 2.1.
236. S.11; see above, section 2.2.
237. S.23; see above, section 2.6.
238. S.83.
239. Condition K; see above, section 2.2.10.
240. Ss.83, 85 and 86.

241. See the Water Re-organisation (Successor Companies) (Transfer of Loans) Order 1989, S.I. 1989 No.1532.
242. Ss.84 and 85.
243. S.86. On 2 August 1989 the Government announced its 'green dowry' policy, whereby £1,024 million was injected into the ten water companies and £4.4 billion of debt was written off, DoE News Release, 1989/423.
244. Ss.87 and 88.
245. S.89.
246. Ss.91 and 95.
247. S.90.
248. Ss.86, 87, 88 and 93.
249. S.92.
250. S.97.
251. S.98.
252. S.98(10).
253. S.98(3) and (4).
254. S.98(5)–(7).
255. Ss.99 and 100.
256. S.10; see Companies Act 1985 (Modifications for Statutory Water Companies) Regulations 1989, S.I. 1989 No.1461.
257. S.102.
258. Which includes anything contained in any records, accounts, estimates or returns, s.189(1).
259. S.174(1).
260. S.174(2) and (3).
261. S.174(5).
262. Currently £2,000.
263. S.175.
264. S.176.
265. S.32.
266. See particularly above, section 2.2.12.
267. S.33; see above, section 2.5.
268. For example, s.151 (compulsory purchase powers), s.152 (restriction on disposals of land) and s.155 (compulsory works powers) only apply to land acquired after the transfer date within their functions.
269. S.188(1).
270. S.185(2).
271. S.188(4)–(6).
272. S.188(3).

CHAPTER 3

Water supply

Before the enactment of the 1973 Water Act, responsibility for the supply of water lay with water companies, local authorities and joint water boards, which were comprised of local authority representatives. Prior to the reorganisation which took place under that Act, there were 187 undertakers including 29 statutory water companies. Although after 1974 the overall responsibility for water supply was taken over by ten water authorities, the 29 statutory water companies continued to supply water in their own areas on the water authorities' behalf. Local authorities' powers were confined to certain public health responsibilities.

The principal provisions on water supply were contained in the Water Act 1945 (the 'Waterworks Code'), which consisted of a set of model provisions intended to be adopted, with the necessary modifications, by each undertaker in that individual undertaker's local empowering Act. In this way each undertaker had its own code which could differ from that of a neighbouring undertaker. These differences were inherited by the ten water authorities from 1974. As a result, not only was there a lack of uniformity from undertaker to undertaker, but in many areas a variety of statutory requirements applied.

In 1986 the Government released a discussion paper on water and sewerage law and, following consultation, a set of revised proposals for clarifying and modernising water and sewerage law.[1] Many of these proposals have been enacted by the Water Act 1989 and they apply equally to all undertakers. It is intended that, after a transitional period of three years, all local Act variations would be automatically repealed unless demonstrably needed for some purely local reason.

3.1   General duties of water undertakers

3.1.1   WATER SUPPLY

Every water undertaker is under a general duty to develop and maintain an efficient and economical system of water supply within its area, and to ensure that all such arrangements have been made for: (a) providing supplies of water to premises in that area and for making such supplies available to persons who demand them; and (b) maintaining, improving and extending the water undertaker's water mains and other pipes, as are necessary to ensure that it is and continues to be able to meet its obligations.[2]

The NRA has a general duty[3] to conserve and secure the proper use of water resources, but this duty does not relieve water undertakers of the responsibility to develop and use resources in order to fulfil their general duty under this section.[4]

Water undertakers may make agreements between themselves for the transfer of bulk supplies of water. Where undertakers are unable to reach agreement, the Director is given power to order a transfer of water and to determine the conditions under which it is to be made.[5] In doing so, the Director need only have regard to the desirability of the undertaker's recovering the expenses of complying with its obligations under this section and to securing a reasonable return on its capital, but must consult the NRA where such an order could affect any of its functions.[6]

3.1.2   REQUISITIONING OF WATER MAINS

Following a request in the form of a notice served on an undertaker by an owner or occupier of any premises in a particular locality, or by a local authority within whose area the whole or any part of that locality is situated,[7] a water undertaker is under a duty to provide a water main to be used for providing supply of water for domestic purposes. This duty only applies where the premises to which the supply of water would be provided consist or will consist of buildings or parts of buildings, and where certain financial requirements are met.[8]

This duty only relates to the bringing of a water main to a locality and is particularly relevant to developers of housing estates and developments because it will guarantee that water mains will be available in time and at a cost which may be reasonably determinable.

A water main is defined[9] as meaning any pipe vested in an undertaker, which is used or to be used by a water undertaker for the purpose of making a general supply of water available to customers or potential customers of the undertaker, as distinct from for the purpose of providing a supply to particular customers.[10]

The water undertaker must then come to an agreement with the person requiring the provision of the main on the places where service pipes are to be connected to the water main.[11] A 'service pipe' is defined[12] as being so much of a pipe which is, or is to be, connected with a water main and is, or is to be, subject to water pressure from that main, or as would be so subject but for the closing of some valve.

The water undertaker must provide a water main within a period of three months from the determination of the places where service pipes are to connect with the water main, or the date on which the financial requirements are satisfied, whichever is the later.[13]

An undertaker may demand that the person or persons who have required the provision of the main give undertakings which bind them to pay to the undertaker, in respect of each of the twelve years following the provision of the main, an amount not exceeding the relevant deficit (if any) for that year on that main. The relevant deficit is the amount by which the water charges payable for the use during that year of the water main are exceeded by the annual borrowing costs (as calculated over a period of twelve years) on the expenditure reasonably incurred by the water undertaker as if the sum concerned had been borrowed by that water undertaker. The costs reasonably incurred in providing a water main include those in providing such other water mains, tanks, service reservoirs and pumping stations as it is necessary to provide in consequence of the provision of a new main, and a reasonable proportion of the costs incurred in providing any consequential additional capacity in an earlier water main.[14]

A water undertaker may also require security to be provided for the discharge of obligations imposed by the undertakers to be given by the owner or occupier of premises.[15] Where any sums have been deposited with a water undertaker by way of security for the discharge of any obligation, the undertaker must pay interest[16] on the sum at quarterly intervals.[17]

Any dispute between a water undertaker and another person as to the undertakings or security required by that undertaker or the amount required to be paid in pursuance of an undertaking is to be referred to a sole arbitrator.[18]

These requirements relating to water main requisitions do not affect the powers of water authorities to make charges for new connections which reflect the undertakers' increased infrastructure costs of new supplies,[19] but are designed to ensure that undertakers receive the full extra costs incurred by requisitions of water mains.

In relation to water supply the term 'domestic purposes' means water supplied for drinking, washing, cooking, central heating and sanitary purposes. Where the premises are occupied as a house, the expression includes water supplied for the purposes of a profession carried on in that house and for such purposes outside the house (e.g. washing of vehicles and watering of gardens) as are connected with the occupation of the house and may be satisfied by a supply of water drawn from a tap inside the house without the use of a hosepipe. It does not include the use of a bath having a capacity of more than two hundred and thirty litres, the business of a laundry, or of preparing food or drink for consumption otherwise than on the premises.[20]

3.1.3   DUTY TO MAKE CONNECTIONS TO WATER MAINS

It is also the duty of a water undertaker to connect any premises within its area which include a building or a proposed building to an existing water main for the purpose of providing water for domestic purposes at the expense of the owner or occupier of those premises,[21] who serves a notice on it to that effect.[22] The notice must be accompanied or supplemented by all such information as the undertaker may reasonably require and it is the responsibility of the owner or occupier to ensure that a service pipe to the premises is brought to such a position as to enable connection to the water main.[23] The undertaker is then required to make the necessary connections, including, in certain circumstances, the provison of service pipes from the water main to connect with the service pipe provided by the owner or occupier.[24]

A water undertaker may impose certain conditions which must be met prior to the connection of premises to a water main.[25] A condition may be imposed by an undertaker if it serves a counter-notice on an occupier or owner of premises within fourteen days from the date of the service of the original notice,[26] and may include one or more of the following:

1.   That security be provided for the discharge of obligations relating to the repayment of the reasonable costs incurred by the undertaker.
2.   That any outstanding water charges or expenses incurred in the making of a disconnection be paid by the owner or occupier.

3. That a meter[27] for use in determining charges be installed and connected either by the undertaker or in accordance with specifications approved by the undertaker.[28]
4. That pipes and plumbing which are the responsibility of the owner or occupier comply with approved specifications.
5. That separate service pipes be provided to separate houses or buildings or, where different parts of a building are separately occupied, to each of those parts.
6. That in certain circumstances premises be provided with a cistern which has a float-operated valve.[29]
7. That all water fittings are installed and operated correctly in accordance with regulations made by the Secretary of State.
8. That any notice requiring steps to be taken to prevent the recurrence of damage, contamination, waste, misuse or undue consumption of water be complied with.[30]

Where any sums have been deposited with a water undertaker by way of security for the discharge of any obligation, the water undertaker must pay quarterly interest at a rate approved or determined by the Director.[31]

Any dispute between a water undertaker and another person as to the terms of any condition relating to meters or the specifications for service pipes and plumbing is to be referred to a sole arbitrator.[32]

Where a service pipe has already been fully laid when the notice is served on an undertaker, the undertaker has fourteen days to connect the service pipe from the day on which the notice was served or the conditions satisfied, whichever is the latest. Where the undertaker is required to lay a section of service pipe to connect the main to premises,[33] the time period for compliance is generally twenty-one days.

3.1.4   DUTY TO SUPPLY WATER FOR DOMESTIC PURPOSES

In addition to providing a new main and connecting premises to an existing main, a water undertaker is under a duty to provide a domestic supply of water to premises consisting in the whole or any part of a building[34] if, either, those premises were connected to a main prior to 1 September 1989,[35] or a demand for such a supply is made by an owner or occupier of premises newly connected to a main.[36] Until there is an interruption of this duty[37] an undertaker must provide a supply of water to premises as is sufficient for domestic purposes and maintain the connection between the main and the service pipe. This duty does not require an undertaker to provide a supply of water from a trunk main[38] or from a main used solely for water for non-domestic purposes, or while necessary works are being carried out.[39]

Where a demand for a supply of water has been made in relation to premises connected after 1 September 1989, the undertaker may make that supply conditional upon one or more of the following:[40]

1. That any outstanding charges in connection with a supply which has been cut off due to non-payment, have been paid.
2. That, in certain circumstances, premises be provided with a cistern which has a float-operated valve.[41]
3. That all water fittings are installed and operated correctly in accordance with regulations made by the Secretary of State.
4. That any notice requiring steps to be taken to prevent the recurrence of damage, contamination, waste, misuse or undue consumption be complied with.[42]

3.1.5 SUPPLY OF WATER FOR NON-DOMESTIC PURPOSES

Following a request from an owner or occupier, a water undertaker is bound to provide a new supply of water for non-domestic purposes to premises which do not consist of the whole or any part of a building, if this can be done without prejudicing current or probable future obligations to supply water for domestic and non-domestic purposes and probable future obligations to supply water for domestic purposes, or if it can be done without incurring unreasonable expenditure.[43]

Where terms and conditions for the provision of such a supply cannot be agreed upon between the undertaker and a potential customer, or in cases of a dispute over whether the duty is owed or not, the matter will be determined by the Director or by an arbitrator appointed by him or her. Where a charges scheme is in force under section 76, those charges are to be considered conclusive and final and no reference may be made to the Director. In instances where no scheme is in force however, the Director, in determining the appropriate charges, must have regard to the deservability of the undertaker recovering the expenses of complying with its obligations and of securing a reasonable return on its capital.[44]

3.1.6   PROVISION OF WATER FOR FIRE-FIGHTING

At the request of a fire authority or an owner or occupier of a factory or place of business, every water undertaker is under a duty to fix fire hydrants to its mains at appropriate places for the purpose of extinguishing fires.[45]

The expenses incurred in complying with this obligation shall be borne by the fire authority or the owner or occupier of a factory or place of business, as the case may be. The undertaker is required to maintain the fire hydrants and allow any person to take water from them for extinguishing fires. Special provisions relate to charging for water used for fire-fighting.[46]

3.1.7   PROVISION OF WATER FOR OTHER PUBLIC PURPOSES

Subject to reasonable terms and conditions, a water undertaker must supply water from mains or pipes with appropriate capacity[47] for cleansing sewers and drains, cleansing and watering highways and supplying any public pumps, baths or wash-houses.[48] No provision is made for settlement of disputes, although the Director may resolve matters by the exercise of his or her enforcement powers.[49]

3.1.8   CONSTANT SUPPLY AND PRESSURE

In respect of water in a water undertaker's mains or other pipes which are used for providing domestic water supplies or which have fire-hydrants fixed on them, it is the duty of that undertaker to ensure that the water is laid on constantly and at such a pressure as will cause the water to reach the top of the top-most storey of every building within its area.[50] This duty does not require an undertaker to provide a supply of water at a height greater than that to which it will flow by gravitation,[51] or to maintain the constancy or pressure during the carrying out of necessary works.

A water undertaker may require that any premises the supply of water to which need not, in accordance with provisions in the Act or made under the Act, be laid on constantly at pressure,[52] or a house[53] to which water is required to be delivered at a height greater than 10.5 metres below the draw-off level of the supplying service reservoir or tank, be provided with a cistern having a float-operated valve. In the latter case the water undertaker may require that the cistern be capable of holding sufficient water to provide an adequate supply to the house for a period of twenty-four hours.[54]

3.1.9   RECORDS OF UNDERGROUND WORKS

The NRA and every water undertaker must keep records of the location of every resource main,[55] water main, discharge pipe[56] and other underground works[57] vested in it and ensure that such records are available, free of charge and at all reasonable times, for inspection by the public.[58] Until 1 September 1999, a water undertaker need not keep records of any underground works laid or completed before 1 September 1989, unless those particulars were shown on a map kept by the water authority or statutory water company.[59] 'Records' includes computer records and other non-documentary forms, although the information to be made available to the public must be in map form.[60]

Water and sewerage undertakers are required by their Instruments of Appointment to prepare and review underground asset management plans which monitor the performance of their systems and plan the future programmes of repairs, renewals and extensions. Such plans are not available to the public but must be furnished to the Director General of Water Services.

3.2   Enforcement of duties

The duties to provide a water main for the supply of water for domestic purposes,[61] to make a connection to an existing water main for a supply of water for domestic purposes[62] and to supply water for domestic purposes[63] are actionable by the person to whom the duty is owed, if loss or damage occurs as a result of the breach and the undertaker cannot show that all reasonable steps were taken and all due diligence exercised to avoid that breach.[64]

The general duty under section 37 with respect to the provision of water supply, the duties to provide water for fire-fighting and other public purposes,[65] the duty to maintain constancy and pressure of water supplies[66] and the duty to maintain records[67] are enforceable under section 20 of the Act.[68] These duties are not actionable by an individual; they are not owed to a specific person or group of persons. A person who suffers damage as a result of the failure by a water undertaker to fulfil any of these obligations cannot make a claim.[69] The only remedy is to persuade the Secretary of State or, as the case may be, the Director, to exercise his or her powers under section 20.[70]

However, any failure by a water undertaker to comply with a provisional or final order is actionable in civil proceedings by any person who sustains loss or damage as a result of that failure to comply,[71] and is enforceable by the Secretary of State in civil proceedings for an injunction or other appropriate relief.[72] In an action for damages, it is a defence for the undertaker to show that it took all reasonable steps and exercised all due diligence to avoid contravening the order.[73]

The duty to provide a supply of water for non-domestic purposes in certain circumstances[74] is to be treated as a breach of contract by the undertaker, and actionable by civil suit.

In addition to being enforceable under section 20, breaches of the duties to provide a supply of water for fire-fighting purposes and to maintain the constancy and pressure of water supplies constitute criminal offences unless the undertaker can show that it took all reasonable steps and exercised all reasonable diligence to avoid the commission of the offence.[75]

An undertaker which is guilty of an offence is liable on summary conviction in the Magistrates' Court to a fine not exceeding the statutory maximum,[76] or on conviction on indictment in the Crown Court to an unlimited fine.

3.3   Ownership of and responsibility for water supply pipes

Subject to an agreement to the contrary, every relevant pipe[77] which has been laid in exercise of any works powers[78] by the NRA or a water undertaker shall vest in the NRA or the water undertaker which laid or constructed them.[79]

Service pipes[80] from premises to a water main, including that part in a street, are generally the responsibility of their individual owners, or in the case of common supply piples, their joint owners. However, water undertakers are responsible for carrying out repairs at the expense of the owner to service pipes under a street and may also repair individual and common service pipes at the expense of the owner if they suspect that a waste of water is occurring.[81]

Service pipes are often the most problematic aspect of water supply. They have sometimes been installed at a time when demand for water was lower than now, and consequently are inadequately sized for present-day conditions; many are reduced in capacity by internal corrosion or made of unsuitable materials such as lead, and allow leakage through external corrosion. The shared use of common supply pipes often leads to considerable supply difficulties, particularly for customers at the end of such pipes or who live in areas where pressure is generally unsatisfactory.[82]

An exception to service pipes being owned individually or in common by customers occurs where a water undertaker has been required to connect any premises which include a building or a proposed building to an existing water main for the purpose of providing a supply of water for domestic purposes.[83] In this situation, the undertaker is obliged to provide, at the expense of the person requiring the connection, to lay so much of the service pipe as is necessary in a street.[84] In addition, where:

(a) the water main is situated in a street;
(b) the premises consisting of a building together with any land occupied with it abut on the part of the street where the main is situated; and
(c) the service pipe to those premises will enter the premises otherwise than through an outer wall of a building abutting on the street and is to have a stopcock fitted by the undertaker on the premises;

the undertaker is required to lay the service pipe at the expense of the person requiring the connection, in the land between the boundary of the street and that stopcock.[85]

These rules also apply where a main is situated alongside a street, but within eighteen metres of the middle of the street, as if the street included the land between the main and the boundary of the street so long as that land is not part of the premises to be supplied.[86] The general vesting principles also do not apply in cases where the connection is made in consequence of a requirement imposed by a local authority on a private supply of water[87] and the undertaker lays a service pipe in land owned or occupied by a person who is certified by the local authority to have unreasonably refused his or her consent to the laying of the service pipe.[88]

In certain circumstances, a water undertaker may require the provision of a separate service pipe for a house or other building which is separately occupied and which is already supplied with water but does not have a separate service pipe.[89]

A house is defined as meaning any building or part of a building which is occupied as a dwelling-house, whether or not a private dwelling-house, or which, if unoccupied, is likely to be so occupied.[90]

Separate provisions are made where the supply of water to two or more houses was provided before 15 April 1981 wholly or partly by the same service pipe and continues to be so provided. The undertaker may only require the provision of separate service pipes where the pipes have become defective, charges remain unpaid, the house is converted into a larger number of houses, or there has been or is likely to be an interference with the existing service pipe.[91] In other cases, the undertaker may serve a notice on the consumer[92] requiring the provision of a separate service pipe and stating that if the person fails to comply with the notice within three months, it may itself carry out the works and recover the expenses reasonably incurred in doing so from that person.[93]

3.4   Powers to disconnect service pipes and cut off supplies

In certain circumstances, a water undertaker may disconnect a service pipe which is connected to one of its mains,[94] or may otherwise cut off a supply of water to any premises if:

(a) it is reasonable for the disconnection to be made or the supply to be cut off for the purpose of carrying out any necessary works;[95]

(b) the occupier of the premises is liable (whether in his or her capacity as occupier or under any agreement with the undertaker) to pay charges due to the undertaker in respect of the supply of water to these premises, and has failed to do so within seven days of being served with a notice requiring him or her to pay such charges;[96] or

(c) notice specifying the time after which a supply of water to those premises will no longer be required has been served on the undertaker by a consumer and that time has passed.[97]

Where an undertaker cuts off or reduces a supply of water in order to carry out necessary works, it owes a duty to the consumer to carry out those works with reasonable despatch and to ensure that any supply of water for domestic purposes is not interrupted for more than twenty-four hours unless an emergency supply has been made available within a reasonable distance of the premises. Any breach of this duty by an undertaker is actionable in civil proceedings by any person who sustains loss or damage as a result of the breach.[98]

Where an undertaker has served notice on a person requiring payment, and that person within the period of seven days serves a notice on the undertaker that he or she disputes his or her liability to pay the charges in question, the undertaker may not cut off the supply until either, the undertaker is able to enforce a judgment against that person for the payment of the charges, or, that person is in breach of an agreement entered into since the service of the notice, for the purpose of avoiding or settling proceedings by the undertaker for the recovery of those charges.[99]

Undertakers are also bound by their Instruments of Appointment, which require that they have in force an approved code of practice relating to disconnections. The conditions of appointment, which are enforceable by the Director, in effect require the undertaker to obtain a judgment for debt arrears before exercising its powers to disconnect a supply.

Where an undertaker disconnects a service pipe or cuts off a supply to any inhabited house for a period of more than twenty-four hours, it must within forty-eight hours of the time the supply was cut off serve notice that it has cut off that supply on the local authority in whose area the house is situated.[100]

A water undertaker which:

(a) cuts off a supply of water to any premises where it has no power to do so;[101]
(b) in disconnecting any such pipes or cutting off any such supply, fails without reasonable excuse to comply with any statutory requirements in pursuance of which it disconnects the pipe or cuts off the supply; or
(c) fails, without reasonable excuse, to serve a notice on a local authority as required by section 49(8);

commits an offence and is liable, on summary conviction, to a fine not exceeding level 3 on the standard scale.[102]

3.5   Powers to prevent misuse, etc., of water

A water undertaker has the right to exercise certain powers when it has reason to believe that water which has been or is to be supplied is being or is likely to be wasted, or having regard to the purposes for which it is supplied, misused or unduly consumed.[103] It may also exercise its powers where it has reason to believe that damage to persons or property is being or is likely to be caused by any damage to, or any defect in, any water fitting used in connection with the supply of water which is not a service pipe belonging to the undertaker.[104] The powers exercisable by a water undertaker in these circumstances are equivalent to its powers in relation to the prevention of contamination of water.[105]

3.6   Offences in relation to water supply

Any owner[106] or occupier of premises commits an offence if he or she intentionally or negligently causes or allows any water fitting[107] for which he or she is responsible[108] to be or remain out of order, in need of repair, or constructed or used so that water supplied is or is likely to be wasted, or having regard to the purposes for which it is supplied, misused or unduly consumed.[109] Any person who uses water supplied to any premises for a purpose other than the one for which it is supplied to those premises[110] also commits an offence.[111]

A person found guilty of either of these two offences is liable, on summary conviction, to a fine not exceeding level 3 on the standard scale,[112] and the undertaker is entitled to recover from that person a reasonable amount in respect of any water wasted, misused or improperly consumed in the commission of the offence.[113]

The Secretary of State may make regulations for preventing the waste, undue consumption and misuse of water and for securing that water fittings are safe and do not cause or contribute to the erroneous measurement of any water or the reverberation of any pipes.[114]

3.7   Rights and powers of work

In order properly to carry out their functions water and sewerage undertakers need compulsory purchase and works powers. The rights and powers with respect to water supply are in most instances identical to those in respect of sewerage services.

3.7.1   COMPULSORY ACQUISITION

The Secretary of State may authorise[115] a water and sewerage undertaker to purchase land compulsorily anywhere in England and Wales which is required for, or in connection with, the carrying out of its functions.[116]

The procedure for compulsorily acquiring land is laid down in the Acquisition of Land Act 1981,[117] and the Compulsory Purchase Act 1965.[118] The undertaker or the NRA must give notice of the intended acquisition or creation of rights to all persons with an interest in the land in question and must place notices in a newspaper circulating in that locality. If objections are made the Secretary of State may hold a local inquiry before deciding whether to authorise the acquisition of the land or any interests in the land.

Compensation must be paid to persons with an interest in land where that land or an interest in that land is compulsorily acquired. The rules for assessing compensation are contained in the Land Compensation Act 1961,[119] the Compulsory Purchase Act 1965[120] and the Land Compensation Act 1973.[121]

In default of an agreement about compensation between the undertaker and a person with an interest in the land to be acquired, the matter is to be determined by the Lands Tribunal.

3.7.2   WORKS POWERS

Schedule 19 to the Water Act 1989 confers on the NRA and water and sewerage undertakers powers to lay pipes and sewers and carry out related works. The powers conferred on water and sewerage undertakers are exercisable both inside and outside the undertakers' areas.[122]

3.7.2.1 *Street works*[123]

With respect to works undertaken in streets, the NRA and every water and sewerage undertaker has power, for the purpose of carrying out its functions, to do the following:[124]

1. To lay a relevant pipe[125] in, or under or over any street and to keep that pipe there.
2. To inspect, maintain, adjust, repair or alter any relevant pipe.
3. To carry out in a street any such works as are requisite for securing that the water in any relevant waterworks[126] is not polluted or otherwise contaminated.[127]
4. To carry out any works requisite for, or incidental to, the above purposes, including:

    (a) breaking up or opening a street;
    (b) tunnelling or boring under a street;
    (c) breaking up or opening a sewer, drain or tunnel;
    (d) moving or removing earth and other materials;
    (e) erecting and keeping in a street notices indicating the position of accessories for its relevant pipes which are used to control the flow of water in those pipes.

A stopcock fitted to any service pipe in a street must be fitted as near as practicable to the boundary of the street and the highway authority must be consulted prior to the fitting of a stopcock in a highway.[128]

In exercising these powers, it is the duty of the NRA and every undertaker to do as little damage as possible and to pay compensation for any loss caused or damage done in the exercise of those powers.[129] Any dispute as to whether compensation should be paid or the amount of such compensation is to be determined by a single arbitrator appointed by agreement between the parties to the dispute or, in default of agreement, by the Secretary of State.[130]

In carrying out street works, the bodies must give notice to the relevant highway authority specifying the works to be undertaken, whereupon the highway authority is to specify what requires to be done to protect the authority's apparatus, at the undertaker's or the NRA's expense.[131] In addition, the undertaker must obtain consent for proposed works with respect to a street[132] under the control or management of or maintained by a railway company[133] or navigation authority,[134] or which forms part of a level crossing.[135]

Failure to obtain the necessary consent before carrying out such works is a criminal offence and carries a penalty on summary conviction of a fine not exceeding level 3 on the standard scale.[136]

3.7.2.2 Works in relation to certain undertakings

The various works powers conferred on undertakers may only be exercised in relation to certain undertakings with the consent of persons carrying on those undertakings if the works will either interfere with and adversely affect, directly or indirectly, works or property vested in those persons, and the use of such works or property,[137] or prejudice the exercise of any statutory power conferred on those persons.[138]

The relevant undertakings are the following:[139]

1.   The undertakings of the National Rivers Authority, the Civil Aviation Authority, the British Coal Corporation and the Post Office.
2.   The undertaking of any water undertaker or sewerage undertaker.
3.   Any undertaking consisting in the running of a telecommunications code system within the meaning of Schedule 4 of the Telecommunications Act 1984.[140]
4.   Any airport to which Part V of the Airports Act 1986 applies.
5.   The undertaking of any public gas supplier within the meaning of Part 1 of the Gas Act 1986.
6.   The undertaking of the Central Electricity Generating Board or of any Area Board or their successors under the Electricity Act 1989.
7.   The undertaking of any navigation, harbour or conservancy authority or of any internal drainage board.[141]
8.   The undertaking of the British Railways Board, London Regional Transport or any other person authorised by any enactment to construct, work or carry on a railway.

9.   Any public utility undertaking carried on by a local authority.[142]

Before any power is exercised which interferes with any sluices, floodgates, groynes, sea defences or other works used for draining, preserving or for improving any land under any local statutory provision, and for irrigation purposes, consent must be obtained from any person who uses them.[143]

A consent by any of those bodies or persons may be given subject to reasonable conditions, but may not be unreasonably withheld.[144] Any dispute as to whether anything done or proposed to be done interferes or will interfere with an undertaking, whether any consent is being unreasonably withheld, or whether a condition attached to a consent is reasonable, is to be determined by a single arbitrator.[145]

3.7.2.3 Works on private land

In relation to land other than streets, the NRA and water and sewerage undertakers have powers to lay relevant pipes (whether above or below the surface) and to keep those pipes there, to inspect, maintain, adjust, repair or alter any such pipes, to carry out all such works as are requisite for securing that the water in any relevant waterworks is not polluted or otherwise contaminated,[146] and to carry out any works requisite for, or incidental to, the purposes of such works.[147]

A water undertaker may only lay a service pipe in private land where there is already a service pipe laid or it is required to lay the pipe under section 42.[148]

The powers to inspect, repair, etc., a service pipe are exercisable irrespective of the person to whom the pipe belongs, but the expenses incurred in exercising those powers are recoverable from the person to whom the pipe belongs only if and to the extent that that person has agreed to pay them.[149]

The powers in relation to private land may only be exercised after reasonable notice has been given to the owner and occupier of the land where the power is to be exercised.[150] The minimum period capable of constituting reasonable notice is three months, where the power is exercised for the purpose of laying a relevant pipe (unless it is laid in substitution for an existing pipe of the same description), or forty-two days, where the power is exercised for the purpose of altering an existing pipe.[151] These specified minimum periods do not apply, in the case of any notice given before 1 September 1990, to the exercise of powers in an emergency, or to any notice given for the purpose of laying or altering a service pipe or complying with a duty to provide a water main[152] or sewer.[153]

The owner or occupier on whose land any work is undertaken may not object to the exercise of these powers, but may claim compensation in certain circumstances, in the following cases:[154]

1. If the value of any interest in any relevant land is depreciated by virtue of the exercise of the powers. The person entitled to that interest is entitled to compensation from the NRA or undertaker who carried out the works of an amount equal to the amount of depreciation.

2. Where the person entitled to any interest in land sustains loss or damage through the exercise of the powers where that loss or damage would entitle him to compensation for disturbance, if his interest in that land had been compulsorily acquired under section 151.[155]

3. For any damage to or injurious affection of any other land which is not land where the power is exercised on land held with that land.

Any question of disputed compensation is to be referred to the Lands Tribunal.[156]

Where any person is entitled to compensation, that compensation is off-set by any enhancement in the value of the interest in that land, or any other land which is contiguous or adjacent to that land and is land to an interest in which that person is entitled in the same capacity.[157] Thus, in *Rush & Tompkins Ltd.* v. *West Kent Sewerage Board* (1963) 14 P & CR 469, a compensation figure of £1,480 for laying a sewer was cancelled out by the enhancement of the value of the applicant's land by some £3,800, because the construction of the sewer made the land more readily saleable as industrial land.

The Secretary of State may make regulations requiring the NRA or undertakers to make advance payments on account of compensation that will become payable in respect of the exercise of their powers.[158]

The Director General of Water Services is under a duty to investigate any complaint made or referred to him or her with respect to the exercise of works powers by an undertaker on private land.[159] He or she need not investigate any such complaint if it appears to him or her to be vexatious or frivolous, he or she is not satisfied that the complaint has been brought to the attention of the undertaker and that undertaker has been given a reasonable opportunity of investigating and dealing with it, or the complaint was first made to him or her or a customer service committee more than twelve months after the exercise of the powers in question first came to the notice of the complainant.[160] Where the Director investigates such a complaint, the undertaker must provide the Director with all such information and assistance as he or she may reasonably require[161] and the Director must consider any representations made by the undertaker or the complainant.[162] If, after investigation, the Director is satisfied that the undertaker has failed adequately to consult the complainant about the exercise of its powers or has acted unreasonably so as to cause the complainant to sustain loss or damage or be subjected to inconvenience, he or she may direct the undertaker to pay to the complainant an amount up to a maximum of £5,000 in respect of that failure, loss, damage or inconvenience.[163] The Director may not direct an undertaker to make a payment in respect of which compensation is otherwise payable, unless the amount of any such compensation fails to reflect the fact that it was not reasonable for the complainant to be caused such loss, damage or inconvenience.[164]

Following its appointment, every undertaker was required to submit to the Secretary of State for his approval a code of practice with respect to its exercise of works powers on private land.[165]

The Secretary of State may at any time, by regulations, approve any code of practice or any modifications of that code submitted to him or her, or withdraw his or her approval.[166] In doing so he or she is bound by the general duties imposed on him or her[167] and must consult with such persons as he or she considers appropriate. A contravention of the code of practice does not affect the various works powers, is not enforceable under section 20, nor does it of itself give rise to any civil or criminal liability, but is to be taken into account by the Director in any determination of a complaint.[168]

3.7.2.4 Other works powers

The NRA or an undertaker may only carry out works below the high water mark in accordance with and subject to such restrictions as may, before the works are commenced, have been approved by the Secretary of State, in a notice to that effect.[169]

Where the NRA or a water undertaker is exercising any of its works powers or carrying out the construction, alteration, repair, cleaning or examination of any reservoir, well, borehole or other work belonging to or used by it, it may cause the water in any relevant pipe or in any such reservoir, etc. to be discharged into any available watercourse.[170]

In so doing it must:

(a) cause as little loss[171] and damage as possible in the exercise of such powers;

(b) pay compensation for any loss caused or damage done in the exercise of those powers;[172]

(c) take all necessary steps to secure that any water discharged by it is as free as may be reasonably practicable from mud and silt; solid, polluting, offensive or injurious substance; and any substances prejudicial to fish or spawn, or to spawning beds or food of fish.[173]

If the NRA or a water undertaker fails to take all such necessary steps it commits an offence and is liable, on summary conviction, to a fine not exceeding level 3 on the standard scale.[174]

These powers to discharge water do not authorise a discharge which damages or injuriously affects the works or property of any railway company or navigation authority, or floods or damages any high-way,[175] but they provide a defence to a prosecution of an offence of pollution of controlled waters.[176]

Except in an emergency, no discharge may be made through any pipe with a diameter exceeding 229 millimetres unless a specified procedure is followed.[177] In the case of a discharge by the NRA, consent must be obtained in such manner as may be prescribed. In the case of a discharge by a water undertaker, consent must be obtained from the NRA and any navigation authority which carries out functions in relation to the part of the watercourse where the discharge is made or within three miles downstream from the discharge.[178]

Any person who is an occupier of premises which abut on any watercourse or is an officer of an association of owners or occupiers of such premises may request that their name and address be entered in a register kept by the NRA and every water undertaker pursuant to these requirements.[179] Where an application is made for a consent to discharge, it must be accompanied and supplemented by all reasonable information and the applicant must serve a copy of the application and any consent given on that application to every person who is registered with the applicant in respect of any premises within three miles downstream from the proposed discharge.[180] However, there is no provision for such persons to make objections or representations.

A consent may be related to a particular discharge or to discharges of a particular description and may be made subject to reasonable conditions, but a consent may not be reasonably withheld.[181]

An application with respect to a particular discharge must be determined within a period of seven days from the day the application was made, but if not so determined, the consent applied for shall be deemed to be given unconditionally. Applications for consent in other cases must be determined within three months from the day the application was made.[182] Any dispute as to whether or not a consent should be given or over the reasonableness of conditions is to be referred to the arbitration of a single arbitrator.[183]

Where any such discharge is made in an emergency the NRA or water undertaker must, as soon as practicable after making the discharge, serve a notice on every person to whom it would have been required to serve an application for consent, stating that the discharge has been made and giving such particulars of it and of the emergency as the persons served with the notice might reasonably require.[184] A failure to comply with the requirements of paragraph 9 of Schedule 19 (consents for discharges) or of any condition of a consent is an offence and renders the offender liable to a fine not exceeding level 3 on the standard scale.[185]

3.7.3   POWERS IN RELATION TO LAND

Where the NRA or a water undertaker proposes to carry out any engineering or building operations[186] or to discharge water into any inland water or underground strata, it may apply to the Secretary of State[187] for an order conferring compulsory powers with respect to these matters.[188] Such an order may:

(a) confer power compulsorily to acquire land, including power to acquire interests in and rights over land by the creation of new rights and interests, and power to extinguish any such rights;[189]
(b) apply any of the powers in relation to land and works powers (under Part IV of the Act) which would not otherwise apply;
(c) amend or repeal any local statutory provision;[190]
(d) make any authority granted by the order subject to conditions, and contain such supplemental, consequential and transitional provision as the Secretary of State considers appropriate.[191] Nothing in an order may exempt the NRA or a water authority from restrictions imposed in relation to the abstraction and impounding of water under Part IV of the Water Resources Act 1963;[192]
(e) grant authority for discharges of water by the NRA or a water undertaker where they have no powers to take water or require discharges to be made, from the inland water or other source from

which the discharges authorised by the order are intended to be made.[193]

The procedure with respect to application for and consideration of such orders is specified in Schedule 20. The applicant must submit a draft order to the Secretary of State, publish notices containing specified information with respect to the application in the London Gazette and a local newspaper circulating in the relevant locality, and serve a copy of the notice on specified persons and authorities.[194]

The notice must specify where a copy of the draft order may be inspected free of charge within twenty-eight days of the first publication of the notice and state that any person may, within that period, by notice to the Secretary of State, object to the making of the order.[195] The Secretary of State must consider any objections received by him or her[196] within the specified time period, either by causing a local inquiry to be held, or affording to the objector and to the applicant an opportunity of appearing before and being heard by a person appointed by him or her for that purpose.[197] The Secretary of State may then determine the application either by making the order in the terms applied for, or with such modifications as he or she thinks fit, or refusing the application. However, he or she may not make any modifications which he or she considers likely to adversely affect any persons unless he or she is satisfied that additional notice has been given by the applicant.[198]

As soon as practicable after an order has been made, the applicant must publish a notice of the making of the order in a local newspaper containing specified particulars, and serve copies on certain persons and authorities.[199] The various enactments relating to compulsory acquisition are to apply to an order made under this section with adaptations relating to the right of a person aggrieved to question the validity of an order conferring powers of compulsory acquisition in the High Court.[200] Compensation is payable in respect of depreciation, loss, damage or injurious affection caused by the exercise of powers pursuant to an order[201] and provision is made for the assessment of that compensation.[202]

The NRA and water and sewerage undertakers have power to make byelaws with respect to any waterway[203] owned or managed by them and with respect to any land held or managed with the waterway.[204] The NRA may also exercise such powers with respect to any inland waters,[205] and associated land, to which there is a public right of navigation, if navigation is not for the time being subject to the control of any navigation, harbour or conservancy authority, or where such an authority is unable for the time being to carry out its functions.[206] Such byelaws may be used for the following purposes:[207]

1. The preservation of order on or in any such waterway, waters or land.
2. The prevention of damage to anything on or in any such waterway, waters or land, or to any such land.
3. Securing that persons resorting to any such waterway, waters or land so behave as to avoid undue interference with the enjoyment of the waterway, waters or land by others.

More particularly the byelaws may do the following:

1. Regulate sailing, boating and fishing and other forms of recreation.
2. Prohibit the use of the waterway or inland waters in question by boats which are not registered in accordance with the byelaws, and make reasonable charges in respect of the registration of such boats.
3. Require the provision of such sanitary appliances as may be necessary for preventing pollution.[208]
4. Provide for a contravention of the byelaws to constitute a summary offence punishable on summary conviction in a Magistrates' Court, by a fine to a maximum of level 5 on the standard scale.[209]

The NRA has similar powers to make byelaws preventing the use of boats and other recreational uses on inland waters[210] and in respect of waterways.[211]

Byelaws made under this section by a water and sewage undertaker are to cease to have effect at the end of ten years from the day on which they were made, but the Secretary of State may, by order, provide for them to continue for a specified period.[212]

Special rules apply with respect to the acquisition of mineral rights by the NRA and undertakers and with respect to the working of mines and minerals where pipes, sewers or other related works are affected.[213]

The NRA or undertaker, in compulsorily acquiring any land, is not entitled to any mines or minerals lying under that land unless it is specifically provided for in the conveyance or compulsory order.[214]

Where the owner of any mines or minerals underlying any

works or undertakings proposes to work those mines or minerals, he or she must give notice of his or her intention to do so to the NRA or undertaker at least thirty days before commencing work. After receipt of the notice, the NRA or the undertaker may have the mines or minerals inspected to determine whether the working of the underlying mines or minerals is likely to damage any part of their undertaking. If so, they may serve a notice to this effect on the owner within the period of thirty days and pay compensation[215] to the owner of the minerals for any restriction imposed.[216] If any damage is caused by the working of the mines or minerals otherwise than as authorised, the owner must repair the damage forthwith or repay the NRA or undertaker for expenses incurred in so repairing it.[217]

A person designated by the NRA or an undertaker may enter land or mines to carry out inspections or undertake works.[218]

Any person with an interest in land may require an undertaker to remove or alter the location of mains and other pipes which would otherwise interfere with the development of that or adjacent land.[219] The undertaker must comply with any such reasonable requirement[220] but is entitled to recover the costs of any resulting works from the person serving the notice.[221]

3.7.4   OFFENCE OF INTERFERENCE WITH WORKS, ETC.

Subject to certain defences, any person who, without the consent of the NRA or a water undertaker:

(a) intentionally or recklessly interferes with any resource main, water main or other pipe, or any structure, installation or apparatus[222] belonging to the NRA or the undertakers; or
(b) by any act or omission negligently interferes with any such property or work so as to damage it or to affect its use or operation,

is guilty of an offence and liable, on summary conviction, to a fine not exceeding level 3.[223]

It is a defence to show that the act or omission was done in an emergency to prevent loss or damage to persons or property or, with respect to the opening or closing of a stopcock, the consent of every affected consumer has been obtained and, in the case of opening a stopcock, that that stopcock was closed by a person other than the undertaker.[224]

A further offence is committed where any person, without the consent of the NRA or water undertaker:

(a) attaches any pipe or apparatus to a main or pipe vested in or used by the NRA or a water authority;
(b) makes any alteration in a service pipe or in any apparatus attached to any such pipe; or
(c) uses any pipe or apparatus which has been attached or altered in contravention of (b).[225]

Both of these offences also constitute the breach of a duty owed to the NRA or water undertaker, and any such breach which causes loss or drainage is actionable in civil proceedings by the NRA or water undertaker.[226]

3.7.5 POWERS OF ENTRY TO PREMISES, ETC.

Any person designated in writing by the NRA or an undertaker may enter the premises for any of a number of specified purposes. Entry may be made:

(a) to determine whether it would be appropriate for the NRA or the undertaker to acquire any land or any right over land or any right over land for purposes connected with their functions;
(b) to determine whether it would be appropriate for the NRA or the undertaker to apply for an order conferring compulsory powers for carrying out works under section 155.[227]

For these purposes the designated officer is empowered:[228]

(a) to carry out experimental borings or other works for the purpose of ascertaining the nature of the sub-soil, the presence of underground water in the sub-soil or the quantity or quality of any such water;
(b) to install and keep monitoring or other apparatus on the premises; and
(c) to take away and analyse samples of water, land or articles.

These powers may not be exercised to determine whether, where or how a reservoir should be constructed, or whether, where or how a borehole should be sunk for the purpose of abstracting water from or discharging water into any underground strata, unless the Secretary of State has given his or her written authorisation. Before giving an authorisation the Secretary of State must be satisfied that notice of the proposal has been given to the owner and occupier of the premises in question, and must have considered any representations or objections made to him or her by those persons within fourteen days of receipt of the notice.[229]

Further powers of entry are given in paragraph 10 of the Schedule 19 to the Act. Entry may be made:[230]

(a) to carry out any survey or test to determine whether it is appropriate and practicable for the NRA or an undertaker to exercise any power conferred by the Schedule, and how any such power should be exercised; and

(b) to exercise any power conferred by the Schedule.

The power to carry out surveys and tests includes the power to carry out experimental borings and to take away and analyse samples of water, effluent, land or articles.

Further power of entry is conferred for the purpose of carrying out tests and undertaking work in relation to the installation, maintenance, etc., of meters.[231]

Except in an emergency,[232] or where a warrant has been obtained from a justice of the peace,[233] none of these powers of entry may be exercised except at a reasonable time and after seven days' notice of the intended entry has been given to the occupier of the premises.[234]

Powers of entry are also given with respect to the prevention of damage, contamination and waste of water supplies,[235] and to the exercise of trade effluent functions by a sewerage undertaker.[236]

Any person designated in writing by the Secretary of State, the Minister of Agriculture or the NRA, may enter any premises or vessel to ascertain whether any provision of any enactment, subordinate legislation, instrument or byelaw is or has been contravened, and to determine whether and if so, in what manner, any power or duty imposed on them should be exercised or performed. The designated person may carry out inspections, measurements and tests on any entered premises or vessel, take away samples of water, effluent, land or articles, carry out experimental borings or other works, install and keep monitoring or other apparatus there, and exercise any power or duty conferred on the Secretary of State, the Minister or the NRA.[237]

Except in an emergency, or where a warrant has been obtained from a justice of the peace, entry may not be made except at a reasonable time, but no prior notice need be given unless the premises or vessel is used for residential purposes, or the entry is to be with heavy equipment, where seven days' notice of the intended entry must be given to the occupier.[238] These powers of entry apply to all functions of the NRA contained in the Water Act or other enactments.[239]

Powers of entry are also given to local authorities in relation to monitoring of water supplies,[240] to Drinking Water Inspectors,[241] to persons designated in regulations made to prevent contamination, waste, etc., with respect to water fittings[242] and to designated persons for purposes connected to mining operations.[243]

The Act gives powers to officers of the NRA or undertakers to apply to a justice of the peace for a warrant authorising a designated person to exercise certain powers of entry in relation to specified powers and in accordance with the warrant and, if need be, by force, where:

(a) the exercise of the power in relation to the premises has been refused; or
(b) such a refusal is reasonably apprehended;[244]
(c) the premises are unoccupied; or
(d) the occupier is temporarily absent from the premises;
(e) an application for admission to the premises would defeat the object of the proposed entry.[245]

A warrant continues in force until the purposes for which the warrant was issued have been fulfilled.[246] The exercise of the power of entry pursuant to a warrant is controlled by section 179. A person so entering must produce evidence of his or her designation and other authority, must leave the premises as effectually secured against trespassers as he or she found them, and must pay full compensation to any person who has sustained loss or damage as a result of the entry.[247]

Any person who intentionally obstructs another person acting in the exercise of any power under a warrant commits an offence.[248]

Any person who, without having been designated or authorised, purports to be entitled to enter any premises in exercise of any power commits an offence.[249]

3.8   Water resources

The NRA is under a general duty to take such action as it considers necessary or expedient, and, in accordance with any directions made by the Secretary of State, to conserve, redistribute or otherwise augment water resources in England and Wales, and to secure the proper use of water resources, but, without prejudice to water undertakers' own duties, to develop resources in order to carry out their public water supply functions.[250] It is to achieve this partly by entering into arrangements with water undertakers to provide for the proper management and operation of the waters, reservoirs, apparatus or other works belonging to, operated by or available to water undertakers. These agreements, known as 'water resources management schemes', may include provisions with respect to the construction or installation of reservoirs, apparatus or other works, requiring payments to be made by the NRA to the water undertaker and the reference of questions arising from the agreement to be made to the Director or the Secretary of State.[251] A copy of the agreement must be sent to the Secretary of State, who may enforce the obligations of a water undertaker under section 20.[252]

These agreements are directly relevant to the NRA's duties with respect to its setting and monitoring of minimum acceptable river flows. The NRA may, if it thinks it appropriate to do so, and must if directed by the Secretary of State, submit a draft statement to him or her for approval in relation to any inland water,[253] containing provision for determining or amending the minimum acceptable flow for that inland water.[254] After appropriate consultation,[255] the NRA is to submit a draft statement setting out the control points at which the flow in the water is to be measured, the method of measurement and the flow which is to be the minimum acceptable flow at each control point.[256]

Before submitting a draft statement, the NRA must publish a notice stating its general effect and serve copies on various bodies, specify a place where a copy may be inspected during a period of twenty-eight days and stating that within that period written objections may be made to the Secretary of State. Upon the receipt of any objections, the Secretary of State must either hold a local inquiry or afford the objector and the NRA an opportunity of being heard by a person appointed by him or her.[257]

In determining the flow, the NRA must have regard to the following:

1.   The flow of water in the inland water from time to time.
2.   In the light of the duties of the NRA under sections 8 and 9 of the Water Act 1989 (general environmental duties),[258] the character of the inland water and its surroundings.
3.   Any water quality objectives established under Chapter I of Part III of the Water Act in relation to the inland water or any other inland water which may be affected by the flow in the inland water in question.[259]

Copies of any minimum acceptable flow must be kept at the offices of the NRA and be available for public inspection free of charge.[260]

The NRA must keep under review any approved statement and at least once every seven years submit any new draft statements or proposals for amendment which it considers appropriate.[261]

The NRA and undertakers must provide each other with all necessary information about the flow, level or volume of any inland water or any water contained in any underground strata, about rainfall or any fall of snow, hail or sleet or about the evaporation of any water. They must provide reasonable facilities for the inspection and the taking of copies of such records and make them available free of charge to local authorities, county councils, joint planning boards and internal drainage boards, and to all other persons on payment of such reasonable fees as the NRA may determine.[262] The duty of a water undertaker to provide such information is enforceable by the Secretary of State under section 20.[263]

Third parties who hold information concerning the flow, level or value of inland waters (other than land-locked lakes or ponds) are obliged to allow the NRA access to them, and any person who without reasonable excuse fails to do so, commits an offence and is liable on summary conviction, to a fine not exceeding level 1.[264]

This section and the duty to exchange information concerning pollution[265] are intended to ensure that the flow of information between the bodies concerned is maintained so that water management on an overall catchment basis may be carried on.

The NRA also has functions with respect to the control of abstraction[266] and impounding of water. Subject to certain exceptions, no person may abstract water from any source of supply or cause or permit any other person so to abstract it, except in pursuance of a licence granted by the NRA.[267] Contravention of this restriction or non-compliance with a condition imposed in a licence is an offence.[268] The general restriction on abstracting water does not apply where the quantity does not exceed five cubic metres, or, with the consent of the NRA, is less that twenty cubic metres and does not form part of a continuous operation where in total more than twenty cubic metres is abstracted.[269] There is also an exception for abstractions made by an occupier of land contiguous to an inland water for domestic purposes and agricultural purposes other than spray irrigation, provided that the abstraction is less than twenty cubic metres in any twenty-four hour period.[270] A further similar exception relates to the abstraction of water from underground strata for domestic purposes. Both these latter exceptions do not come into effect until 1 September 1990.[271]

The Water Resources Act 1963 and regulations made under that Act contain detailed provisions on the procedures for applying for, publication and determination of abstraction licences, their form and effect and the transfer of licences. In determining an application for an abstraction licence, the NRA must have regard to the need to ensure that the proposed abstraction will not reduce the flow below any satisfactory minimum acceptable flow or reduce it further if it is already below that level.

No person may begin to construct or alter any impounding works[272] at any place in an inland water unless authorised by a licence granted by the NRA to obstruct or impede the flow at that point by means of impounding works.[273] Again, the Water Resources Act 1963 provides for applications, appeals, variations and revocations of licences.

Where one or more licences are in force authorising water abstracted under the licences to be used for spray irrigation, the NRA may, by reason of exceptional shortage of rain or other emergency, serve a notice on the licence holder reducing for a specified period the quantity of water to be abstracted.[274]

In pursuance of its general powers as to charging, the NRA may make charges on persons granted licences and may make an agreement with any person, on his or her application, providing for exemption from, or reduction of, charges.[275] With respect to applications for or variations of abstraction licences, the NRA may require the payment to it of charges as determined under a charges scheme. Except where such a scheme is made before the 1 September 1991, a scheme must have the approval of the Secretary of State and the consent of the Treasury.[276] Before submitting a scheme, the NRA must give public notification and allow an opportunity for public representations and objections. In considering such a scheme, the Secretary of State must consider any representations made to him or her, the desirability of the NRA recovering its reasonable expenses incurred in carrying out its water resource functions, and the need to ensure that no undue preference is shown and that there is no undue discrimination in the fixing of charges.[277] The revenue raised from abstraction licences may not be used in relation to the NRA's other functions, but may be used for other water resources responsibilities as well as for financing the costs of the abstraction licence system.

The NRA is given powers under the Water Resources Act 1963 to acquire and dispose of land either by agreement or compulsorily,[278] to carry out works in relation to its water resources functions,[279] and to enter into agreements to facilitate its water resource functions.[280]

3.9   Drought

On the application of either the NRA or a water authority, the Secretary of State may, if he or she is satisfied that by reason of an exceptional shortage of rain a serious deficiency of supplies of water in any area exists or is threatened, and subject to certain rights of objection, make by statutory instrument, a general drought order.[281]

An order made on the application of the NRA may authorise it to do the following:

1. Take water from any source specified in the order subject to specified conditions or restrictions.[282]
2. Discharge water to any place specified in the order subject to specified conditions or restrictions.
3. Prohibit or limit the taking by any person (including a water undertaker) of water from a specified source if it is satisfied that the taking seriously affects the supplies of water available.[283]
4. Suspend or modify, subject to specified conditions, any restriction or obligation to which any authority or person is subject as respects the taking of water from any source, the discharge of water, the supply of water, or the filtration or other treatment of water.
5. Suspend or vary, or attach conditions to, any consent specified in the order for the discharge of effluent by any person, including an undertaker.[284]

An order made on the application of a water undertaker may make provision:[285]

(a) authorising the water undertaker to take water from any specified source subject to specified conditions or restrictions;
(b) authorising the water undertaker to prohibit or limit the use of water for any specified purpose;[286]
(c) authorising the water authority to discharge water to any specified place subject to specified conditions or restrictions;
(d) authorising the NRA to prohibit or limit the taking by any person of water from a specified source if it is satisfied that the taking seriously affects the supplies available to the water undertaker;
(e) prohibiting or limiting the taking by the NRA of water from a specified source if the taking of water from that source is determined, in accordance with provision made in the order, seriously to affect the supplies available to the water undertaker;
(f) suspending or modifying, subject to any conditions, any restriction or obligation to which any undertaker or any other person is subject as respects the taking of water from any source, the discharge of water, the supply of water or the filtration or other treatment of water;

(g) authorising the NRA to suspend or vary, or attach conditions to, any specified consent for the discharge of any effluent, including that of the undertaker which applied for the order.

A general drought order expires at the end of six months, although the Secretary of State may extend it for one further period of six months.[287]

The procedure for applications with regard to general drought orders is contained in Schedule 14 to the Act.[288] The applicant for an order must cause notice of the application to be served on specified persons, depending on the contents of the order sought, and must publish a notice in a local newspaper and in the London Gazette. The notice must state the general effect of the application, specify the area affected and a place where a copy of the proposed order may be inspected within seven days, and also that objections may be made to the Secretary of State within that period.[289]

Before making an order, the Secretary of State, if there have been objections which have not been withdrawn, must either cause a local inquiry to be held[290] or afford an opportunity to the objector and if the objector avails himself of the opportunity, to the applicant, of appearing before and being heard by a person appointed by the Secretary of State for that purpose.[291] In situations where an order is required to be made urgently, the Secretary of State may dispense with these requirements, but must still consider any objections before making an order.

After a drought order has been made, the applicant must publish a notice to that effect in a local newspaper and in the London Gazette, stating a place where a copy of it may be inspected.[292]

Where the Secretary of State is further satisfied that the deficiency of water is such as to be likely to impair the economic or social well-being of persons in an area, he or she may make an emergency drought order.[293] In addition to the provisions which may be made in a general drought order,[294] an emergency drought order may authorise a water undertaker:

(a) to prohibit or limit the use of water for such purposes as it thinks fit;
(b) to supply water in its area or in any place within its area by means of stand-pipes or water tanks, and to erect or set up and maintain stand-pipes or water tanks in any street in that area.[295]

Where powers have been conferred on any person by an emergency order, the Secretary of State may give directions as to the manner in which, or the circumstances in which, any of those powers is or is not to be exercised, and that person is under a duty to comply with the directions.[296]

The procedure for the making of an emergency drought order is the same as that for a general drought order.[297] An emergency drought order expires after three months unless extended by the Secretary of State, who may do so for a maximum period of a further two months.[298]

A drought order which authorises the taking of water from a source from which water is supplied to an inland navigation,[299] or which suspends or modifies a restriction on the taking of such water or an obligation to discharge compensation water into such water,[300] may include provision for prohibiting or limiting the taking of water or suspending or modifying any obligation to which a navigaton authority is subject as regards the discharge of water from the inland navigation.[301]

A drought order may authorise the NRA or a water undertaker to enter and occupy any land and to execute any works required for the performance of any duty or the exercise of any power imposed or conferred by or under the order, but every such order must contain a requirement that the NRA or undertaker give to the occupier of the land and any other specified persons, not less than twenty-four hours' notice of any intended entry.[302]

A drought order may also contain provision relating to the making of applications for warrants of entry,[303] and may make different provision in relation to different persons, circumstances or localities.[304] Undertakers may, despite an interruption or dimunition of the supply of water, still recover any fixed or minimum charge as if there had been no such interruption or dimunition.[305]

In certain circumstances compensation is payable by the NRA or an undertaker for any loss or damage sustained by reason of anything done in pursuance of any drought order.[306] For both general and emergency orders, compensation is payable in respect of the entry upon or occupation or use of land to the owners and occupiers of land and all other persons interested in the land or injuriously affected by the entry, occupation or use, for loss or damage sustained.[307]

The following compensation is additionally payable but only with respect to general drought orders:[308]

1. Compensation for loss or damage sustained in respect of the taking of water from a source or its taking from a source otherwise

than in accordance with a restriction or obligation which has been suspended or modified, to the owners of the source and all other persons interested in the source or injuriously affected by the taking of water.[309]

2. Compensation for loss or damage sustained in respect of waters being discharged or not discharged to any place or its being discharged otherwise than in accordance with a restriction or obligation which has been suspended or modified, to the owners of the place of discharge and to all other persons interested in the place of discharge, or injuriously affected by the discharge or lack of discharge.[310]

3. Compensation for loss or damage sustained in respect of the imposition of a prohibition or limitation on the taking of water from a source, to any persons to whom the prohibition or limitation applies.[311]

4. Compensation for loss or damage sustained in respect of a power to make discharges of sewage effluent or trade effluent in pursuance of any consent, to any person who has been exercising that power.[312]

A claim for compensation is made by serving a notice on the body which applied for the drought order stating the grounds of the claim and the amount claimed.[313] The claim must be made no later than six months after the end of the period for which the order authorises the power in respect of which compensation is claimed.[314] Provision is made for questions as to the right of a claimant to compensation, and as to the amount of compensation recoverable, to be finally determined by the Lands Tribunal.[315]

3.10   Charging

3.10.1   CHARGING FOR SERVICES

Water undertakers and sewerage undertakers have power to fix charges for any services provided in the course of carrying out their functions and to demand and recover charges fixed from any persons to whom they provide services.[316] This power is to be exercised by or in accordance with a charges scheme or by or in accordance with agreements with the persons to be charged.[317]

In fixing charges, undertakers are bound by the conditions in their Instruments of Appointment which provide formulae for the calculation of charges.[318]

Section 76 provides for water or sewerage undertakers to fix their charges by means of charges schemes. Condition D of the Instruments of Appointment of water and sewerage undertakers requires undertakers to have in effect by 1 April 1990 charges schemes setting out their standard tariffs for domestic water supplies and sewerage services.[319]

With respect to non-domestic water supplies, the Director[320] may determine charges in the absence of agreement except where there is a charges scheme in force setting out the charge for the case in question.[321] Where there is no charges scheme in force, the Director must in making a determination have regard to the desirability of the undertaker recovering the expenses of complying with its obligations under section 46 and of securing a reasonable return on its capital.[322] Similarly, with regard to charges for consents to discharge trade effluent, paragraph 3(4) of Schedule 8 provides that questions about the payment of charges shall not be determined by the Director where a charges scheme is in force.[323]

Subject to any agreement to the contrary, supplies of water provided by a water undertaker and sewerage services provided by a sewerage undertaker are treated as being supplied or provided to the occupier for the time being of any premises.[324] There is no definition of 'occupier' in the Act, but it is to be presumed that it refers to a person who has actual control and possession of premises.

An undertaker may not charge for becoming or taking steps for the purpose of becoming the person who provides a supply of water or sewerage services for domestic purposes.[325] It may, however, make a charge for connections to a water supply or public sewer of premises which have never at any previous time been connected to a supply of water or a sewer used for drainage for domestic purposes.[326]

No charges may be made for the declaration of vesting of a sewer or any agreement to make such a declaration under Part II of the Public Health Act 1936[327] or for the drainage of any highway or the disposal of the contents of any drains or sewer used for draining any highway.[328] In addition, no charge may be made in respect of water taken for the purpose of extinguishing fires or taken by a fire authority[329] for any other emergency purposes, water taken for testing fire-fighting apparatus or training persons for fire-fighting, or making water available for these purposes.[330]

The Director General of Water Services may, by order, fix maximum charges which a person who is not a water or sewerage undertaker may recover in respect of water supplies or sewerage services provided by him or her with the help of services provided by a water or sewerage undertaker.[331] Water services and sewerage services are provided to a person with the help of services provided by an undertaker if:[332]

(a) a facility for that person to have access to a supply of water provided by an undertaker in pipes, or to make use of sewerage services provided by an undertaker, is made available to that person otherwise than by the undertaker;

(b) that person is provided with a supply of water in pipes by a person to whom the water is supplied, directly or indirectly, by a water undertaker; or

(c) that person is provided with sewerage services by a person who, for the purpose of providing those services, makes use of sewerage services provided, directly or indirectly, by a sewerage undertaker.

3.10.2 METERING

Section 80 provides that the charges of water or sewerage undertakers may not be fixed by reference to a rating valuation list[333] after 31 March 2000. It is therefore up to water and sewerage undertakers to find alternative means of charging, and the most attractive alternative appears to be the use of metered charges which relate charges to volume of water supplied or sewage discharged. Whatever method is chosen it must comply with the undertakers' conditions of appointment, particularly the prohibition on undue discrimination against and undue preference towards any class of customers or potential customers.[334]

In the non-domestic sector, roughly 30 per cent of water currently supplied in England and Wales is metered. Since 1981 a scheme has been available whereby domestic consumers may opt for a metered system, but since then fewer than 100,000 consumers have opted for metering from over 18.5 million consumers in England and Wales.

In 1988, the Government introduced the Public Utility Transfers and Water Charges Act 1988. In addition to paving the way for the privatisation of the water industry, the Act introduced a special regime of trials in relation to compulsory water metering. The aim of these trials was to give the water industry power to test whether metering of domestic water supply might serve as a suitable alternative to the present system of charging based on rateable value. For the purpose of the trial schemes, water undertakers in fixing charges must have regard to the cost of providing their services and cannot show undue preference towards or discrimination against any class of customer.

The provisions of this Act have been largely re-enacted by the Water Act 1989.

The Secretary of State may make regulations supplementing the provisions of the Water Act with respect to the installation of meters,[335] with respect to the connection, disconnection, use, maintenance, authentication and testing of meters, and with respect to any related matters.[336]

Where an undertaker has fixed any charges in relation to any premises by reference to volume or has given notice of its intention of so fixing any charges within the period specified in the notice[337] and there is a service pipe, drain or private sewer connecting those premises to a water main or public sewer, the Act gives the undertaker certain powers of entry to carry out works.[338]

Any person designated in writing by the undertaker may enter those premises, or any land associated with those premises to do the following:[339]

1. Carry out surveys or tests to determine whether the carrying out of specified works is practicable, whether it is necessary or expedient for any other works to be carried out, and how much any such works should be carried out.
2. Carry out any specified works.
3. Inspect, examine or test any meter on those premises or any pipes or apparatus installed in respect of any meter.
4. Ascertain from any meter the volume of water supplied to, or effluent discharged from, those premises.

Upon entering the premises, the designated person may carry out the following specified works:[340]

1. The installation and connection of meters.
2. The installation and connection of separate service pipes in connection with the installation of meters, where the premises comprise a house which is one of two or more houses to which the supply of water is wholly or partly by the same service pipe.[341]
3. The carrying out of any other works appearing to the undertaker to be necessary or expedient, including the installation and connection of pipes and the alteration and removal of any plumbing.

Certain powers are also given with respect to the carrying out of works in a street.[342]

Except where a warrant has been obtained from a justice of the peace[343] entry to premises may only be made at a reasonable time and after seven days' notice of the intended entry has been given to the occupier of the premises.[344]

Generally, undertakers are required to meet the cost of the installation, connection, maintenance, repair, disconnection and removal of meters and any works connected with those activities.[345] However, the undertaker is entitled to recover the following from any other person:

1. Any expenses incurred for the purpose of enabling a condition imposed on the connection of premises for the first time to a water main to be satisfied.[346]
2. Any sums which it is entitled to recover in pursuance of terms or conditions determined in relation to a supply of water for non-domestic purposes.[347]
3. Any sums which it is entitled to recover from that person in respect of the provision of separate service pipes.[348]
4. Any expenses incurred in relation to a meter used for determining charges for the carrying out of a sewerage undertaker's trade effluent functions.
5. Any expenses incurred in consequence of an occupier opting to be charged by reference to volume.
6. A proportion of the expenses incurred in positioning a meter or any pipe in a place other than that reasonably proposed by the undertaker.[349]

An undertaker must make good, or pay compensation for, any damage caused by it in connection with the carrying out of the above works.[350]

Any dispute over the exercise of any power to carry out work on any premises, as to who should bear any expenses, whether compensation should be paid or in relation to other matters dealing with meters, is to be determined by a single arbitrator.[351]

Charges which are fixed by reference to volume may be imposed so that a person is made liable to pay charges after that person has ceased to be the occupier of premises in circumstances where:[352]

(a) he or she fails to inform the undertaker of the ending of his or her occupation at least two working days before he or she ceases to occupy them; and
(b) the charges relate to a period ending with whichever of the following first occurs:
  (i)   the twenty-eighth day after he or she informs the undertaker;
  (ii) any day on which the meter would normally have been read;

(iii)   any day on which another person informs the undertaker that he or she has become the new occupier of the premises.

Where different services are provided in relation to the same premises by different undertakers, and one undertaker has obtained a reading from a meter which is relevant to the determination of charges by the other undertaker, and they have agreed to bear the reasonable proportion of expenses of obtaining and disclosing the reading, the undertaker who obtained the reading must disclose the reading to the other undertaker.[353]

Any person who intentionally or recklessly interferes with a meter so as to prevent it from making an accurate recording, or carries out any work which he knows will affect the operation or require the disconnection of a meter, is guilty of an offence and is liable on summary conviction to a fine not exceeding level 3 on the standard scale.[354] An undertaker which carries out any works made necessary by the commission of an offence is entitled to recover any expenses reasonably incurred from the person who committed the offence.[355]

It is a defence to show that the person had the consent of the undertaker who uses the meter. Where an application is made to an undertaker for such a consent, the undertaker must give notice of its decision as soon as reasonably practicable after receiving the application and may make it a condition of consent (but only where it is reasonable to do so) that the undertaker itself carries out some or all of the works. The undertaker may then carry out the works and recover any expenses reasonably incurred by it in doing so. Compensation is payable by an undertaker for any loss or damage sustained in consequence of a failure to comply with any obligation imposed on it, or a failure to exercise reasonable care in carrying out any works.[356]

3.11   Consumer protection

3.11.1   DUTIES OF THE DIRECTOR AND SECRETARY OF STATE

In exercising various powers and in performing various duties the Secretary of State for the Environment and the Director General of Water Services are bound to take account of certain consumer interests.[357]

With respect to the Secretary of State, the powers and duties concerned are as follows:

1. Any powers or duties in relation to the appointment and regulation of water and sewage undertakers.
2. The making of regulations presenting standards of performance in connection with water supply and the provision of sewage services.[358]
3. The approval of a code of practice with respect to the exercise of works powers on private land.[359]

With respect to the Director, the powers and duties are as follows:

1. The determination of payment of interest and repayments of capital, and payment of interest on sums deposited with a water undertaker, in respect of water mains requisition.[360]
2. The determination of matters relating to the financial conditions of sewer requisition.[361]
3. The determination of interest to be paid on sums deposited with an undertaker for the discharge of any obligation relating to a request to move pipes, etc. on private land.[362]

These powers and duties must be exercised or performed in a manner that they consider is best calculated:

(a) to ensure that the interests of every customer or potential customer of an undertaker are protected as respects the fixing and recovery by that company of charges for services and any other amounts required to be paid, and in particular to ensure that there is no undue preference or undue discrimination shown towards customers or potential customers in rural areas;
(b) to ensure that the interest of such persons are protected as respects the other terms on which any services are provided by undertakers, and as respects the quality of those services;
(c) to ensure that the interests of those persons are further protected as respects benefits that could be secured for them by the application in a particular manner of any of the proceeds of a disposal of that company's protected land or interest in or right over that land;
(d) to promote economy and efficiency on the part of any such company;
(e) to facilitate effective competition between persons holding or seeking appointments as undertakers.[363]

The Secretary of State and the Director, in ensuring that the interests of customers are protected as respects the quality of services provided, are to take into account in particular the interests of those who are disabled or of a pensionable age.[364]

3.11.2 CUSTOMER SERVICE COMMITTEES

Following the transfer date of 1 September 1989, the Director of Water Services was required to establish customer service committees and allocate them to the companies as water and sewerage undertakers.[365] Ten such committees were formed, consisting of a chairman appointed by the Director, after consultation with the Secretary of State,[366] and between ten and twenty members appointed by the Director.[367] In appointing members the Director must have regard to the desirability of the persons appointed having experience of, or having shown capacity in, some matter relevant to the functions of undertakers in the area in question, and the desirability of the committee including disabled persons and one or more persons with experience of work among, and the special needs of, disabled persons.[368]

Provision is made in Schedule 4 for the establishment of sub-committees, remuneration, expenses, pensions, staff and various financial matters.

The duties of customer service committees are specified in section 27. They are required:

(a) to keep under review all matters appearing to the committee to affect the interests of customers and potential customers, to counsel each company allocated to it about such of those matters as appear to affect the interests of those persons, and to make such companies representations about any matters which the committee considers appropriate;

(b) to investigate any complaint and, if appropriate, to make representations to the company in respect of the complaint which is made or referred to the committee by a customer or potential customer, which complaint does not appear to be vexatious or frivolous, and which relates to the carrying out by a company of its functions;

(c) to refer to the Director every complaint which he or she is required to investigate in relation to works on private lands[369] and any assertion that a company has or is contravening any condition of its appointment or any enforceable statutory or other requirements;

(d) to refer to the Director any complaint which the committee is unable to resolve.[370]

The Director of Water Services in turn is required:

(a) to consider whether any complaint referred to him or her should be referred to a customer service committee instead of being dealt with by him or her;

(b) to consider whether any assertion that a company has or is contravening a condition of its appointment or any enforceable or statutory or other requirement should be referred to the Secretary of State;

(c) to consider any such complaint which is not referred by him or her to the Secretary of State;

(d) to consider any complaints referred to him or her by a customer service committee;

(e) to consider any complaint made to him or her that a committee has failed to perform any duty imposed on it;[371]

(f) to investigate a complaint with respect to the exercise of works powers on private land.[372]

The Director must make such arrangement as he or she considers appropriate for facilitating the transmission of information between customer service committees.[373]

3.11.3 OTHER SAFEGUARDS

The Water Supply and Sewerage Services (Customer Service Standards) Regulations 1989[374] provide for customers of water and sewerage undertakers to be entitled to payment or credit in circumstances where an undertaker fails to meet specified minimum standards of service in relation to the supply of water or provision of sewerage services to domestic premises. A payment or credit of £5 must be made where the undertaker gives notice of a proposed visit to domestic premises but fails to keep the appointment, where a claim for payment is made within three months.[375]

A payment on credit of £5 must also be paid to a customer if an undertaker fails within a specified period either to respond to a query concerning the correctness of an account or to a request to change the arrangements by which a customer pays his or her accounts to which the undertaker is not prepared to accede, or to deal with a written complaint about the quality, pressure or adequacy of a supply of water or about sewerage services.[376]

The regulations require that customers be given a detailed statement at least once a year of the rights provided by the regulations[377] and that any disputes be referred to the Director for determination.[378] Customers who are in default in paying their bills for more than six weeks are not entitled to payments or credits, unless there is an agreement or court order in force regarding the payment of the money owed.[379] Payments or credits made under the regulations do not affect the other legal rights or liabilities of the customer or undertaker.[380]

Where a supply of water to domestic premises is cut off, interrupted or reduced to carry out necessary works,[381] the undertaker is required to give the consumer notice of the proposal for carrying out the works, and before the supply is cut off to notify him in writing of the time by which the supply will be restored. Where the supply to domestic premises has been interrupted or cut off to allow emergency works to be carried out, the undertaker must take all reasonable steps to notify affected customers of that fact, where an alternative supply may be obtained, the time by which it is proposed to restore the supply, and the telephone number of an office from which further information may be obtained.[382] A payment or credit of £5, or a multiple of £5 in certain circumstances, must be paid by an undertaker where the supply of water to domestic premises is not restored within specified periods.[383] It is an offence for a water undertaker to disconnect a service pipe or otherwise cut off a supply of water to any premises where it has no authority to do so.[384]

Customer safeguards are also included in the undertakers' Instruments of Appointment. In addition to safeguards, remuneration of charges and increases in charges, each undertaker must have a code of practice on the following:

1. Its relations with customers and customer service committees.
2. Procedures on disconnection.
3. Procedures on leakage.
4. Levels of service information and service targets.

The Director is required to keep under review the activities connected with the functions of undertakers, to collect information about the undertakers and the way in which they carry out their functions and to advise and assist the Secretary of State for the Environment and the Director General of Fair Trading.[385] He or she may also publish information and advice, subject to considerations of confidentiality, for the benefit of customers,[386] and is required to make an annual report of his activities to the Secretary of State, which is laid before Parliament and published.[387]

Notes

1. 'Water and sewerage law: consultation paper', DoE, Welsh Office, March 1986; 'Water and sewerage law review: the Government's revised proposals', DoE, Welsh Office, May 1988.

2. S.37(1). The Secretary of State has made the Water Supply and Sewerage Services (Customer Service Standards) Regulations 1989 which supplement this duty by establishing overall standards of performance with respect to particular aspects of the duty. See below, section 3.11.3.

3. Under s.125.

4. S.125(2).

5. S.39(1).

6. S.39(3) and (4). Agreements made continue in force: Sch.26, para.5 before 1 September 1989.

7. Or, in appropriate circumstances, by the Commission for New Towns, the Development Board for Rural Wales, a development corporation, or an urban development corporation, S.40(2)(d) and (e).

8. S.40(1).

9. S.189(1).

10. The definition includes references to a tunnel or conduit which serves or is to serve the main in question and to any accessories for the main, s.189(4).

11. In default of agreement the decision is to be made by a single arbitrator of the places at which it is reasonable, in all the circumstances, for service pipes to premises in the locality to connect with that water main, s.40(4) and (5).

12. S.189(1).

13. S.40(3).

14. S.40(5). An 'earlier water main' means any water main which has been requisitioned in the period of twelve years before the provision of the new main.

15. S.41(1)(6).

16. As approved or determined by the Director.

17. S.41(8).

18. S.41(9).

19. See below, section 3.10.1.

20. S.189(3) and (4).

21. S.44(5).

22. S.42(1).

23. S.42(6).

24. S.42(3)–(5).

25. S.42(1).

26. S.43(2).

27. Meaning any apparatus for measuring or showing the volume of water supplied to, or of effluent discharged from, any premises, s.43(8).

28. The power to require the installation of a meter may be exercised even if the undertaker has no immediate intention of fixing charges on those premises with reference to volume, but an undertaker may not require the alteration or removal of any pipe laid or plumbing installed before 1 April 1989, s.43(4).

29. The circumstances are listed in s.51(5).

30. See s.63.

31. S.43(3).

32. S.43(6). An undertaker may approve specifications and publish them in such manner as it considers appropriate, s.43(5).

33. Under s.42(3)–(5).

34. The duty is owed only in respect of a supply to a building and not to land associated with the building; 'building' and 'premises' are not defined. In West Mersey Urban District Council v. Fraser [1950], 2 K.B. 119, it was held that premises referred to property with a degree of permanency on the particular site it occupied. The word could therefore include a permanently moored houseboat.

35. That is, the 'transfer date', and there has been no interruption of the domestic supply duty in relation to those premises since the transfer date (s.45(2), as defined in s.45(4)).

36. S.45(1).

37. There is an interruption of the domestic supply duty if that supply is cut off by the undertaker in consequence of a failure to pay outstanding charges (s.49) or a failure to

take the necessary steps to prevent damage, contamination, waste, misuse or undue consumption (s.63). It is not interrupted if the supply is cut off in order to carry out works, or if there is a change of occupier or owner of the premises, s.45(4).

38. A trunk main is a main which is used to convey water from a source of supply to a filter or reservoir or between filters or reservoirs, or to convey water in bulk between different places outside the area of the undertaker, s.189(1).

39. S.45(5).

40. S.45(6).

41. See s.51(5).

42. See s.63.

43. S.46(1)–(3).

44. S.46(6).

45. S.47.

46. See below, section 3.10.1.

47. That is, if the pipe or main has a fire hydrant fixed on it.

48. S.48.

49. S.20(5).

50. S.51(1).

51. From a service reservoir or tank chosen by the undertaker.

52. That is, a supply of water for non-domestic purposes through mains or other pipes which do not have fire hydrants fixed to them, or in accordance with modifications to the duty made by the Secretary of State on application of the Director or a water undertaker, s.51(4).

53. As defined in s.51(10).

54. S.51(5). If the cistern is not provided or repaired in accordance with a notice given by the water undertaker, it may itself provide a cistern or carry out any necessary repairs and recover the expenses incurred from the owner of the premises, s.51(6).

55. Meaning any pipe, not being a trunk main, which is used for the purposes of conveying water from one source of supply to another, between a source of supply and a regulating reservoir, or for the purposes of giving or taking a supply of water in bulk, Sch.19, para.1(6). A trunk main as defined in s.189(1) is a particular type of water main.

56. Meaning a pipe used by a water undertaker to discharge water during the carrying out of works, Sch.19, para.1(6).

57. Other than a service pipe as defined in s.189(1).

58. S.165. Any modification of the records should be made as soon as reasonably practicable after the completion of the works which make the modification necessary, and should incorporate the dates of the modification and the completion of the works, s.165(4).

59. S.165(5).

60. S.165(3). There is no minimum requirement as to the scale of the maps.

61. S.40; see above, section 3.1.2.

62. S.42; see above, section 3.1.3.

63. S.45; see above, section 3.1.4.

64. The duty under s.40 is owed to the person who required the provision of the main, that in s.42 to the person who served the notice, and that in s.45 to the customer of the water undertaker.

65. Ss.47 and 48; see above, sections 3.1.6 and 3.1.7.

66. S.51; see above, section 3.1.8.

67. S.165; see above, section 3.1.9.

68. Ss.47, 51 and 165 by the Secretary of State, s.48 by the Director, and s.37 by the Secretary of State or, in accordance with a general authorisation given by the Secretary of State, the Director. It may be that a person who relies on a map containing an inaccuracy due to the negligence of the NRA or an undertaker, and consequently suffers loss or damage because of that inaccuracy, may be able to bring a civil action for negligent misstatement.

69. *Clark* v. *Epsom Rural District Council* [1929], 1, Ch.287.

70. *Robinson* v. *Workington Corporation* [1897], 1, Ch.619; s.20(10) states that where any act or omission constitutes a contravention of a statutory requirement enforceable by

that section, the only remedies for that contravention, apart from those under s.20, are those for which express provision is made by or under any enactment.

71. S.22(4) and (5).
72. S.22(7).
73. S.22(6).
74. S.46; see above, section 3.1.5.
75. Ss.47(8) and (9), 51(8) and (9). The duties in s.51 do not apply to existing mains and pipes owned by water undertakers before the transfer date. These are still governed by the provisions of the Water Act 1945 or by any local legislation which has different pressure and constancy requirements, Sch.26, para.11. The equivalent defence in the 1945 Act refers to frost, drought, unavoidable accident or other unavoidable cause. Whether the new defence is stricter than that provided in the 1945 Act awaits judicial interpretation.
76. Currently £2,000.
77. 'Relevant pipe' means in relation to the NRA a resource main or discharge pipe and in relation to a water undertaker a water main (including a trunk main), resource main, discharge pipe and service pipe, Sch.19, para.1.
78. Conferred by Schedule 19 to the Water Act 1989 or otherwise.
79. S.153(2).
80. Meaning so much of a pipe which is, or is to be, connected with a water main for the purpose of supplying water to any premises and is or is to be subject to water pressure from that main, or would be so subject but for the closing of some valve, s.189(1).
81. Sch.19, para.2(7), s.63(7).
82. See 'Water and sewerage law: consultation paper', *op.cit.*, para.2.11.
83. S.42; see above, section 3.1.3.
84. S.42(3)(a).
85. *ibid.*
86. S.42(4).
87. Under s.57; see below, section 5.4.7.
88. S.42(3)(c) and s.153(4)(a).
89. S.50(1).
90. S.189(1).
91. S.150(2).
92. As defined in s.66(1).
93. S.50(3). The duty on an undertaker to make connections to water mains under s.42 (see above, section 3.1.3) shall apply as if the consumer had by notice required the undertaker to connect the separate service pipe. The consumer will also be presumed to have made a demand under ss.45 (see above, section 3.1.5) for a supply of water for domestic purposes, and insofar as those premises were provided with water for other purposes, to have requested the undertaker to provide the same supply as was provided before the service of the notice. Any works carried out by the undertaker are necessary works for the purposes of ss.45 to 49 (see above, sections 3.1.4–3.1.7 and this section 3.4) and s.51 (see above, section 3.1.8), s.50(5).
94. Subject to any terms or conditions determined in relation to a supply of water for non-domestic purposes, s.46.
95. This power includes the power to reduce a supply of water. 'Necessary works' is defined in s.66(1). Except in an emergency, the power is exercisable only after the undertaker has served reasonable notice on the consumer of the proposal for the carrying out of the necessary works, s.49(2).
96. Any expenses reasonably incurred by the water undertaker are recoverable from the person in respect of whose liability the power is exercised, s.49(5). Where a supply of water is provided also to other premises wholly or partly by the same service pipe, the undertaker may only cut off the supply if the same person is the occupier of the premises in relation to which the charges are due and of the other premises, s.49(6).
97. S.49(1). No person is liable to a water undertaker for any expenses incurred in exercising this power (s.49(7)) or for water charges made by reference to volume after the expiry of the notice (s.77(4)).

98. S.49(3).
99. S.49(4).
100. S.49(8). Customer service committees must also be kept informed of the general situation with respect to disconnections; see below, section 3.11.2.
101. Either under s.49, s.63 or any other enactment.
102. Currently £400, s.49(9).
103. S.63(1)(d).
104. S.63(1)(a).
105. See below, section 5.4.11.
106. As defined in s.189(1).
107. 'Water fittings' includes pipes (other than water mains), taps, cocks, valves, ferrules, meters, cisterns, baths, water closets, soil pans and other similar apparatus used in connection with the supply of water, s.66(1).
108. That is, any water fitting which is not the responsibility of a person other than the owner or as the case may be, the occupier, s.61(4).
109. S.61(1).
110. Unless it is used to extinguish a fire.
111. S.61(2).
112. Currently £400.
113. S.61(3).
114. S.62(1)(c) and (d).
115. An authorisation for the NRA may also be made by the Minister of Agriculture.
116. S.151(1). This authorisation may include the acquisition or extinguishment of any interests and rights over land.
117. 1981, Ch.67. Except in the case of acquisition of mineral rights where Sch.21 to the Water Act 1989 applies.
118. 1965, Ch.56.
119. 1961, Ch. Ss.5–16.
120. 1965, Ch.56. Where the compulsory acquisition is of a right over land by the creation of a new right, the Compulsory Purchase Act 1965 applies, with the modifications set out in Schedule 18 to the Water Act 1989, s.151(6).
121. 1973, Ch.26, ss.44–51.
122. Sch.19, para.1(3).
123. 'Street' means 'any length of a highway (other than a waterway), road, land, footway, alley or passage, any square or court, and any length of land laid out as a way whether it is for the time being formed as a way or not, irrespective of whether the highway, road or other thing in question is a thoroughfare or not' (s.1(3), Public Utilities Street Works Act 1950) and includes, where the street is a highway which passes over a bridge or through a tunnel, that bridge or tunnel, s.189(5), Water Act 1989.
124. Sch.19, para.2(1).
125. As defined in para.1(1).
126. That is, any waterworks which contain water which is or may be used by a water undertaker for providing a supply of water to any premises, Sch.19, para.1(2).
127. See also s.154.
128. 'Highway' is defined in the Highways Act 1980, Sch.19, para.2(3).
129. Sch.19, para.2(4).
130. Sch.19, para.2(5).
131. The procedure for notification is contained in Part I of the Public Utilities Street Works Act 1950, Ch.39.
132. Not being a highway maintainable at public expense within the meaning of the Highways Act 1980.
133. Meaning the British Railways Board, London Regional Transport or any other person authorised by any enactment to construct, work or carry on a railway, Sch.19, para.3(6).
134. Defined as meaning any person who has powers under any enactment to work, maintain, conserve, improve or control any canal or other inland navigation, navigable river, estuary, harbour or dock, s.189(1).

135. Except in the case of an emergency as defined by the Public Utilities Street Works Act 1950, Ch.39.
136. Currently £400, Sch.19, para.3(5).
137. S.160(1).
138. S.160(2).
139. S.160(3).
140. A procedure where works involve the alteration of telecommunications apparatus is specified in para.23 of Sch.2 to the Telecommunications Act 1984, s.160(80).
141. These bodies are defined in s.189(1). Undertakers must also consult an internal drainage board before constructing or altering any inland water (as defined in the Water Resources Act 1963, other than one that forms part of a main river for the purposes of the Land Drainage Act 1976, s.160(9)) or constructing or altering any works on or in any such inland water, s.160(5).
142. That is, the council of a district or of a London Borough or the Common Council of the City of London, s.189(1).
143. S.160(4).
144. S.160(6).
145. S.160(7).
146. See also s.154.
147. Sch.19, para.4(1).
148. See above, section 3.1.3.
149. Para.4(3).
150. Para.4(4).
151. Para.4(5).
152. Under s.40; see above, section 3.1.2.
153. Under s.71. Sch.19, para.4(6).
154. Para.6(1)–(3).
155. See above, section 3.7.1.
156. Which is to apply the provisions of ss. 2 and 4 of the Land Compensation Act 1961 in determining such compensation, para.6(4). In relation to the assessment of compensation for depreciation, the rules set out in s.5 of the Land Compensation Act 1961 apply as they apply to compensation for the compulsory acquisition of an interest in land, para.6 (5). Modified rules apply where the interest in land in respect of which compensation is payable is subject to a mortgage, para.6(6).
157. Para.6(7).
158. Para.6(8). The Water and Sewerage (Works) (Advance Payments) Regulations 1989 (S.I.1989 No.1379) provide that the amount of the advance payment is 90 per cent of the amount which the parties have agreed as the amount of compensation or, where no such agreement has been reached, 90 per cent of the compensating authority's estimate of the compensation.
159. S.162(1).
160. S.162(2).
161. This duty is enforceable by the Director under s.20; see s.162(10)(a).
162. S.162(3).
163. S.162(4).
164. S.162(5).
165. This duty is enforceable by the Secretary of State under s.20; see s.162(10)(b).
166. S.162(7).
167. Under s.7.
168. S.162(8).
169. Sch.19, para.7.
170. Para.8(1).
171. Which is deemed to include any extra expenditure incurred by any water or sewerage undertaker or public authority other than the one making the discharge for the purpose of properly carrying out its statutory functions, para.8(3).
172. Any dispute as to whether compensation should be paid, or as to the amount of any such compensation, is to be referred to the arbitration of a single arbitrator, para.8(4).

173. Para.8(5).
174. Currently £400.
175. Para.8(8).
176. That is, the powers are deemed to be 'prescribed enactments' in terms of s.108(1)(e).
177. Para.9.
178. Para.9(1).
179. Para.9(2).
180. Para.9(3).
181. Para.9(5).
182. Para.9(4).
183. Para.9(9).
184. Para.9(7).
185. Currently £400, para.9(8).
186. 'Engineering or building operations' includes: (a) the construction, alteration, improvement, maintenance, or demolition of any building or structure or of any reservoir, watercourse, dam, weir, well, borehole or other works; and (b) the installation, modification or removal of any machinery or apparatus, s.189(1).
187. Or the Minister of Agriculture if the applicant is the NRA, s.155(7).
188. S.155(1) and (2).
189. For general powers of compulsory acquisition under s.155, see above, section 3.7.1.
190. As defined in s.189(1).
191. S.155(4).
192. S.155(5).
193. S.155(6). However, such an order does not of itself grant those powers to the NRA or a water undertaker.
194. Sch.20, para.1.
195. Para.1(2).
196. Except where the objection relates exclusively to matters that may be dealt with in the assessment of compensation, para.4(2).
197. Para.4(1).
198. Para.3.
199. Para.5.
200. Para.6.
201. Except where a licence to abstract water or to obstruct or impede the flow of an inland water under the Water Resources Act 1963 is granted or deemed to be granted to the NRA or undertaker in question and injurious affection is caused by engineering or building operations in accordance with the provisions of that licence (para.7).
202. Para.8.
203. 'Waterway' is defined in the National Parks and Access to the Countryside Act 1949 as including lakes, rivers and other waters including reservoirs which are suitable or which can be reasonably rendered suitable for sailing, boating, bathing or fishing, together with any associated land.
204. S.158(1).
205. Defined in the Water Resources Act 1963 as including tidal and non-tidal rivers, estuaries, and arms of the sea.
206. For the procedure for making byelaws, see below, section 5.10.5.
207. S.158(3).
208. For the NRA's powers to control the discharge of effluent from vessels under s.114, see below, section 5.6.
209. Currently £2,000.
210. S.79 of the Water Resources Act 1963, as amended by Sch.13, para.21.
211. S.113 of the Transport Act 1968, as amended by Sch.25, para.38.
212. S.158(5).
213. S.159. With respect to these matters, Sch.21 is to have effect and in the case of compulsory acquisition of mineral rights, etc., is to have effect instead of Sch.2 to the Acquisition of Land Act 1981.

214. Sch.21, para.1. The NRA or undertaker is, however, entitled to such parts of mines or minerals as it may be necessary to dig or carry away in carrying out its works.
215. Compensation is to include payments for the severance by the undertaking of the land lying over the mines, the interruption of continuous working of the mines and the mines being worked in accordance with restrictions. Payment must also be made for any minerals not compulsorily purchased which cannot be got or won because of the position of any undertaking or of any restriction imposed, para.4.
216. Where the working of mines or minerals is prevented in this way, the owner of the mine or minerals may cut and make such airways, headways, gateways or water levels as are required for the ventilation, drainage and working of mines and minerals which are not underlying any undertakings, para.3.
217. Para.2.
218. Para.5.
219. S.161.(1). Other than pipes, etc., which are in, under or over any street.
220. The question of whether a requirement is reasonable may be finally determined by the Director in the exercise of his or her enforcement powers, s.161(8).
221. S.161(5).
222. 'Apparatus' does not include a meter, s.167(7). For the offence of tampering, etc., with meters, see below, section 3.10.2.
223. S.167(1). Currently £400.
224. S.167(2).
225. S.167(3). It is a defence under (c) to show that the person did not know and had no grounds for suspecting that the pipe or apparatus in question had been illegally attached or altered.
226. S.167(5). The amount recoverable in such an action includes a reasonable amount in respect of any water wasted, misused or improperly consumed in consequence of the commission of the offence, s.167(6).
227. See above, section 3.7.3.
228. S.156(1)–(3).
229. S.156(4) and (5).
230. Sch.19, para.10(1)–(3).
231. Sch.10, para.1; see above, section 3.10.2.
232. 'Emergency' is only defined in relation to works undertaken pursuant to para.10 of Sch.19. For the purposes of any power exercised under that paragraph, 'emergency' includes, in relation to street works, any circumstances requiring the carrying out of emergency works within the meaning of the Public Utilities Street Works Act 1950; and in relation to other works powers includes any danger to property and to any interruption of a supply of water provided to any premises by any person and to any interruption of the provision of sewerage services to any premises, Sch.19, para.10(5).
233. Under s.178.
234. S.156(6), Sch.19, para.10(4), Sch.10, para.1(6).
235. S.64; see above, section 3.5 and below, section 5.4.11.
236. S.287 of the Public Health Act 1936 and s.10 of the Public Health (Drainage of Trade Premises) Act 1937; see below, section 5.9.
237. S.147(1) and (2).
238. S.147(3).
239. S.147(4).
240. S.59(2).
241. S.60(4); see below, section 5.4.6.
242. S.62(4); see above, section 3.5, and below, section 5.4.11.
243. Sch.21, para.5; see above, section 3.7.3.
244. A warrant may not be issued where the exercise of a power has been refused or a refusal is reasonably apprehended, unless the justice of the peace is also satisfied that notice of the intention to apply for the warrant has been given to the occupier, or that the giving of such notice would defeat the object of the proposed entry, s.179(4).
245. A warrant may not be issued for the purpose of determining whether, where or how a

reservoir or borehole should be constructed or sunk unless the Secretary of State has given his or her written authorisation, s.178(5); see s.156(4).

246. S.178(6).
247. A failure to comply with any requirements of the warrant or s.179 does not absolve the relevant body from its obligations to pay compensation, s.179(7).
248. S.179(8). On summary conviction, that person is liable to a fine not exceeding level 3 on the standard scale (currently £400).
249. S.180(1). That person is liable, on summary conviction, to a fine not exceeding level 4 on the standard scale (currently £1,000).
250. S.125.
251. S.126.
252. S.126(3); see above, section 2.5.
253. 'Inland water' includes rivers, streams and other water sources, tidal and non-tidal, natural or artificial, but does not apply to land-locked lakes or ponds within the meaning of s.2(3) of the Water Resources Act 1963.
254. S.19(1) and (2). Or, where the NRA considers it would be appropriate, containing provisions relating to the level or volume of an inland water, s.22 of the Water Resources Act 1963.
255. The NRA must consult with any water undertaker having a right to abstract water from an inland water or from underground stata which may be affected by the draft statement, with any internal drainage board, any navigation, conservancy or harbour authority in whose district the inland water is situated or which exercises functions in relation to that water, and with the Central Energy Generating Board, s.19(4)(a)–(f) of the Water Resources Act 1963.
256. S.19(3).
257. Sch.7, Water Resources Act 1963.
258. See below, section 6.1.
259. See below, section 5.2.
260. Sch.7.
261. S.20.
262. S.130.
263. S.130(6); see above, section 2.5.
264. Currently £50, s.130(3).
265. Under s.119.
266. As defined in s.135 of the Water Resource Act 1963.
267. S.23.
268. S.49.
269. S.24(1A).
270. S.24(2).
271. Sch.13, para.6(5).
272. Meaning: (a) any drain, weir or other works in an inland water by which water may be impounded; and (b) any works for diverting the flow of an inland water in connection with the construction of any such work, s.36(6).
273. S.36.
274. S.45.
275. *ibid.*
276. S.129 of the Water Act 1989.
277. S.60.
278. S.65 of the Water Resources Act 1963.
279. Ss.67 and 69.
280. S.81.
281. S.131(1).
282. S.131(3).
283. A prohibition or limitation may be imposed so as to have effect in relation to a source from which a person to whom the prohibition or limitation applies has a right to take water whether by virtue of an enactment or instrument, an agreement or the ownership of land, s.133(2). This power and the power to suspend, or vary, or attach conditions to

any consent for the discharge of effluent, must be exercised so as to ensure, so far as reasonably practicable, that the supplies of water available to the water undertaker are not seriously affected, s.133(3).

284. S.131(3). Where the NRA exercises the power to restrict the discharge of effluent by a sewerage undertaker, the sewerage undertaker may itself modify any consents or agreements relating to the discharge by other persons of trade effluent so as to enable it to comply with any requirements or conditions imposed on it with respect to discharges from sewers or works of the undertaker, s.133(4).

285. S.131(4).

286. This power may be exercised in relation to consumers generally, a class of consumer or a particular consumer. The undertaker must give notice of the prohibition or limitation to those who are or may be affected. The prohibition or limitation may not come into operation under seventy-two hours after such notice has been given, s.131(5).

287. S.131(9).

288. S.131(8).

289. Sch.14, para.1.

290. He or she may do so in any case on his or her own account, para.2(6).

291. The Secretary of State may require an objection to be in writing, and may disregard an objection if it relates exclusively to matters of compensation, para.2(4).

292. Para.2.

293. S.132(1).

294. Except a provision authorising a water undertaker to prohibit or limit the use of water for a specified purpose, s.132(4)(a).

295. Any works carried out under the authority of an emergency order are included in the definition of emergency works in s.39(1) of the Public Utilities Street Works Act 1950, s.132(8).

296. S.132(6). The duty on any water or sewerage undertaker is enforceable under s.20.

297. S.132(9), Sch.14.

298. S.132(10).

299. Which includes any canal or navigable river.

300. 'Compensation water' means water which the NRA or an undertaker is under an obligation to discharge in accordance with the provisions of a licence under the Water Resources Act 1963 into a source of supply, or under any local statutory provision into any river, stream, brook, or other running water or into a canal, s.135(1).

301. S.133(1).

302. S.133(5) and (6).

303. Under ss.178 and 179; see above, section 3.7.5.

304. S.133(7).

305. S.133(8).

306. Sch.14, Part II.

307. Para.5.

308. Para.6.

309. Para.6(2).

310. Para.6(3).

311. Para.6(4).

312. Para.6(5).

313. Para.7(1).

314. Para.8(1).

315. Paras.7(2) and 8(2)–(4).

316. S.75(1).

317. S.75(2). In relation to a sewerage undertaker's trade effluent functions any agreement must be in accordance with s.7 of the Public Health (Drainage of Trade Premises) Act 1937; see below, section 5.9. An undertaker may enter into an agreement with a consumer despite the existence of a charges scheme, s.76(4)(a).

318. See above, sections 2.2.1–2.2.3.

319. See above, section 2.2.3.

320. Or an arbitrator appointed by the Director, s.46(5).

321. S.46(4) and (6).
322. S.46(6)(c).
323. See below, section 5.9.
324. S.79(1).
325. S.79(1). In relation to the drainage of premises 'domestic purposes' means those purposes mentioned in s.71(2)(a); see below, section 4.1.
326. S.79(2). A limit has been placed on the amount recoverable from these infrastructure costs by Condition C of the Instruments of Appointment of undertakers.
327. S.79(3); see below, section 4.1.
328. S.79(4).
329. As defined in the Fire Services Act 1947.
330. S.81(1). Charges may be made, however, in respect of work carried out for the benefit or at the request of persons receiving supplies of water for these purposes, s.81(2).
331. S.82(1).
332. S.82(2).
333. That is, a list maintained for rating purposes under the Local Government Finance Act 1988 or the General Rate Act 1967, s.80(3).
334. See above, section 2.2.4.
335. 'Meter' means any apparatus for measuring or showing the volume of water supplied to, or of effluent discharged from, any premises, s.78(4).
336. S.78(2).
337. A notice may relate to particular premises or to any description of premises and must be published in the locality in which the premises to which it relates are situated, in such a manner as the undertaker considers appropriate for bringing it for the attention of those persons likely to be affected. A copy must also be served on the Secretary of State, Sch.10, para.1(5).
338. Sch.10, para.1.
339. Para.1(4).
340. Para.1(3).
341. See s.50. Sch.10 does not prevent an undertaker exercising its power by virtue of s.50(3)(b) to impose a condition under s.43(1)(c) or (d) where it has, under s.50, required the provision of a separate service pipe to any premises; see para.1(7).
342. Para.1(2). See Sch.19, para.2(1)(d), 2(4) to (6), (8) and (9), and para.3; see also above, section 3.7.2.1. All of the works carried out by a water undertaker are considered necessary for the purposes of s.45 to 51; see above, sections 3.1.4–3.1.8. Para.1(7).
343. Under s.178.
344. Para.1(6).
345. Para.2(1).
346. Under s.43(1)(c) or (d), except in certain situations where separate service pipes are required for two or more houses which were supplied by a common supply pipe prior to 15 April 1981. Para.2 (proviso).
347. Under s.46; see above, section 3.1.5.
348. S.50(3)(b).
349. Para.2(5).
350. Para.2(4).
351. Para.5.
352. S.77(3).
353. Para.4. This duty is enforceable by the Secretary of State under s.20.
354. Currently £400, para.3(1).
355. Para.3(6).
356. Para.3(2)–(5).
357. S.7(1).
358. Ss.38 and 68.
359. S.162(7).
360. Ss.41 and 43.
361. S.72.
362. S.161.

363. S.7(5). In addition to protecting the consumer's interests, the Secretary of State and the Director must secure that the functions of water and sewerage undertakers are properly carried out as respects every area of England and Wales, and that undertakers are able (in particular by securing reasonable returns on their capital) to finance the proper carrying out of the functions of such undertakers, s.7(2).
364. S.7(4).
365. S.6(1)–(3).
366. The chairman may hold office for a term not exceeding four years, s.7(6).
367. S.6(4).
368. S.7(5).
369. S.162.
370. S.27(1). The only remedy for a breach by a customer service committee of any of these obligations is to make a complaint to the Director, s.27(3).
371. S.27(2).
372. S.162.
373. S.27(4).
374. S.I.1989/1159.
375. Reg.3. The right to payment is subject to certain exceptions set out in Reg.3(3).
376. Regs.4 and 5.
377. Reg.8.
378. Reg.11.
379. Reg.9.
380. Reg.10.
381. Under s.49.
382. Reg.6.
383. Reg.7 except where the supply is interrupted or cut off because of drought.
384. S.49(9).
385. S.26.
386. S.34.
387. S.35.

CHAPTER 4

Sewerage services

4.1 General duties of sewerage undertakers

Every sewerage undertaker is under a duty to provide and maintain a system of public sewers (whether within its area or elsewhere) and to cleanse and maintain those sewers so as to ensure that the area is and continues to be effectually drained. It must also make provision for the emptying of those sewers and such provision as is necessary to effectually deal, by means of sewage disposal works or otherwise, with the contents of those sewers.[1] In performing these duties, the undertaker is required to have regard to its existing and likely future obligations to allow for the discharge of trade effluent[2] into public sewers and to the need to provide for the disposal of trade effluent which is so discharged.[3]

This general duty is enforceable by the Secretary of State or, with the consent of or in accordance with a general authorisation given by him or her, the Director, under section 20.[4] A plaintiff will normally need to prove negligence by an undertaker in an action for damages in a case of sewer flooding: *Smeaton* v. *Ilford Corporation.*[5]

The Secretary of State, on the application of the Director, may make regulations for determining standards of performance in connection with the provision of sewerage services.[6]

Schedule 8 to the Act generally transfers the functions and powers exercised by water authorities in respect of the provision of sewerage services to sewerage undertakers from water authorities.[7]

The terms 'drain' and 'sewer' are defined in the Public Health Act 1936. A 'drain' means a drain used for the drainage of one building or of any buildings or yards, appurtenant to buildings within the same curtilage. 'Sewer' does not include a drain as so defined, but otherwise includes all sewers and drains used for the drainage of buildings and yards appurtenant to buildings.[8] A sewer does not necessarily carry only sewage: it may, for example, be used to carry flood- or rainwater.[9]

A public sewer is a sewer which is vested in a sewerage undertaker in its capacity as such.[10] A reference to a pipe, main, drain, or sewer in the Water Act 1989 includes reference to a tunnel or conduit which serves or is to serve as the pipe in question and to any accessories for the pipe.[11] Sewers become vested in a sewerage undertaker when it constructs them at its own expense, when they are vested in it in pursuance of statutory arrangements,[12] under an agreement,[13] or a declaration of vesting.[14]

A sewerage undertaker may at any time declare that a sewer within its area or serving part of its area, being a sewer whose construction was completed after 1 October 1937, is to become vested in it as from a specified date.[15] The undertaker must give notice to the owner of the sewer of its proposal to make such a declaration and allow a period of two months for an appeal to be made to the Secretary of State, who may allow or disallow the proposal and may specify conditions, including the payment of compensation by the undertaker.[16] An owner of a sewer may apply to an undertaker requesting it to make such a declaration.[17]

The main sewers laid by an undertaker automatically form part of the public sewerage system and are maintainable at the expense of its customers generally, but the sewers and drains on a development site are normally laid by a developer. Although individual drains become the responsibility of property owners once the buildings are sold, the private sewers built by the developer may be 'adopted' by the sewerage undertakers into the public system.[18] Unadopted sewers normally become the shared responsibility of the owners of the properties they serve. Where an undertaker considers that a proposed drain or sewer is likely to be needed to form part of the general system, it may require the drain or sewer to be constructed to specified standards to enable it to be adopted.[19] Where an undertaker refuses to enter into an agreement to adopt a sewer, or imposes conditions to which the person constructing or proposing to construct it objects, that person may appeal to the Secretary of State who may uphold the refusal to grant the application, or enter into any agreement into which the undertaker might have entered.[20]

It is the duty of a sewerage undertaker to provide a public sewer for the drainage of premises[21] for domestic purposes where the owner or occupier of such premises[22] requires that undertaker by written notice to provide a sewer, and certain financial conditions are met.[23]

'Domestic purposes' means:[24]

(a) the removal, from the buildings and from land occupied with and appurtenant to the buildings, of the contents of lavatories;
(b) the removal, from the buildings and from such land, of water which has been used for cooking or washing, not being water used for the business of a laundry or of a business of preparing food or drink for consumption otherwise than on the premises; and
(c) the removal, from the buildings and such land, of surface water.[25]

The undertaker is given a period of six months, from the day the financial conditions are satisfied or the day on which the places at which connections to the public sewer are to be made are agreed, or whichever is the later, to comply with this duty.[26] A sewerage undertaker has a discretion as to the point requisitioned sewers should be brought, so as to ensure the most efficient and economical drainage of new developments, having regard to the existing public sewer layout.[27] In default of agreement as to the places at which it is reasonable, in all the circumstances, for drains or private sewers to connect to a public sewer, the matter is to be determined by a single arbitrator.[28]

In considering a similarly worded section in the Water Act 1973, the court in *William Leech (Midland)* v. *Severn Trent Water Authority*[29] held that the phrase 'as to enable drains and private sewers to be used for the drainage of premises in that locality to communicate with the public sewer' implied effective communication, which meant the water authority had to provide a pump if it was not possible to discharge into a public sewer by gravity. The Court of Appeal also held that the authority was required to make the actual connection itself and that it was not entitled merely to bring the sewer onto the land, leaving the owner to make the connection.

The financial conditions are satisfied in relation to the requirement for the provision of a public sewer if such undertakings and security as the undertaker may have reasonably required have been given or provided for the discharge of any obligations imposed by those undertakings on the person or persons who required the provision of the sewer.[30]

The undertakings referred to are those which bind the person or persons who require the sewer to pay to the undertaker, in respect of each of the twelve years following the provision of the sewer, an amount not exceeding the relevant deficit (if any) for that year or that sewer.[31] The relevant deficit for any year on a public sewer is the amount (if any) by which the drainage charges[32] payable for the use during that year of that sewer are exceeded by the annual borrowing costs of a loan of the amount required for the provision of that sewer.[33] The annual borrowing costs of a loan required for the provision of a sewer is the amount repayable each year if an amount equal to the costs incurred in providing the sewer (except those incurred in the provision of additional capacity)[34] had been borrowed by the undertaker of terms requiring interest to be paid and capital to be repaid in twelve equal annual instalments.[35]

These financial provisions are designed to make requisitioners pay the full cost of investment in new sewers over a twelve-year period, rather than having new sewers subsidised by existing customers, as was the situation under the previous legislation.

The costs of providing a new sewer include the costs reasonably incurred in providing other sewers and pumping stations consequential on the provision of that sewer, and a reasonable proportion of costs incurred in providing such additional capacity in an earlier public sewer[36] as is now used as a consequence of providing the new sewer.[37] This allows for the situation where a developer requisitions a sewer for a small development with the intention of expanding the development later. Under the previous legislation, if the undertaker laid an oversize sewer for the first development, it was unable to recover the extra expense.[38] The Water Act now allows an undertaker to recover a reasonable proportion of the cost of oversized pipes from subsequent developers if their development follows within twelve years of the original requisition.

On any sum which is deposited with a sewerage undertaker by way of security for the discharge of any financial obligations, that sewerage undertaker must pay quarterly interest at a rate approved by the Director.[39] Any dispute between an undertaker and another person as to the undertakings or security required by the undertaker or the amount required to be paid in pursuance of any such undertaking is to be determined by a single arbitrator.[40]

The duty of a sewerage undertaker to provide a public sewer is a duty owed to the persons requiring its provision, and any breach of this duty which causes those persons to sustain loss or damage is actionable, unless the undertaker can show that it took all reasonable steps and exercised all due diligence to avoid the breach.[41]

The owner or occupier of any premises, or the owner of any private sewer is entitled to have his or her drains or sewer made to connect with an undertaker's public sewers and thereby to discharge effluent waste and surface water from the premises or sewer.[42] For the purpose of exercising this right, the owner or occupier of any premises may break open any street, and examine, repair or renew any such drain or private sewer.[43] He or she must, however, give notice of the proposal to the undertaker, who may refuse to permit the connection to be made unless certain conditions are complied with.[44]

An undertaker receiving such a proposal by an owner or occupier may give notice to him or her that it intends itself to make the connection. However, it is not bound to make the connection until either the cost of the work, as estimated by the undertaker, has been paid to it, or security for such payment has been given to its satisfaction.[45]

Every sewerage undertaker must keep records of the location and other relevant particulars, i.e. whether it is a drain, sewer or disposal main, the descriptions of effluent for the conveyance of which it is used, whether it is a sewer to which a declaration of vesting or an agreement to adopt has been made,[46] of the following:

1. Every public sewer or disposal main, any outfall pipe or other pipe which is a pipe for the conveyance of effluent to or from any sewage disposal works, whether of an undertaker or not, and is not a public sewer,[47] which is vested in the undertaker.
2. Every sewer in relation to which a declaration of vesting has been made.[48]
3. Every drain or sewer in relation to which an agreement under section 18 of the Public Health Act 1936 has been made.[49]

Any modification of the records must be made as soon as reasonably practicable after the completion of works which made the modification necessary, and the date of the modification and the completion of the works must be entered in the records.[50] The undertaker must ensure that up-to-date copies of these records are provided free of charge to local authorities at all times,[51] and that the information, in the form of sewer maps, is available for public inspection free of charge at its office. The duty of a sewerage undertaker to keep such records is enforceable by the Secretary of State under section 20.[52]

It is an offence (apart from the lawful discharge of trade effluent) to throw, empty or turn, or suffer or permit to be thrown, or emptied or to pass, into any public sewer or into any drain or sewer communicating with a public sewer:

(a) any matter likely to injure the sewer or drain, or to interfere with the free flow of its contents, or to affect prejudicially the treatment and disposal of its contents; or

(b) any chemical refuse or waste stream, or any liquid of a temperature higher than 110 degrees Fahrenheit, being refuse or stream which, or a liquid which, when so heated, is dangerous, or the cause of a nuisance or prejudicial to health, either alone or in combination with the contents of the sewer or drain.[53]

On the advice of a sewerage undertakers and consistent with any directions given by it, a local authority must reject plans deposited with it under building regulations for a building or an extention of a building which it is proposed to erect over any sewer or drain shown on a map kept by it, in such a manner as would result in its interfering with the use of the drain or sewer or obstruct access to the drain or sewer.[54]

A local authority[55] may perform any of the sewerage functions of a sewerage undertaker upon agreement with, and on behalf of, that authority, but such an arrangement does not affect the availability to any person of any remedy against the undertaker in respect of the carrying out of the undertaker's sewerage functions or of any failure to carry them out.[56]

4.2   Trade effluent functions

The occupier of any trade premises within the area of a sewerage undertaker may, with the consent of that undertaker, discharge any trade effluent from the premises into the public sewers. Trade premises are any premises used or intended to be used for carrying on a trade or industry, and trade effluent means any liquid, either with or without particles of matter in suspension, which is wholly or in part produced in the course of any trade or industry carried on at trade premises, but does not include domestic sewage.

The sewerage undertaker may refuse consent, or give consent either unconditionally or subject to such conditions as it thinks fit with respect to certain criteria. Any person aggrieved by a refusal or failure to give consent may, within two months, appeal to the Director General of Water Services for a determination.

Where trade effluent contains prescribed substances in excess of a background concentration, or results from prescribed processes, or if either asbestos or chloroform is present in a concentration greater than a background concentration, it is subject to special controls, with consents being granted by the Secretary of State rather than by an undertaker.[57]

4.3   Rights and powers of works, etc.

The rights and powers of a sewerage undertaker are substantially the same as those given to water undertakers, with the necessary adaptations relating to their differing functions.

4.4   Consumer protection

The Secretary of State and the Director General of Water Services exercise powers of control and enforcement over the sewerage functions of undertakers to the same extent as in relation to undertakers' water supply functions.

Notes

1. S.67(1).
2. 'Trade effluent' is defined to mean any liquid, with or without particles of matter in suspension in it, which is wholly or in part produced in the course of any trade or industry carried on at trade premises but does not include domestic sewage, Public Health (Drainage of Trade Premises) Act 1937, s.14(1). For the disposal of trade effluent into sewers, see below, section 5.9.
3. S.67(2).
4. S.67(4).
5. [1954] Ch.450.
6. S.68. Such regulations may relate to individual undertakers or to undertakers as a whole. See the Water Supply and Sewerage Services (Customer Service Standards) Regulations 1989 (S.I.1989 No.1159); see also above, section 3.11.3.
7. The Act does not consolidate the law relating to drains and sewers, but makes some significant amendments, principally to the Public Health Act 1936.
8. S.343(1), Public Health Act 1936.
9. *Hutton v. Esher Urban District Council* [1974], Ch.167 (CA).
10. S.189(1), Water Act 1989.
11. S.189(4).
12. Under Schs.2 or 5.
13. S.18, Public Health Act 1936.
14. *ibid.*, s.17.
15. *ibid.*
16. *ibid,* s.17(3).
17. *ibid.,* s.17(2).
18. *ibid.,* s.18.
19. *ibid.,* s.19.
20. *ibid.,* s.18(4).
21. That is, premises on which there are buildings or premises on which there will be buildings when proposals made by any person for the erection of any buildings are carried out, s.71(1)(b).
22. And certain other bodies in respect of New Towns and development areas, s.71(3).
23. S.71(1).
24. S.71(2)(a).
25. Where a person is proposing to erect buildings on premises the term applies to these purposes once the buildings have been erected, s.71(2)(b).
26. S.71(4), unless extended by agreement.

27. S.71(5).
28. S.71(6).
29. [1980] J.P.L. 753.
30. S.72(1). No security can be demanded if a public authority requires the provision of the sewer.
31. S.72(2).
32. That is, the aggregate of any charges imposed by the undertaker in relation to such premises where there are buildings, and charges reasonably attributable to the use of that sewer for the disposal for domestic purposes of those premises or to the disposal of effluent drained for domestic purposes from those premises, s.72(7). As to charges generally, see above, section 3.10.
33. S.72(3).
34. Meaning works carried out for the purpose of enabling the sewer to be used for purposes in addition to those for which it is necessary to provide the sewer in order to comply with a requirement, s.72(6).
35. S.72(4). The appropriate interest rate is determined by the undertaker with approval of the Director, or the Director in default of determination, but once determined or approved may not be altered, s.72(9)(b).
36. That is, any sewer requisitioned within the previous twelve years.
37. S.72(5).
38. Although it was able to upgrade a sewer later at the developer's expense.
39. S.72(8) and (9).
40. S.72(10).
41. S.71(7) and (8).
42. S.34(1), Public Health Act 1936.
43. ibid., S.34(2).
44. ibid., S.34(3).
45. ibid., S.36.
46. S.166(2).
47. Sch.19, para.1.
48. Under s.17, Public Health Act 1936.
49. See s.166(1).
50. S.166(6).
51. This information is to be made available in the form of a map for inspection by the public free of charge at the office of the local authority, s.166(4).
52. S.166(8).
53. S.27, Public Health Act 1936.
54. S.18, Building Act 1984.
55. Or the Commission for the New Towns, a development corporation for a New Town, the Development Board for Rural Wales or an Urban Development Corporation, s.73(5).
56. S.73.
57. Trade Effluent (Prescribed Processes and Substances) Regulations 1989.

CHAPTER 5

Water quality

5.1   Measurement and standards of water quality

Water quality cannot be measured or evaluated meaningfully without consideration of the use for which the water is used. Quality standards for water that is used for water supply abstraction will obviously be different from those applicable to water intended to be suitable for shellfish production, and both may differ from the desired water quality for trout fishing, irrigation, swimming or water cooling for industrial processes. Evaluation of water (whether in streams, lakes or elsewhere) must therefore consider both the concentrations of various constituents in that water and the particular use or uses that it is intended to be put to.

In general, measurements of water quality are based on a comparison with composition and properties of water in its natural state, whether that natural state be in a watercourse in upland areas, an estuary, or in the coastal sea. For this reason, water pollution at common law is defined not in terms of scientific standards but by reference to the natural quality of water in a watercourse.[1] Liability for water pollution arises in consequence of an alteration to the natural quality of a particular water, irrespective of whether that water was naturally of a high or low quality. In both international law and in European Community legislation,[2] 'pollution' is determined with reference to the effect of human interference on the aquatic environment.

A large number of parameters may be used to describe and measure water quality characteristics. Given that water quality is usually subject to changes with or without human interference, the choice of which parameters should be measured and which methods of analysis should be employed, involves a complex matrix of variables.

Generally, water quality can be evaluated with reference to its physical, chemical and biological characteristics. Physical characteristics include its temperature, colour and content of suspended solids; chemical characteristics take account of the content of specified chemicals such as ammonia, heavy metals, etc., in the water; while biological characteristics consider such properties as the bacteriological content and the existence of pathogens in the water.

In measuring and assessing these characteristics, a number of different types of analysis may be used, either alone or in conjunction with each other.[3] The first is to measure directly the concentrations of specific constituents of water, such as calcium, magnesium, lead, iron, mercury and chromium. These may be particularly important in areas of water supply because of their potential effects on public health. In other situations, concentrations of certain ions or compounds may be of interest. Although all containing sulphur, the effects of sulphates, sulphites and sulphides on water are all different. Other important chemical groups in evaluating water quality include organic nitrogen, ammonia, nitrites, nitrates and phenols. The various methods in this category are all intended to permit direct and quantitative measurements of selected parameters. In addition, they enable direct comparisons of water characteristics to be made.

A second category of methods of measuring water quality is based on the evaluation of characteristics that cannot be related directly to concentrations of one or more chemicals or chemical groups. For example, turbidity is a measure of scattering of light or particles present in the water, and is particularly important in assessing the visual acceptability of drinking water. Measurement of turbidity cannot be achieved simply by measuring the concentration of a specific constituent. Instead, it has been necessary to develop an arbitrary scale which measures the extent to which the water exhibits a cloudy appearance, and is based on a comparison with standards prepared to contain known concentrations of specific suspended materials which are known to cause turbidity. Other analytical processes based on arbitrary scales have been developed for colour, alkalinity and acidity, suspended solids concentrations and dissolved solids.

Another category of water quality measurements relates to the measurement of factors associated with a particular quality characteristic. For example, it would be extremely time-consuming and expensive to determine the wide variety of types and numbers of pathogenic organisms that may be present in drinking water supplies. Instead, the procedure used is to measure the number of 'indicator organisms' – specifically the coliform group of bacteria present in the water. Coliforms indicate the extent to which water has been contaminated by fecal matter, and have been found to bear a clear association with the probability that pathogens may be present in the water, either then or in the future. Other examples of tests based on associated factors include the measurement of chemical factors and of conductivity to estimate dissolved solids in water.

A fourth method of water quality assessment is to measure the effects caused by constituents rather than the identity or concentration of the constituents themselves. For example, oxygen demand is important in determining the effects of effluent discharges on aquatic life. The biological oxygen demand (BOD) test measures directly the amount of oxygen actually consumed by living organisms under conditions approximating those that may exist in a receiving water. In doing so, it measures the effect of the various constituents of effluent or oxygen resources without directly identifying any of those constituents. Other tests based on measuring the effects of constituents include hardness, colour, fish assaying and turbidity.

5.2   Classifications of water and water quality objectives

A new feature introduced by the Water Act is the power given to the Secretary of State to classify the quality of 'controlled water',[4] and to set water quality objectives in relation to one or more of the classifications.[5] The system of classification is designed to ensure that priorities are identified which can provide the basis for planned programmes of upgrading and improvement. In doing this, the Secretary of State is to take account of the different uses to which rivers and estuaries are put, the different standards different users require, and the standards specified in EC Directives.[6]

The requirements in such classifications are to be one or more of the following:

1. General requirements as to the purposes for which the waters to which the classification is applied are to be suitable.
2. Specific requirements as to the substances that are to be present in or absent from the water, and as to the concentrations of substances which are or are required to be present in the water.
3. Specific requirements as to the other characteristics of those waters.

Monitoring of water quality may be by means of prescribed methods and frequent samples.[7]

The Surface Waters (Classification) Regulations 1989,[8] the first of such classifications, set water quality standards with regard to the classification (after treatment) as drinking water. The Regulations contain a list of 211 mandatory parameters in respect of which water quality is determined.[9]

Before exercising his or her power to set water quality objectives, the Secretary of State must publish notice of his or her proposal in an appropriate manner to bring it to the attention of persons likely to be affected by it. The notice must specify a period of at least three months from the date of publication within which representations or objections may be made. He or she must then consider any representation or objection duly made.[10] The Secretary of State may review water quality objectives, if requested to do so by the NRA, after it has consulted with water undertakers and other persons if considered appropriate, or if at least five years have elapsed since the previous classification.[11] A water quality objective for any waters is the satisfaction by those waters and at all times after each date specified in the notice of classification, of the requirements specified in the notice.[12]

5.3   Role of European Community law[13]

Until 1987 the power of the European Community to make laws with respect to environmental matters was derived from the general power conferred by member states in their accession to the Treaty of Rome 1957.[14] Since that date, explicit reference to a Community environmental policy has been introduced by the Single European Act 1987,[15] which amended the Treaty of Rome by adding new articles.[16] Now the objectives of action by the Community relating to the environment are to preserve, protect and improve the quality of the environment; to contribute towards protecting human health; and to ensure a prudent national utilisation of natural resources.[17] Action by the Community is to be based on the principles that preventative action should be taken, that environmental damage should as a priority be rectified at source, and that the polluter should pay.[18]

The principal form of Community legislation relevant to environmental matters are Directives, which are said to be binding 'as to the result to be achieved . . . but shall leave to the national authorities the choice of form and methods.'[19] Directives therefore allow some degree of flexibility by member states in their implementation, but normally require some form of positive act of implementation within a time specified in the Directive. Unless the substance of a Directive is already part of the law of the United Kingdom, its implementation is brought about by the enactment of a statute or the passing of subordinate legislation in the form of regulations.[20] In England and Wales it has been the practice of the Government to issue circulars through the Department of the Environment to water authorities, and now undertakers as well, for the enforcement of Directives.[21] Whether this practice is sufficient to implement Directives in the absence of a direct legal obligation on undertakers to comply with the circulars, is a nice point. In a decision relating to the implementation of the Bathing Water Directive in the Netherlands,[22] the European Court held that a member state is free to implement a Directive through measures adopted by regional or local authorities, but that the overriding requirement was that effect must be given to the Directive by means of national provisions of a binding nature. Thus, mere administrative changes, which could be altered at any time, did not constitute implementation of the Directive by the Dutch Government.

Whether the advice given in circulars issued by the Department of the Environment is of a binding nature depends on whether a court could issue an administrative order of mandamus compelling an undertaker to adhere to the provisions of a circular. The issue remains untested, but, with the prospect of water quality objectives and standards being formalised by governmental regulations,[23] the difficulty of showing a legally binding obligation will be overcome in that respect. In addition, the European Court has developed a judicial doctrine of 'direct effect', whereby Directives and other European Community legislation are capable of conferring rights upon individuals even without formal implementation in national legislation. This doctrine permits an individual to compel a member state to comply with an obligation imposed on it by Community legislation, and enables that individual to obtain a remedy in the national courts rather than a mere declaratory judgment in the European Court.

However, for the doctrine to be applicable, the measure at issue must be clear and unambiguous, unconditional and not dependent upon further action being taken by either the Community or member states.[24] Given the fact that Community Directives on environmental matters contain a degree of discretion in their forms and manner of implementation, it is a matter of some debate whether the doctrine of 'direct effect' is applicable to such Directives.[25]

The Community has adopted a number of Directives on water

quality and the prevention of pollution, which generally fall into two categories. First, those which deal with the control of particular types of pollutants[26] and secondly, those which are concerned with the prevention of pollution of water used for particular purposes.[27]

5.4   Water supply quality

Water undertakers are required to supply only water which is wholesome when they supply water to any premises for domestic purposes.[28] A reference to 'domestic purposes' means a reference to the drinking, washing, cooking, central heating and sanitary purposes for which water supplied to premises may be used. It includes the purposes of a profession carried on in a house and such purposes outside the house (including the washing of vehicles and the watering of gardens) as are concerned with the occupation of the house and may be satisfied by a supply of water drawn from a tap inside the house and without the use of a hosepipe.[29] 'Domestic purposes' do not include the use of a bath having a capacity of over 230 litres, the business of a laundry or a business of preparing food or drink for consumption otherwise than on the premises.[30] In addition, they must ensure, so far as reasonably practicable, that there is no deterioration in the quality of water which is supplied from time to time from any source or combination of sources used for domestic water supplies.[31]

The former duty is limited by the proviso that water shall not be regarded as unwholesome at the time of supply where it has ceased to be wholesome only after leaving the undertaker's pipes.[32] However, this proviso does not apply and consequently water is to be regarded as unwholesome, if:

(a) it has ceased to be wholesome after leaving the undertaker's pipes but while still in a pipe subject to water pressure from a water main; and

(b) the reason for its deterioration in quality is due to the failure of a water undertaker to take such steps as are laid down in regulations for the purpose of securing the elimination, or reduction to a minimum, of any prescribed risk that the water would cease to be wholesome after leaving the undertaker's pipes.[33]

The Secretary of State is given wide powers in section 53 to specify in regulations what is required of water undertakers to comply with their general duty to supply wholesome water. In addition to being enforceable by the Secretary of State,[34] regulations may also provide for criminal sanctions. Further powers are given to the Secretary of State in section 65 to make regulations prescribing technical requirements and standards for the purpose of determining the wholesomeness of water.

5.4.1 WHOLESOMENESS

The term 'wholesomeness' has been considered in a number of cases,[35] but for the first time, standards of wholesomeness have been defined and laid down in regulations. The Water Supply (Water Quality) Regulations 1989[36] are concerned with the quality of water supplied in England and Wales for drinking, washing and cooking and with arrangements for the publication of information about water quality. They give effect in part to certain EC Directives on drinking water quality.[37]

Although in some cases tougher standards are set[38] than in those Directives, Part II of the Regulations prescribes standards of wholesomeness in respect of water supplied by water undertakers for certain domestic purposes, and in particular it provides that water is to be regarded as wholesome if it contains concentrations or values in respect of various elements, organisms and properties which are consistent with prescribed maximum, and in some cases, minimum, concentrations or values.[39]

In general, water must not contain any element, organism or substance (other than a specified parameter) at a concentration or value which would be detrimental to public health; nor may it contain any combination of elements, organisms or substances (whether or not specified parameters) which would be detrimental to public health.[40]

It must not contain concentrations or values of forty-four listed parameters in excess of the prescribed concentrations or values for those parameters.[41] Water is not unwholesome solely by reason of a sodium concentration exceeding the specified limit,[42] if 80 per cent of the results of analysis of all samples taken in accordance with the Regulations within the preceding thirty-six months from sampling points within the water supply zone in question demonstrate a concentration of sodium within the relevant specified maximum.[43] Water will also not be unwholesome solely be reason of the presence in it of total coliforms,[44] if 96 per cent of the results of analysis of a specified number of samples established the absence of such coliforms.[45]

Samples taken from water supplied to the water supply zone in question in respect of a further ten parameters[46] must also establish that the average concentration or value of those parameters over the preceding twelve months did not exceed the specified limits.[47]

Where water has been softened or desalinated and is to be supplied for drinking or cooking, requirements relating to that water's hardness and alkalinity are also specified.[48]

In addition, water supplied for drinking, washing and cooking will be considered unwholesome if, on transfer from a treatment works or service reservoir for supply for drinking or cooking, it contained a concentration of specified biological parameters[49] in excess of the prescribed concentrations.[50]

5.4.2   RELAXATION OF THE REQUIREMENTS OF WHOLESOMENESS

In certain circumstances the Secretary of State, or, in the case of private water supplies, the Secretary of State or the appropriate local authority, may relax the requirements relating to standards of wholesomeness.[51]

5.4.2.1 *Public supplies*

Upon the written application of a water undertaker, the Secretary of State may authorise a relaxation of the requirements where he or she is satisfied:

(a) that the authorisation is necessary, as an emergency measure, to maintain a supply of water for human consumption;

(b) that the authorisation is called for by reason of exceptional meteorological conditions; or

(c) that the authorisation is called for by reason of the nature or structure of the ground in the area from which the supply emanates.[52]

On making its application to the Secretary of State for an authorisation, a water undertaker must serve a copy on either the Common Council of the City of London, a London Borough Council, or a district council if any premises in relation to which the authorisation is sought fall within the area of those authorities.[53]

The Secretary of State is, however, restricted in his or her discretion to authorise a relaxation.[54] He or she may not relax the requirements so as to give rise to a risk to public health which he or she considers unacceptable, and he or she may not relax the requirements so far as they relate to certain specified parameters.[55]

An authorisation must specify, where relevant, the extent to which the prescribed concentration or value of any parameter is authorised to be contravened[56] and the date on which it ceases to have effect.[57] It may relate to particular sources or particular supply areas or zones and may include conditions relating to the steps to be taken to improve the quality of such water and the monitoring of its quality.[58]

The Secretary of State may at any time modify or revoke an authorisation, whether or not it is expressed to be given for a specified period. However, unless its immediate modification or revocation is required for public health reasons, the Secretary of State must give at least six months' notice to the water undertaker and the appropriate local authority of his intention to revoke or modify an authorisation.[59]

A water undertaker must notify the Secretary of State as soon as the circumstances which gave rise to the application for the authorisation cease to exist, and, despite the requirement of six months' notice, the Secretary of State must thereupon revoke the authorisation.[60]

5.4.2.2 Private supplies[61]

In relation to a private supply of water for domestic purposes, either the Secretary of State or the appropriate local authority[62] may authorise a relaxation of the requirements on the application of either:

(a) the owner or occupier of the premises where the source of the private supply is situated;
(b) any other person who exercises powers of management or control in relation to that source; or
(c) the owner of any premises served by that supply.[63]

The powers of modification and revocation of an authorisation are adapted as appropriate, but where a private supply serves, or is to serve, more than 500 persons at any one time, the authority must consult the Secretary of State and comply with any directions given by him or her.[64]

5.4.3   MONITORING OF WATER SUPPLIES BY WATER UNDERTAKERS

Water supplies are monitored by water undertakers with reference to samples taken from consumers' taps. Water undertakers must identify in respect of each of its water supply zones[65] such number and location of consumers' taps as will in its opinion ensure that the samples taken[66] are representative of the quality of water within that zone.[67]

In relation to certain parameters, the Secretary of State may authorise the taking of samples from points other than consumers' taps.[68]

Water undertakers are required to take a minimum number of samples (the 'standard number') each calendar year in respect of a variety of properties, elements, organisms and substances listed in Tables in Schedule 3 to the Regulations.[69]

Where the analysis of samples has shown that a prescribed concentration or value has been contravened or where changes in an undertaker's practices may have had an effect on the quality of water, the specified number of samples to be taken is increased in that and the following year,[70] until such time as an analysis of samples shows that there has been no contravention of the prescribed concentration or value in the relevant period.[71]

A water undertaker must also take a standard number of samples in respect of specified organisms and substances[72] at treatment works and at reservoirs which store treated water.[73]

In relation to any source of water which has not been used at any time since 15 July 1985 or any source which has not been used for six months preceding the date on which the undertaker proposes to supply water from it, additional samples must be taken.[74]

In taking, handling, transporting, storing and analysing samples, water undertakers must comply with certain requirements as to the procedures for and conditions of, such taking, handling, etc.[75]

Any person designated in writing for the purpose by a water undertaker may enter any premises[76] to monitor, record and take tests of the quality and wholesomeness of water supplied for domestic purposes, and to take away such samples of water, effluent, land or articles as the undertaker considers necessary.[77]

5.4.4   WATER TREATMENT

The Water Supply (Water Quality) Regulations 1989 also deal with the treatment of water and regulate the substances, processes and products that may be used by water undertakers in connection with the supply of water.

5.4.4.1 *Treatment of raw water*

Before supplying water from any source for the purposes of drinking, washing and cooking, the water must be disinfected, which means that it must be subjected to a process which removes or renders inactive pathogenic micro-organisms.[78]

In addition, water supplied from any surface water[79] must be subjected to such further treatment as is necessary to secure compliance with the EC Directive on the quality of surface water intended for the abstraction of drinking water.[80]

Surface water will be regarded as being of sufficient quality[81] if it is abstracted from waters classified as suitable for abstraction for supply (after treatment) as drinking water in the Surface Waters (Classification) Regulations 1989.[82]

These Regulations contain a list of twenty-one mandatory parameters in respect of which water quality is determined.[83]

5.4.4.2 *Contamination from pipes*

In certain circumstances there may be a risk that water supplied by a water undertaker would cease to comply with the requirements relating to copper, lead or zinc after it leaves the undertaker's pipes, because either copper or lead is the major component, or zinc is a component, of pipes attached to the undertaker's pipes.[84] In these situations the water undertaker must treat the water in such a way as will, in its opinion, eliminate the risk or reduce it to a minimum, unless such treatment is unlikely to achieve a significant reduction, is not reasonably practicable, or relates only to water supplied in an insignificant part of a water supply zone.[85]

In addition, where the risk relates to lead, the undertaker must, upon receiving a written request from an owner of premises, remove its part of any pipe when the remainder of that part which connects directly to a tap used for the supply of drinking water is removed.[86]

5.4.4.3 *Control of substances, products and processes*

Before a water undertaker applies any substance or product to, or introduces any substance or product into, water for drinking, washing or cooking, it must obtain approval from the Secretary of State,[87] unless:

(a) the undertaker is satisfied that the substance or product either alone or in combination with any other substance or product in the water, is unlikely to affect the quality of the water; or

(b) the undertaker can demonstrate that the substance or product has been used in the period of twelve months preceding the Regulations being made on 6 July 1989; or

(c) the substance or product was listed in the 15th Statement of the Committee on Chemicals and Materials of Construction for Use in Public Water Supply and Swimming Pools.[88]

The Secretary of State may include in the approval such conditions as he or she thinks fit and may, subject to six months' notice, or, unless he or she is satisfied that it is necessary in the interests of public health, without notice, revoke or vary any approval or notice given previously by him or her.

In the same way, the Secretary of State may, by notice in writing, require a water undertaker to make an application to him or her for approval of the use of any process.[89] The Secretary of State may refuse the application or impose such conditions as he or she thinks fit, and after having given notice, make revoke or vary such approval.

At least once each year, the Secretary of State must issue a list of all substances, products and processes in relation to which an application for use has been granted, refused, revoked or modified or the use of which has been prohibited.[90]

A water undertaker, who applies or introduces any substance or product or uses any process in contravention of a notice or the conditions of an approval, commits a criminal offence, unless it can show it took all reasonable steps and exercised all due diligence to avoid the commission of the offence.[91]

Any person who knowingly or recklessly makes a false statement in relation to providing information or making an application commits an offence.[92]

5.4.5   RECORDS AND INFORMATION

For each water supply zone, a water undertaker must prepare and maintain records containing information about the quality of water supplied in that zone.[93] Entries relating to the results of analysis must be entered in the records within twenty-eight days from the day in which the result is first known to the undertaker.[94] Records must be revised and updated at least once a year and in relation to results of samples, must be kept for at least five years.[95]

These records must be available for public inspection free of charge at all reasonable times[96] and facilities to take copies of any part of a record must be made available.[97]

Each year a water undertaker must supply information in standard form[98] to a local authority concerning the general quality of water supplied to premises in the authority's area including the results of samples taken in respect of each parameter.[99]

In addition, it must notify local authorities and district health authorities immediately following the occurrence of any event, which by reason of its effect or likely effect on water supplied by it, gives rise or is likely to give rise to a significant risk to the health of persons residing in the authority's area.[100]

Water undertakers are required to publish an annual report[101] containing information about the quality of water supplied by them, the extent to which the specified criteria have been complied with, details of any relaxations allowed, and any action taken by the Secretary of State to enforce the requirements of the Act or Regulations.

5.4.6   FUNCTIONS OF LOCAL AUTHORITIES

Every local authority is under a duty to take all such steps as it considers appropriate to keep itself informed about the wholesomeness and sufficiency of water supplies supplied to premises in its area, including every private supply to any such premises.[102]

5.4.6.1 *Public supplies*

In fulfilling this duty, a local authority may take and analyse, or cause to be analysed by a person designated by it in writing, such samples of water supplied to premises in their area as it reasonably requires.[103] In doing so, it is bound to comply with the requirements imposed on water undertakers relating to the handling, storage, transporting and analysis of samples.[104]

Where there is anything which appears to a local authority to suggest:

(a) that any supply by a water undertaker for domestic purposes to any premises in its area is, has been or is likely to become unwholesome;
(b) that the unwholesomeness of any supply is, was or is likely to be such as to cause a danger to life or health; or

(c) that a water undertaker has failed or is likely to fail to ensure that there is no deterioration in the general quality of water in respect of a source or combination of sources;

it is requested to notify the water undertaker of the fact.[105]

In these circumstances, and where:

(a) it is not practicable at reasonable cost for a water undertaker to provide wholesome water to any particular premises by means of pipes;

(b) it is practicable at reasonable cost for the undertaker to provide a supply otherwise than in pipes to those premises; and

(c) the unwholesomeness of the supply of water is such as to cause a danger to life or health;[106]

a local authority is under a duty to require that the water undertaker provide a supply otherwise than in pipes.[107] In this situation, the local authority is liable for any charges payable to the undertaker in respect of the water supply, but may recover the amount of the charges from the owner or occupier of the premises to which the supply is provided.[108]

If a local authority is not satisfied that all necessary remedial action has been taken by a water undertaker after the undertaker has received notification of an unwholesome supply, it must inform the Secretary of State who has powers of enforcement under the Act,[109] of the contents of the notification, and must itself comply with any directions given by the Secretary of State.[110]

Given the financial and manpower resources of local authorities, the duties imposed on water undertakers themselves and the functions and powers exercised by the Drinking Water Inspectorate of HMIP,[111] it is difficult to see what particular role local authorities can play in the monitoring of public water supplies that is not duplicated elsewhere.

5.4.6.2 Private supplies[112]

However, local authorities are given the primary responsibility for ensuring the quality of domestic private water supplies. Where a local authority is satisfied in relation to any premises in its area which is supplied with water for domestic purposes by means of a private supply that any water so supplied is not, was not, or is likely not to be, wholesome,[113] it may serve a notice in relation to that supply on one or more of the relevant persons.[114] Any such notice must give particulars of the matters in respect of which the notice is served, specify the steps which are required to be taken to ensure the water supply is or becomes wholesome, and specify a period of at least twenty-eight days within which any representations or objections concerning the notice must be received by the authority.[115] There appears to be no restriction on who may make representations or objections in respect of a notice.

The authority may also in serving the notice specify the steps it intends to take itself, require a relevant person to make payments to another relevant person or to the authority for reasonable expenses incurred, or undertake to make payments for expenses reasonably incurred by relevant persons in taking any steps specified in the notice.[116] It may require a supply of water to be provided to premises specified in the notice by a water undertaker or any other person in preference to the current private supplier.[117]

A notice served by a local authority will not take effect until the end of the period specified in the notice within which representations or objections may be made.[118] If any representations or objections made by the person served with the notice are received by a local authority, it must submit the notice to the Secretary of State for confirmation. On receipt of a notice the Secretary of State must consider whether the notice should be confirmed and whether, if it is confirmed, it should be confirmed with or without modifications. For this purpose, he or she may hold a local inquiry or give the local authority and persons who made representations or objections an opportunity to be heard by a person appointed by the Secretary of State for that purpose.[119]

If any person who is required by virtue of a notice to take any step in relation to any premises fails to take that step within the period specified, a local authority may take that step itself, and recover any expenses reasonably incurred in taking that action.[120] There is no right to bring a civil action against a person who fails to comply with a notice issued by a local authority, but any sum required to be paid to any person in such a notice is recoverable from the person who was required to pay it.[121]

A requirement in a notice which is expressed to bind those premises in relation to the owners and occupiers from time to time, binds successive owners or occupiers of those premises as a local land charge.[122]

Notices may be modified or revoked by a local authority subject to requirements as to the consideration of representations and objections.[123]

5.4.7   POWERS OF LOCAL AUTHORITIES

In addition to its remedial powers in relation to private supplies and its supervisory powers in relation to public supplies, a local authority may serve on any person a notice requiring him or her to furnish such information as is reasonably required by it to exercise any of its powers or duties in relation to water quality.[124] A person who fails to comply with the requirements of such a notice is guilty of an offence and liable on summary conviction to a fine not exceeding level 5 on the standard scale.[125]

Any person designated in writing for the purpose by any local authority may enter any premises to determine whether, and if so, in what manner, any power or duty conferred or imposed on that authority should be exercised or performed, to exercise any such power or perform any such duty, or to carry out inspections, measurements and tests.[126] Generally, entry to premises may only be made at a reasonable time and after twenty-four hours' notice of the intended entry has been given to the occupier of the premises.[127] Exceptions are in cases of emergency or where the authority obtains a warrant from a justice of the peace to exercise its powers in certain circumstances.[128]

Where it is necessary for a local authority to carry out remedial action in respect of private water supplies, it is given powers equivalent to water undertakers with respect to the laying of pipes and carrying out of works.[129] Where a local authority exercises works powers on private land the provisions concerning complaints to the Director[130] do not apply. Any complaint would have to be made to a local government ombudsman under the Local Government Act 1974.

5.4.8   ENFORCEMENT OF WATER SUPPLY QUALITY OBLIGATIONS

The following duties and obligations imposed on water undertakers in respect of water quality are enforceable by the Secretary of State:

1. To supply only water which is wholesome at the time of supply when supplying water to any premises for domestic purposes.[131]
2. To ensure, so far as reasonably practicable, in relation to each source or combination of sources from which it supplies water to premises for domestic purposes, that there is, in general, no deterioration in the quality of the water which is supplied from time to time from that source or combination of sources.[132]

3. To provide a supply of water for domestic purposes otherwise than in pipes, when required to do so by a local authority for reasons of danger to life or health, and where it is practicable at reasonable cost to provide such a supply.[133]
4. To take and analyse or cause to be analysed the specified number of samples of the water within each of its water supply zones.[134]
5. To take and analyse or cause to be analysed the specified number of samples of water in relation to treatment works, reservoirs, changes in practice or new sources, and to collect and analyse such samples in accordance with the Regulations.[135]
6. To comply with the requirements relating to the treatment of water, and regulations on the substances, processes and products that may be used in connection with the supply of water.[136]

Enforcement can be undertaken by the Secretary of State when he or she is satisfied that a company is contravening any one or more of these statutory requirements, and is effected by means of provisional or final orders.[137] In determining whether to make a provisional or final order, the Secretary of State is required to have regard, in particular, to the extent to which any person is likely to sustain loss or damage in consequence of anything which, in contravention of the statutory requirement in question, is likely to be done, or omitted to be done, before a final order may be made.[138]

For those obligations and duties which are enforceable by the Secretary of State by means of provisional or final orders under section 20, no other or alternative remedies are available except those for which express provision is made in an enactment and those that are available in respect of act or omission otherwise than by virtue of it being a contravention of any enactment.[139]

However, the failure by a water undertaker to comply with a provisional or final order is actionable in civil proceedings by any person who sustains loss or damage as a result of that failure to comply.[140]

In proceedings brought by a person who suffers damage or loss as the result of a failure by a water undertaker to comply with the provisions of an order, it is a defence for that undertaker to show that it took all reasonable steps and exercised all due diligence to avoid contravening the order. This defence, however, is not available with respect to a breach of the general duty to supply wholesome water.[141] In addition, compliance with a provisional or final order is enforceable by civil proceedings brought by the Secretary of State for an injuction or other appropriate relief.[142]

5.4.9   DRINKING WATER INSPECTORATE

The Drinking Water Inspectorate (DWI) forms part of Her Majesty's Inspectorate of Pollution (HMIP) and has been established by the Secretary of State[143] to act with reference to his or her powers and duties concerning the quality and sufficiency of water under the Water Act, subordinate regulations and any other enactments.

Persons appointed as drinking water inspectors are required to carry out investigations for the purpose of ascertaining whether any duty or requirement imposed on an undertaker has been or is likely to be contravened, and to advise the Secretary of State as to whether, and if so in what manner, his or her powers should be exercised.[144]

A water undertaker must give a drinking water inspector all such assistance and provide all such information as he or she may reasonably require to carry out his or her investigations. Failure to comply with this requirement by a water undertaker is an offence.[145]

Drinking water inspectors have powers, normally after reasonable notice has been given,[146] to enter premises for the purposes of carrying out investigations, inspections, measurements and tests, to take away samples of water, land or articles and to require an undertaker to supply copies of any records kept by it.[147]

In addition to employees of the Department of the Environment, the Secretary of State may appoint consultants to give technical advice regarding drinking water regulations and control.[148]

5.4.10   OFFENCES IN RELATION TO WATER SUPPLY QUALITY

Where a water undertaker supplies water through pipes and that water is unfit for human consumption, that undertaker is guilty of a criminal offence unless it can be shown that there were no reasonable grounds for suspecting that the water would be used for human consumption, or that all reasonable steps were taken and all due diligence exercised to avoid the commission of the offence.[149]

The criteria for establishing whether water is unfit for human consumption are not specified anywhere in the Act or regulations but it appears a much stricter requirement than that water be wholesome when it is supplied for domestic purposes,[150] in that water falling below certain standards of wholesomeness may not be strictly unfit for human consumption. The precise meaning of the term 'unfit for human consumption' remains a matter for interpretation by the courts.

On being found guilty of this offence, an undertaker is liable on summary conviction to a fine not exceeding the statutory maximum and on conviction by indictment to an unlimited fine.[151] Proceedings in respect of this offence may only be instituted by the Secretary of State or the Director of Public Prosecutions.[152]

If any person is guilty of any act of neglect by which the water in any waterworks[153] which is used or likely to be used for human consumption for domestic purposes, or for manufacturing food or drink for human consumption, is polluted or likely to be polluted, he or she is guilty of an offence.[154]

If any owner or occupier of premises intentionally or negligently causes or allows any water fitting[155] for which he or she is responsible to be or remain so out of order, so in need of repair or so constructed or adapted, or to be so used:

(a) that water in a water main or other pipe of a water undertaker is or is likely to be contaminated by the return of any substance from those premises; or
(b) that water that has been supplied by the undertaker to those premises is or is likely to contaminated before it is used;

that person is guilty of an offence and liable on summary conviction to a fine not exceeding level 3 on the standard scale.[156]

5.4.11 POWERS TO PREVENT CONTAMINATION OF WATER

The Secretary of State is given wide powers to make regulations to prevent waste, misuse or contamination of water.[157] A water undertaker has the right to exercise certain powers when it has reason to believe that water or its water main or other pipe is being or is likely to be contaminated by the return of substances from any premises, or that water which is in any pipe connected to its main or pipes or which has been supplied by the undertaker, is being or is likely to be contaminated before it is used.[158]

In an emergency, the water undertaker has power to disconnect the service pipe[159] or to cut off the water supply.[160] As soon as is reasonably practicable after this has been done, the water undertaker must serve a notice on the consumer[161] specifying the steps that need to be taken to secure that contamination would not recur if the supply were restored.[162] A water undertaker who fails to serve this notice is guilty of an offence.[163]

In cases other than emergencies, the water undertaker must serve a notice on the consumer requiring him to take specified steps to ensure that the contamination ceases or does not occur. The notice must specify a period of at least seven days within which the steps are to be taken, and the consequences of any failure to comply with the notice.[164]

Where the situation after serving notice becomes an emergency, or the premises appear to be unoccupied and the specified steps not taken, the water undertaker may cut off the supply of water to those premises in the same way as for an emergency.[165]

If, however, the premises are occupied and the consumer fails to take the required action, the water undertaker itself may take those steps and recover any expenses reasonably incurred.[166]

Any person designated in writing by any water undertaker or local authority may enter any premises for the purpose of ascertaining whether any statutory provision with respect to any water fittings is being or has been contravened, to determine whether any power or duty conferred or imposed by any regulations made under section 62 should be exercised, to exercise or perform any such power or duty and to carry out inspections, measurements and tests and to take away samples of water (and or any water fittings or other articles).[167] Except in an emergency, or where a warrant has been obtained from a justice of the peace,[168] this power of entry may only be exercised at a reasonable time and after twenty-four hours' notice of the intended entry has been given to the occupier of the premises.[169]

Additional powers of entry to disconnect any pipe or cut off any supply because of water contamination are given in section 64, whereby any person authorised in writing by an undertaker may enter the premises to determine whether the power to cut off a supply can and should be exercised, or to exercise that power. However, unless the case is one of emergency or the undertaker has obtained a warrant from a justice of the peace under section 178, seven days' notice must be given before the power of entry is exercised.[170]

5.4.12   FLUORIDATION OF WATER SUPPLIES

Section 172 permits the Secretary of State, with the consent of the Treasury, to indemnify water undertakers against liabilities arising from the fluoridation of water supplies. It formalises the previous practice of the Department of Health to indemnify water authorities and companies in respect of potential liability. Any such indemnity does not provide a defence to liability for the supply of water unfit for human consumption,[171] although proceedings may only be taken in respect of that offence by the Secretary of State or the Director of Public Prosecutions.

5.5   Discharges by sewerage undertakers

The treatment of sewage and the disposal of residues from that treatment affects the environment through discharges of effluent to rivers, estuaries and coastal waters, and through disposal of residual sludges either to sea, land or air.

Many of the water quality problems associated with sewage effluent stem from historic factors. In the second half of the nineteenth century wastes were discharged untreated into the nearest watercourse, and sewers built as early as the 1870s remain in use, many in a poor state. Treatment of sewage discharged into rivers has improved progressively this century, but many sewers still discharge these contents directly into the sea or estuaries. The 1985 DoE River Quality Survey considered the two primary reasons for the overall decline in river quality between 1980 and 1985 to be: (a) the deterioration of sewage works effluents, often due to increased loads; and (b) the increased operation of storm overflows due to the overloading of sewage works.

In relation to sewage sludge there are in principle a number of disposal options – spreading on the land as a 'soil conditioner', disposal in landfill sites, and incineration. The main issue in this respect is the selection of the best practical disposal option as determined by environmental impact and local circumstances. In contrast, effluent disposal from sewage treatment works is more constrained. Its disposal is restricted to rivers or coastal waters in relative proximity to the works in question, and discharges are influenced by variations in climatic conditions as well as daily and seasonal peaks in the volume and composition of effluent reaching and being treated at the works.

Effluent and sludge disposal are closely inter-related. Generally, the greater the treatment of effluent prior to discharge to water, the greater the volume of residual sludge which must be disposed of by other means.

5.5.1   SEWAGE EFFLUENT DISCHARGES[172]

The discharge of inadequately treated sewage effluent into water affects that water by extracting from it dissolved oxygen during its process of bacteriological decay. In situations where there is already a high demand on a river's oxygen content from aquatic life present in that river or where a river has low aeration or is slow moving, the consequences of the added extraction of oxygen by sewage effluent can be significant and serious. When dissolved oxygen is used faster than it can be replenished, its concentration in the water decreases, causing an adverse affect on fish which require a relatively high concentration of oxygen for their metabolic needs. The removal of too much oxygen can lead to the asphyxiation of fish and other aquatic life and enable the growth of micro-organisms that produce by-products causing foul odours.

The particular methods and processes of sewage treatment are the responsibility of individual sewerage undertakers. There are a number of alternative treatment processes available, the selection of which depends on the particular pollutants that are required to be removed and the overall capital and operating costs of the treatment system. Generally, the effluent is first 'screened' by passing the sewage liquid through grids or sieves to remove fabrics, plastics, etc. This is then followed by primary settlement to separate solids (the 'sewage sludge') from the sewage before a process of biological treatment to remove organic material left in the settled sewage. Occasionally, tertiary treatment is undertaken to improve the effluent further. The degree of treatment is determined by the desired quality of the end product, which is determined by the water quality objectives and standards applicable to the receiving waters in question.[173]

5.5.1.1 *Consents under the Water Act 1989*

Sewerage undertakers are subject to the same consent system as industrial dischargers, and are required to obtain consents from the NRA with respect to discharges of treated or untreated sewage effluent from sewage works or directly from sewers.[174]

Under the Control of Pollution Act 1974, annual reports have been rendered to the Department of the Environment and the Welsh Office since 1986 in respect of treatment works which failed to meet the terms of consents granted by HM Inspectorate of Pollution. In that year, of the almost 4,500 works in England and Wales with numerical consents, some 22 per cent were failing their consent conditions. The most frequent reasons for non-compliance included progressive deterioration of old equipment, often beyond the design life of the plant; problems with manning and with the supervision of maintenance crews, and vandalism, (particularly in respect of unmanned works). From the mid-1970s until the early 1980s there was a steady drop in investment by water authorities in sewerage and sewage disposal.[175] Since 1981 there has been an increase in water authority investment.[176] However, the DoE expects relatively little improvement to show in the water quality survey of 1990 and, because of long lead times in investment to an improvement of water quality, there may in fact be a further deterioration in overall quality.

It is generally accepted that the poor performance of sewage works is due not to technical difficulties but more to financial constraints.[177] The privatisation of the industry means that sewerage undertakers are now able to borrow commercially by the methods available to public limited companies, rather than being subject to public sector borrowing constraints.

In December 1988 the Minister for Water announced a capital programme involving expenditure of some £1 billion spread over the ten authorities to bring substandard works into compliance with their discharge conditions by March 1992, wherever practicable.[178]

While these capital improvement schemes were being carried out, HMIP (and since 1 September 1989, the NRA) considered applications, in relation to sewage works which were contravening their conditions, for time-limited discharge consents reflecting their current performance levels. In addition, it was imperative in legal terms that during the process of the flotation of the industry, no sewage works was knowingly contravening the terms of its discharge consent, and thereby acting illegally.

For each plant prone to failure, a time-limited discharge consent has been granted and an agreement made on a costed timetable leading to compliance. For these works, an 'upper tier' limit reflecting current performance levels has been set, normally three times the main consent level. The 'upper tier' represents a maximum level for single samples and is normally assessed on the basis of a series of samples taken over a twelve-month period. A breach of these limits by a sewerage undertaker constitutes an offence.

5.5.1.2 *Bathing Water Directive*[179]

The 1976 Bathing Water Directive provides a mechanism whereby member states are to designate waters as bathing waters on the basis of certain criteria. The aim of the Directive is to protect both the environment and public health by maintaining standards for water used for bathing, other than water used for therapeutic purposes and water used in swimming pools.[180] 'Bathing water' is defined to mean all running or still fresh waters or parts therof, and sea water in which bathing is not prohibited and traditionally practised by a large number of bathers.[181] In England and Wales the Directive applies to coastal bathing waters only, as bathing is neither authorised nor traditionally practised by a large number of bathers in fresh water. For coastal bathing waters the Directive is considered to be relevant to sites with lifeguards, or at which changing huts, car parks or toilets are provided on a substantial scale for bathers.[182] For the designated bathing waters quality standards must be set and enforced on the basis of imperative and guide values set out in the Annex to the Directive. The most significant of these quality standards are concerned with the bacteriological content of water, and in particular coliform values, which indicate the degree of sewage contamination.[183]

Compliance with the specified standards is achieved when samples of water meet the requirements for 95 per cent of samples with regard to imperative values, and 90 per cent of samples with regard to other values, except for certain coliform criteria where compliance of 80 per cent of samples is required.[184] Places and procedures for sampling are also specified by the Directive.[185]

A total of 371 waters have so far been designated as bathing waters under the 1976 Directive, but a significant number still do not meet the required water quality standards laid down by the Directive.[186]

In December 1988 the Minister for Water announced a capital expenditure programme agreed upon with the water industry totalling approximately £1 billion to have all bathing waters comply with the Directive by 1995.[187] Compliance with the Directive is controlled through the system of discharge consents granted by the NRA, principally in relation to discharges from sewage works. For each bathing water, the Directive sets mandatory minimum water quality standards (Imperative 'I' values listed in the Annex) and a number of additional standards for guidance (Guide 'G' values). These water quality standards in turn determine the precise conditions attached to individual consents for discharges. The NRA is required to carry out monitoring and sampling activities as prescribed by the Directive and report through the Department of the Environment to the European Commission.

At present approximately 15 per cent of sewage (liquid effluent with untreated solids) is disposed of directly into the sea by sea outfall, ranging from short outfalls with little pre-treatment to satisfactory long outfalls with full preliminary treatment of grit removal and screening.[188]

5.5.1.3 *Other EC Directives*

Discharges of certain specified dangerous substances from sewage works are subject to special control under the provisions of the Dangerous Substances Directive.[189] A sewerage undertaker must therefore in authorising discharges of trade effluent into sewers[190] have regard to the question of whether or not such discharges should be subject to special controls. In addition, the NRA is required to ensure that consents for discharges from sewage treatment works or sewers include specific emission standards for both list I and list II substances, where:

(a) these receive trade effluent discharges from industrial sectors utilising the listed substances; and
(b) the discharge has, or could have, an appreciable effect on the concentration of the substance in the receiving water.[191]

In granting consents and setting emission standards in conditions attached to those consents, the NRA will also take into account the water quality standards of waters designated under the Freshwater Fish Directive and the Shellfish Directive.[192]

5.5.2   SEWAGE SLUDGE

Some of the most difficult and expensive aspects of sewage treatment involve the treatment and disposal of sludge from the sewage treatment processes. Sludge contains suspended solids removed from sewage by settling and certain growths developed in certain biological treatment processes. Treatment of sludge is usually designed to further break-down biodegradable organic materials, reduce risks to health by pathogenic micro-organisms and facilitate the removal of water to reduce the volume of material to be disposed of.

Approximately one-half of the United Kingdom's sewage sludge is currently spread onto land as a 'soil conditioner',[193] one-third is dumped at sea,[194] 20 per cent is disposed of in landfill sites and 4 per cent is incinerated.

At the Third Ministerial Conference on the Protection of the North

Sea in March 1990, the United Kingdom announced that dumping of sewage sludge would cease by 1998 which allows for the continuation of dumping of sewage sludge, while calling for urgent action to reduce the concentrations of specified substances in the sludge.[195] The substances concerned are those listed in Annex I to the Oslo Convention for the Prevention of Marine Pollution by Dumping from Ships and Aircraft 1972,[196] as well as certain 'Red List' substances[197] and other potentially significant pollutants of the kind listed in Annex II to the Oslo Convention.

The European Commission has issued a draft Directive on municipal waste which would in effect ban the dumping of untreated sewage sludge or sludge treated below a certain level into the sea.[198] The proposed Directive would require secondary biological treatment prior to its dumping into the sea. This would require additional treatment facilities at many treatment works, estimates of the cost of which have varied from £5 billion to £14 billion.

Where sludge is disposed of in landfill sites, the sewerage undertaker must assess whether it contains controlled substances for which a disposal licence must be obtained under Part I of the Control of Pollution Act 1974, or whether it contains substances subject to control under the Groundwater Directive[199] which may in any disposal discharge indirectly into groundwater.

5.5.3   ENFORCEMENT

A discharge in contravention of a condition of consent constitutes an offence.[200] In most cases a prosecution will be brought by the NRA on the basis of scientific analysis of the effluent and the receiving waters, but the Water Act also allows for private prosecutions to be brought.[201]

Under the Control of Pollution Act 1974, the general practice has been for consents granted by the Secretary of State to incorporate a schedule stating the conditions to which discharges are subject. The conditions relate to such aspects as the composition and permitted volumes of discharges, and requirements for monitoring and reporting. The consents contain a statistical compliance table which relate the number of samples taken during the period of a year to the maximum permitted number of samples which may fail to comply to specified limits for various determinants. The table is based on the need for a 95 per cent compliance rate, but incorporates adjustments to take account of normal statistical sampling errors.

In this way, a sewage treatment works will be in breach of its discharge consent where the number of samples which fail to comply with the discharge limits exceeds the permitted number of 'failures' during a year. Therefore, a failure to comply with the discharge limits on one or more occasions may not necessarily constitute an actionable breach of the discharge consent unless the number of such failures is in excess of the permitted number.[202]

It remains to be seen whether this practice will continue with consents granted by the NRA or whether there will be a move towards a dual approach, where two criteria are specified for each consent, one on the basis of a 95 per cent compliance, and the other an absolute maximum that may at no time be exceeded. A breach of either would constitute an offence.

In the past, the approach of the Department of the Environment has been a preference to settle matters relating to breaches of discharge consents by persuasion rather than prosecution. In its Report, the House of Commons Environment Committee stated that they

did not find it realistic for the DoE to leave it to third parties to prosecute water authorities. Despite their fears of frequent prosecution when the Control of Pollution Act 1974[203] was first introduced, the water authorities have in practice enjoyed immunity, despite publications of details about their performance in public registers. Arguably, prosecution of a water authority has become anybody's right, but nobody's job.[204]

In 1986, which was the first year for which the DoE had comprehensive compliance statistics, of the 4,355 numerical discharge consents issued by the DoE, 965 or 22 per cent failed to comply with their consents for 95 per cent of the time.[205] The Environment Committee believed that the situation was in fact more serious than is conveyed by those statistics, because in both 1977 and 1985 there were reviews of consent conditions by the DoE which resulted in an overall relaxation of effluent standards to accommodate earlier widespread non-compliance of sewage effluents.[206] By the time its functions relating to the granting of discharge consents had been transferred to the NRA, the DoE had brought no prosecutions of water authorities for breaches of consents. It remains to be seen whether this approach will be continued by the NRA, but indications are that it will take a more rigorous approach.

There has been one example of a private prosecution of a water authority for breaches of its discharge consent conditions. In *Wales* v.

Thames Water Authority,[207] the Anglers' Co-operative Association brought proceedings against the Authority for failure to comply with the conditions of its consent in respect of the ammonium nitrate content of the effluent discharged from its Aylesbury Sewage Treatment Works. Evidence of the failure to comply was obtained from the register of discharges kept by the Authority. Compliance with the consent was determined on the basis of a 95 per cent compliance table, which effectively meant that there was no breach unless the discharges failed to meet the standard on more than a specified number of occasions. Six breaches of the condition relating to ammonium nitrate were alleged however, and in the period of one year preceding each alleged breach the number of failed samples exceeded the allowance on the compliance table. The Authority pleaded guilty and was fined £1,000 in respect of each of the six offences.

Two important issues remain to be resolved following *Wales*' case. First, is information obtained from the register maintained by the water undertaker or the NRA[208] sufficient as proof of default by a water undertaker without the need for corroboration of the composition or nature of the alleged failed samples?[209] Secondly, can a single discharge failure or a number of failed discharges below the maximum allowed by a compliance table constitute an offence of breach of the conditions of a consent?

5.6   Discharges to water by industry

Industrial waste effluent is generally disposed of by a discharge directly into water subject to consent by the National Rivers Authority or, indirectly, into the sewerage system, subsequently passing to a sewerage undertaker's sewage treatment works and being discharged by that undertaker. Industrial effluent discharged to water from fixed pipelines are generally regarded as well-controlled and not posing a major threat to water quality.[210]

Isolated industrial pollution incidents in contrast to routine discharges of effluent are regarded as a more serious threat to water quality.[211] There are approximately 20,000 pollution incidents per annum, the majority of which are oil spillages, and leakages of sewer and farm wastes.[212] Most of these are minor incidents but some necessarily carry the risk of a major disaster. Certain controls exist currently in the planning system and in the Control of Industrial Major Accident Hazards (CIMAH) Regulations.[213] The CIMAH Regulations relate to production processes and storage of specified dangerous substances, chiefly in the chemical and petrochemical industries, and require certain precautions to be taken against major accidents.

The Government is currently in the process of preparing regulations on the location, construction and maintenance of stores to be used for hazardous substances either adjacent to water or likely to drain into the sewerage system.[214]

In their normal pollution control operations, as well as in emergencies, water pollution control agencies require extensive access to information about chemicals and substances and their potential environmental effects. With regard to pesticides and a number of other chemicals, detailed advice is provided on the label and in their product safety data sheets, but for many chemical substances full information is not available. The Government is currently participating in discussions at the European Community level on more comprehensive provisions for the classification and labelling of substances dangerous to the environment.[215]

Under the Water Act 1989, the principal means of control over discharges into water is the imposition of criminal liability for pollution, backed up by a system of discharge consents,[216] granted either by the National Rivers Authority or, in the case of discharges to sewers, the sewerage undertakers.

5.6.1 OFFENCES

Under section 107 of the Act, subject to certain defences, a person[217] is guilty of an offence if he or she causes or knowingly permits:

(a) any poisonous, noxious or polluting matter or any solid matter to enter any controlled waters; or

(b) any matter, other than trade effluents or sewage effluent[218] to enter controlled waters by being discharged from a drain or sewer in contravention of a relevant prohibition; or

(c) any trade effluent or sewage effluent to be discharged:
  (i)   into any controlled waters; or
  (ii) from land in England and Wales, through a pipe, into the sea outside the seaward limits of controlled waters; or

(d) any trade effluent or sewage effluent to be discharged, in contravention of any relevant prohibition from a building or from any fixed plant onto or into land or into a lake or pond which does not discharge directly or indirectly into a river or watercourse; or

(e) any matter whatever to enter any inland waters so as to tend (either directly or indirectly or in combination with other matter which he or she or another person permits to enter those waters) to impede the proper flow of the waters in a manner leading or likely to lead to a substantial aggravation of:

(i)   pollution due to other causes; or

(ii)   the consequence of such pollution.[219]

A person found guilty of any of the offences specified in section 107 is liable on summary conviction to a term of imprisonment not exceeding three months, a fine not exceeding the statutory maximum (currently £2,000), or both, and on conviction on indictment to a term of imprisonment not exceeding two years, an unlimited fine or both.[220]

5.6.1.1 'Controlled waters'

A wide definition is given to 'controlled waters' in section 103. They consist of all relevant territorial waters, coastal waters, inland waters and ground waters each of which are further defined in that section.

'Territorial waters' are those waters extending seaward for three miles[221] from the base lines from which the breadth of the territorial sea is measured.[222]

'Coastal waters' means waters extending landward from the baselines as far as the limit of the highest tide, or in the case of rivers and watercourses, as far as the fresh-water limit of that river or watercourse, including the waters of any adjoining enclosed dock.[223]

'Inland waters' means rivers and watercourses (including underground and artificial rivers and watercourses) which are not public sewers or sewers or drains which drain into a public sewer above the fresh-water limit,[224] and any lake or pond (including a reservoir and whether natural or artificial, above or below ground) which discharges into a river or watercourse or into another lake or pond which is itself a relevant lake or pond.[225]

'Ground waters' means water contained in underground strata or in any well or borehole or excavation but not in a sewer, pipe, reservoir, tank or other underground works constructed in any underground strata.[226]

5.6.1.2 'Causes or knowingly permits'

There is now a considerable body of case law on the meaning of 'causes or knowingly permits'. The phrase creates two separate offences, one of 'causing' and the other of 'knowingly permitting'.

The distinction was discussed in the case of *McLeod* v. *Buchanan*,[227] where it was stated:

> To cause ... involves some express or positive mandate from the person 'causing' to the other person, or some authority from the former to the latter, arising in the circumstances of the case. To 'permit' is a looser and vaguer term. It may denote an express permission, general permission, general or particular as distinguished from a mandate ... However, the word also includes cases in which permission is merely inferred.

In the light of this it appears that, in order to 'cause' something, there must be an element of control or domination in bringing it about, whilst to 'permit' an occurrence is to be in a position when control over that occurrence can be exercised, but no action is taken either to forbid it or to prevent it from occurring.

The leading case on 'causing' pollution in this context is the House of Lords decision in *Alphacell Limited* v. *Woodward*.[228] The defendants prepared manilla fibres, a raw material for paper manufacturing, operating at a site close to a river. In the course of the process water which was used to wash raw material was piped into settling tanks. Pumps were provided which were designed to switch off automatically when water in the tanks reached a certain level. Any overflow into the river would thus be prevented.

However, on one occasion the pumps became obstructed by leaves and fern as a result of which they failed to switch off automatically. Polluted water from the tanks then overflowed into the river. The defendants were convicted of causing polluting matter to enter a river contrary to section 2(1) of the Rivers (Prevention of Pollution) Act 1951 (which is a predecessor to s.107). The defendants ultimately appealed to the House of Lords which upheld the conviction, holding that it was not necessary to prove that the defendants acted with knowledge, intentionally or negligently. It was sufficient to prove that they had set the process in motion and had therefore caused the pollution in question. The offence was one of strict liability and therefore, if the prosecution can show that the other elements of the offence are present, it need not prove that the accused acted knowingly, intentionally or negligently.[229]

In *Wrothwell Ltd* v. *Yorkshire Water Authority*,[230] a director of the defendant company deliberately poured herbicide known to be toxic to fish into a drain. He expected that it would pass into the public sewerage system and ultimately reach the public sewage treatment works. In fact it passed through pipes directly into a stream causing fish mortality. The company's conviction for causing pollution was upheld. Although the director did not know of the consequence of his action, his act was the cause of the herbicide entering the stream. There was nothing else that could be said to have caused it.

In *Southern Water Authority* v. *Pegram*,[231] the question was whether the chain of causation had been broken. The defendants were pig farmers. A drain which carried rain water on their farm had become blocked. Due to the blockage, the water flowed into a lagoon containing pig slurry, causing one wall of the lagoon to rupture, and the slurry flowed out into a nearby stream. The Divisional Court of the Queen's Bench Division of the High Court held that the defendants were guilty. There was no effective break in the chain of causation linking their activities as pig farmers and the pollution of the river. The amount of rainfall was normal and no party had intervened.

This suggests that there may be a defence if abnormal or unforeseeable weather conditions can be said to have caused pollution.[232]

By contrast, the defendants in *Impress (Worcester) Ltd* v. *Rees*[233] had an oil storage tank close to a river. A trespasser opened a valve on the tank, and oil was released which flowed into the river. It was held that the defendants were not guilty of causing the entry into the river because the acts of the trespasser were sufficiently drastic to break the chain of causation.

Again, in *Price* v. *Cromack*[234], the defendant had entered into an agreement permitting a company to pass effluent onto his land and into two lagoons constructed by the company on his land. Breaches in the retaining walls of the lagoons permitted effluent to flow into a river. It was held that the defendant, who was contractually bound to receive the effluent into the lagoons, had not caused the polluting matter to enter the river because he had done no positive act leading to that result. 'A man cannot be guilty of causing pollution unless at the least he does some positive act in the chain of acts and events leading up to that result.'[235]

However, not every intervention by a third party will break the chain of causation. It is a question of degree in the total circumstances of the case.[236]

The offence of 'knowingly permitting' has generated far fewer reported cases. Lord Wilberforce discussed it briefly in *Alphacell Ltd* v. *Woodward* and said the offence required a failure to prevent the entry in question, in addition to knowledge by the defendant. Thus it was suggested by J. Ashworth in *Price* v. *Cromack* that the defendant there would have been rightly convicted of knowingly permitting effluent to escape from the lagoons into the river.[237]

5.6.1.3 'Poisonous, noxious or polluting'

The term 'poisonous, noxious or polluting' is not defined in the Water Act 1989. It would appear to be broad enough to cover matter which is damaging to flora and fauna even though it is harmless to humans.[238] The three words, poisonous, noxious and polluting, appear to be alternatives in descending order of gravity.[239] Accordingly, an offence may be committed if matter enters the water which is polluting, in that it alters the quality of the water, for example, so that it is less pleasant for cattle to drink, or is no longer of the quality required by an abstractor downstream, even though it does not poison human beings, animals or flora and fauna indigenous to the river. The three words also suggest that it is sufficient for the matter to have the propensity to, for example, poison or pollute, without the necessity for the prosecution to prove that damage has resulted.[240] It may be that where some discoloration has taken place an offence will have been committed if it can be shown that interference with growth of water plants and organisms has occurred by restricting their access to sunlight.

5.6.1.4 'Relevant prohibition'

The concept of a 'relevant prohibition' is a new one brought into water pollution legislation by the Water Act 1989 and applies to offences under section 107(1) (b) and (d).

A relevant prohibition is made either by notice given by the NRA prohibiting a person from making or continuing a discharge either absolutely or unless specified conditions are observed, or by regulations which prohibit a discharge of effluent or matter containing a prescribed substance or a prescribed concentration of such a substance or from a process involving the use of prescribed substances.[241]

Unless the situation is one of emergency, the NRA must give at least three months' notice before the prohibition can take effect. Within the three month period, a person who is served with a prohibition notice may apply for a discharge consent under section 113, in which case the effect of the notice is suspended until the application becomes final, either on the grant or withdrawal of the notice or its determination on appeal.[242]

5.6.1.5 'Trade effluent'

The term 'trade effluent' is given a wide definition. Under section 189, 'effluent' means any liquid, including particles of matter and other substances in suspension in the liquid. By section 124, 'trade effluent' includes any effluent, other than surface water and domestic sewage, which is discharged from premises used for carrying on any trade or industry. The reference to 'any liquid' in section 189 indicates that effluent is not limited to waste liquids. For the purposes of the definition of 'trade effluent', any premises wholly or mainly used (whether for profit or not) for agricultural purposes or for the purposes of fish farming or for scientific research or experiment are deemed to be premises used for carrying on a trade.[243] Discharge of trade effluent into sewers is discussed below in section 5.9.

5.6.1.6 'Sewage effluent'

'Sewage effluent' includes any effluent from the sewage disposal or sewerage works of a sewerage undertaker, but does not include surface water.[244]

Where any sewage effluent is discharged from any sewer or works vested in a sewerage undertaker and the undertaker did not cause or knowingly permit the discharge but was bound (either unconditionally or subject to conditions which were observed) to receive into the sewer or works matter included in the discharge, the undertaker is deemed to have caused the discharge.[245]

5.6.1.7 'Discharged'

The trade and sewage effluent offences involve a discharge. The word 'discharge' may be interpreted to mean only a deliberate release, or alternatively it could be construed to include an accidental escape of trade effluent. It is not clear which meaning is intended, but it would appear from the context that an active meaning is intended. The word 'discharge' is used in defining the trade and sewage effluent offence but is omitted from the 'poisonous, noxious or polluting' offence. Its use in the former case would be superfluous if it carries a passive meaning. Additionally, consents granted by the NRA are specified in Schedule 8 as applying to 'discharges' but the schedule does not refer to the 'entry' of matter into controlled waters.

If the 'discharge' includes an accidental release, then it follows that such accidental releases can be permitted by consent from the NRA. It appears however, that the procedures and provisions concerning the consent system are intended to relate only to deliberate discharges. If this interpretation is correct, it follows that accidental releases of trade and sewage effluent must be charged under section 107(1)(a) as causing or knowingly permitting poisonous, noxious or polluting matter to enter a stream.

Under the equivalent section of the Control of Pollution Act 1974, if an entry into a river fell within the trade and sewage effluent offence, it fell outside the poisonous, noxious or polluting offence, the two offences being mutually exclusive. There is no such provision in the Water Act 1989. It follows that the same fact situation may fall within both offences, but, although they overlap, they are not identical. Thus a person may be guilty of an intentional discharge of trade or sewage effluent under section 107(1)(c) and (d), whether or not the discharge in question is poisonous, noxious or polluting. However, if the entry of trade or domestic sewage is unintentional or accidental the prosecution must prove under section 107(1)(a) that the effluent is in fact poisonous, noxious or polluting.

5.6.1.8 Contravention of conditions of a consent

It is an offence to contravene the conditions of a discharge consent given by the NRA.[246] This offence is entirely new to the Water Act 1989. Its purpose appears to be to enable the NRA to prosecute for breach of conditions, without the possibility of an argument by the defendant that he did not cause or knowingly permit the entry or discharge in question.

In *Severn Trent River Authority* v. *Express Food Group Limited*,[247] it was held that only one offence was committed for each discharge, no matter how many actual conditions had been contravened.

5.6.1.9 Deposits and vegetation in rivers[248]

If, without the consent of the NRA, a person removes from any part of the bottom, channel or bed of any inland waters[249] a deposit accumulated by reason of the action of any dam, weir or sluice, and does so by causing the deposit to be carried away in suspension in the water, he or she commits an offence.[250]

A person also commits an offence if, without the consent of the NRA, he or she causes or permits a substantial amount of vegetation to be deposited, cut or uprooted in or to fall into any inland waters, and fails to take all reasonable steps to remove the vegetation from those waters.[251] These offences do not apply, however, to anything done in the exercise of any power conferred by any enactment relating to land drainage, flood protection or navigation.[252]

5.6.1.10 *Prosecution of an offence*

In any prosecution it is important to distinguish the various ingredients of the offences specified in section 107. Clearly, in relation to the offence in s.107(1)(a) it must be shown that the matter entering the controlled water is poisonous, noxious or polluting. Thus, for example, evidence of fish mortality would be sufficient.

In respect of the offences relating to trade and sewage effluent it need only be shown that there has been a discharge into the waters in cases where no consent has been given by the NRA. On one view, it is sufficient for the prosecution to prove the discharge of effluent into controlled waters. It is for the defence to show that the entry or discharge was within the conditions specified by any consent.[253]

The other view is that the prosecution must at least establish the contents of the matter or discharge.[254] Otherwise it could be virtually impossible for the defence to show that a particular entry or discharge complied with the consent.

This problem will not normally arise where the prosecution is brought, as it will be in most cases, by the National Rivers Authority.[255] In practice, its prosecutions will be based on scientific analysis of samples of effluent or polluted water.

In the past it has been notable that the water authorities sought to secure compliance with the law by persuasion rather than prosecution. Thus, the proportion of polluters who were prosecuted was relatively small.[256] One reason for this was an ambiguity in the interpretation of the legal status of discharge consents. It has been suggested that the standards set in conditions attached to consents were expressed as goals to be achieved rather than specific rates of discharge and parameters that might have reasonably been complied with by dischargers.[257] This 'softly-softly' approach on prosecution for breaches of discharge consents or for pollution incidents was criticised by the House of Commons Environment Committee in its Third Report.[258] The Committee also noted the considerable variation in levels of fines for apparently similar offences around the country, both between and within water authority areas, and also that the costs awarded against polluters were nominal and bore little relationship to the expenses incurred by water authorities in collecting the evidence necessary to mount a successful prosecution.[259]

The Government's view is that it must remain a matter of judgment for the NRA, taking into account the particular circumstances of a case, as to whether prosecution – as opposed to advice and persuasion – is the most effective course of action for it to take.[260] The NRA is under a general duty to exercise the powers conferred on it in such a manner as to ensure, so far as it is practicable by the exercise of those powers to do so, that any water quality objectives set by the Secretary of State under section 105, are achieved at all times.[261] It is arguable that when water quality objectives and their associated standards are set for waters on a statutory basis, the NRA will be under a particular duty to prosecute unauthorised discharges which contravene those standards.

As to the level of fines and costs being imposed when prosecutions are taken, the Government drew the recommendations of the Committee to the attention of the Magistrates' Association,[262] but pointed to the fact that it is up to individual courts to decide on the proper sentence in a particular case.

Generally, compliance with discharge consents from sewage treatment works has in the past been assessed on the basis of conformity with the stated standards for at least 95 per cent of samples taken over a twelve-month period. Alternatively, standards which indicate absolute maxima, a breach of which constitutes an offence, have been more popular with regard to industrial discharges. In the future it appears that a combination of the two approaches may be favoured, with dual standards specified for each discharge, a breach of either resulting in a contravention of the conditions of consent.

The Act lays down a procedure for taking and analysing samples on behalf of the NRA which must be complied with for the results of any analysis to be admissible in legal proceedings in respect of any effluent passing from any land or vessel.[263] On taking the sample, the occupier of the land or the owner or master of a vessel must be notified of the NRA's intention to have it analysed.[264] It must then be divided into three parts and placed in marked sealed containers. One part must be given to the occupier of the land or master or owner of the vessel from which the sample has come, one submitted for analysis, and the third retained for future comparison.

This has implications for private prosecutions which are based on information contained in the register kept by the NRA.[265] Such information is only admissible in court proceedings if the three-way procedure has been followed.[266] If the sample was not taken by or on behalf of the NRA it appears that such samples will be admissible despite the absence of the three-way procedure.

In any legal proceedings it is to be presumed, unless the contrary is shown, that any sample taken at an inspection chamber or manhole or other place provided in compliance with a condition, it is a sample of what was passing from the land or premises to any waters.[267] Where an agreement has been made as to a sampling point for effluent discharge, it is to be presumed in any legal proceedings, unless the contrary is shown, that any sample of effluent taken at such a point, is a sample of what was passing from the land or premises to any waters.[268] Such an agreement is to have effect in respect of the premises despite changes in title or occupier, but may be determined at any time by either party.[269] In default of an agreement, the Secretary of State may, after considering any representations made to him or her by the owner or occupier of the land or premises and any other person who appears to him or her to be interested, fix a point at which samples are to be taken.[270] The NRA must maintain a register containing such particulars as the Secretary of State may direct of sampling points fixed under these provisions, and ensure that the register is available for public inspection at all reasonable hours.[271]

The public registers maintained by the NRA do not include details of pollution incidents and resultant prosecutions. It is intended that the NRA in the future will report[272] both on reported pollution incidents and prosecutions, broken down in the following manner:[273]

1. Industrial pollution – oil.
2. Industrial pollution – chemical.
3. Industrial pollution – other.
4. Farm pollution.
5. Water undertaker sewage treatment works.
6. Other sewage treatment works.
7. Sewerage.
8. Unidentified sources.
9. Other.[274]

The offences under section 107 are triable either way. This means that the defendant has a choice as to whether to be tried in the Magistrates' Court in summary proceedings or in the Crown Court on indictment. The maximum penalty on summary conviction imposed by a Magistrates' Court is a term of imprisonment not exceeding three months or a fine not exceeding the statutory maximum on the standard scale, or both.[275] The statutory maximum is currently £2,000. The maximum penalties which can be imposed on conviction on indictment by a Crown Court are a term of imprisonment not exceeding two years or an unlimited fine, or both.[276] If the case is dealt with by the Magistrates' Court and the Magistrates consider that their powers of sentencing are inadequate, they can commit the defendant to be sentenced by the Crown Court.

Offences relating to deposits and vegetation in inland waters[277] may only be tried in the Magistrates' Court and on conviction the defendant is liable to a fine not exceeding level 4 on the standard scale.[278]

Normally a Magistrates' Court may only try a summary offence if the information has been laid within six months of its commission,[279] but in relation to offences under Part I of Chapter III the time limit for laying of information is extended to twelve months.[280]

In cases where the commission of an offence by a person is due to the act or default of some other person, that other person may be charged and convicted of the offence whether or not the person who actually committed the offence has been proceeded against.[281]

5.6.1.11 *Private prosecutions*

Under the Water Act 1989 there is no restriction on who may bring prosecutions under Chapter I of Part III. Therefore, any individual or organisation may lay any information in respect of the various offences.

In most private prosecutions the prosecuting body will most likely have to place reliance on the entries of analyses of samples contained in the public registers required to be maintained by the NRA.[282] In *Wales v. Thames Water Authority*,[283] a private prosecution was brought by the Anglers' Co-operative Association against the Authority in respect of its effluent discharges from the Aylesbury Sewage Treatment Works. The Authority pleaded guilty and was fined £1,000 in respect of each of the six offences.[284] The case, however, did not consider two important questions. First, whether prosecutors can rely on information contained in registers kept by the NRA without the need for obtaining additional confirmation, and secondly, whether a single failure to comply with the terms of a consent constitutes an offence, as opposed to an annual failure of sampled discharges with respect to the 95 per cent compliance limit.

If, on the laying of an information, a Magistrate considers that the proposed prosecution is frivolous or vexatious, he or she may refuse to issue proceedings and may hear evidence from the proposed defendant at this stage to inform him- or herself of the relevant facts.[285]

At any stage of the prosecution, the Attorney-General or the Director of Public Prosecutions may intervene and take the prosecution over. They then have a discretion, probably not reviewable by the courts, whether to continue or to offer no evidence. It may be that a discharger, faced with what it believes to be a frivolous or vexatious prosecution, can request the Attorney-General or the Director of Public Prosecutions to exercise their powers of intervention.

5.6.2   DEFENCES TO PROSECUTIONS UNDER SECTION 107

Several defences are provided in section 108 to the offences listed in Section 107:

1. The entry or discharge in question complied with a consent (and any conditions to which it is subject) given under Part I of Chapter III of the Water Act 1989[286] or under Part II of the Control of Pollution Act 1974 (the earlier equivalent legislative provision).[287]
2. The entry or discharge in question complied with a licence granted under Part II of the Food and Environment Protection Act 1985 for the deposit of substances and articles in the sea for disposal or the incineration of substances at sea[288] or a disposal licence given under Part I of the Control of Pollution Act 1974 (to dispose of controlled waste on land).[289]
3. The entry or discharge in question complied with any prescribed enactment, any local statutory provision[290] or statutory order which expressly confers power to discharge effluent into water.[291]
4. The entry is caused or permitted or the discharge is made in an emergency in order to avoid danger to life or health, and the person responsible takes all steps as are reasonably practicable in the circumstances for minimising the extent of the entry or discharge and of its polluting effects; and particulars of the entry or discharge are furnished to the NRA as soon as reasonably practicable after it occurs.[292]

    No definition of 'emergency' is given in the Act. It is to be presumed, however, that the term covers a situation where there is reasonable cause to believe that the circumstances are such that there is a likely danger to life or human health. It has also been suggested[293] that the term may apply to accidents resulting from bulk carriage of noxious or polluting substances where spillages are deliberately washed into watercourses to avoid danger or hazard to human health.

5. The discharge of trade or sewage effluent is made from a vessel.[294] Under s.114 the NRA is empowered to make byelaws for prohibiting or regulating the keeping or use on any controlled waters of prescribed vessels which are provided with water closets or other sanitary appliances. The Rivers (Prevention of Pollution) Act 1951 (Continuation of Byelaws) Order 1989[295] provides that the listed byelaws made under the Rivers (Prevention of Pollution) Act 1951 continue to have effect as if made by the NRA under section 114 of the 1989 Act.[296]

6. Water from an abandoned mine[297] is permitted to enter controlled waters.[298]

7. Solid waste from a quarry or mine which has been deposited on land falls or is carried into inland waters, if the deposit is made with the consent of the NRA and no other site for the deposit is reasonably practicable and all reasonably practicable steps are taken to prevent the entry into inland waters.[299]

There is no definition of the term 'reasonably practicable' in the Act but elsewhere it has been suggested that it implies an assessment must be made in which the quantum of risk is placed on one side of the scale and the sacrifice involved in the steps taken to avert the risk is placed on the other, so that if there is a major disparity between the two with the risk of being insignificant in relation to the sacrifice, the onus of proving reasonably practicability is discharged.[300]

8. A highway authority or other person entitled to keep open a drain under section 100 of the Highways Act 1980 for the purpose of draining a highway, is not guilty of causing or permitting a discharge from the drain unless the discharge is made in contravention of a relevant prohibition.[301]

9. A sewerage undertaker is not guilty of an offence in respect of discharge from a sewer or sewerage works which contravenes conditions of a consent if the contravention is attributable to a discharge which another person caused or permitted to be made into the sewer or works and the undertaker was not bound to receive the discharge or was bound to receive it subject to conditions which were not observed and the undertaker could not reasonably have been expected to prevent the discharge into the sewer or works.[302]

10. No offence is committed in respect of a discharge made into a sewerage undertaker's sewer or works if the undertaker is bound to receive the discharge unconditionally or subject to conditions which are observed.[303]

11. In relation to offences under section 4 of the Salmon and Freshwater Fisheries Act 1975[304] and section 68 of the Public Health Act 1875[305] an offence is committed in respect of any entry of matter into any controlled waters which occurs under and in accordance with a consent under the Water Act 1989 or the previous legislation.[306]

5.6.3   THE CONSENT SYSTEM[307]

The various offences of polluting controlled waters are made subject to exceptions in respect of discharges which are in accordance with consents given by either the NRA or the Secretary of State. The system of controlling pollution of water through a system of discharge consents is a key feature of the 1989 Water Act and of Part II of the Control of Pollution Act 1974 which it replaces. It should be noted, however, that compliance with the conditions of a discharge consent, although serving as a defence in criminal proceedings, may not serve as a defence in civil proceedings brought by a person affected by any discharge.[308]

5.6.3.1 *Procedure*

An application for a discharge consent must be made to the NRA and accompanied or supplemented by all such information as it may reasonably require. The Act no longer requires specified information to be given in an application as was the case under section 34 of the Control of Pollution Act. In practice, an informal enquiry should be made of the Authority to determine what information it will require.[309]

Any person who, in making an application for a consent, makes any statement he or she knows to be false in a material particular, or recklessly makes any statement which is false in a material particular, is guilty of a criminal offence, and liable, on summary conviction, to a fine not exceeding the statutory maximum[310] or on conviction on indictment to an unlimited fine.

Proceedings for this offence may only be taken by or with the consent of the Secretary of State, the Minister of Agriculture or the Director of Public Prosecutions.[311]

An application which relates to proposed discharges at two or more places may be treated by the NRA as separate applications for consents for discharges at each of those places.

On receipt of the application the NRA must do the following:

1. Publish notice of the application at least once in each of the two successive weeks in a newspaper circulating in the locality in which the proposed discharge is to be made and in any localities likely to be affected by the proposed discharge.
2. Publish notice of the application in the London Gazette.
3. Send a copy of the application to every local authority or water undertaker within whose area any of the proposed discharges is to occur.
4. In the case of a proposed discharge to coastal waters, territorial waters or beyond the limits of territorial waters, serve a copy of the application on the Secretary of State and the Minister of Agriculture.

Regulations under the Control of Pollution Act 1974 used to require notice of an application to be published in the prescribed form.[312] However, these regulations no longer apply and the notice can be in any form. The NRA is entitled to recover the expenses of publication from the applicant.[313]

The NRA may disregard the publicity provisions if it proposes to give consent and considers that the discharges in question will have no appreciable effect on the receiving waters.[314] There is no definition of 'appreciable effect' given in the Act but advice was given in a Department of Environment Circular[315] on the equivalent provision in the 1974 Act.

Exemption on the ground of 'no appreciable effect' may be given where three criteria are met:

1. The discharge does not affect an area of amenity or environmental significance (a beach, marina, nature reserve, shell fishery, fish spawning area, or site of special scientific interest).
2. The discharge does not result in a major change in the flow of receiving waters.
3. Taken together with previously consented discharges the discharge does not result in such a change in water quality as to:
    (a) damage existing or future uses of the water (whether or not resulting in a change of water quality classification), or
    (b) alter by 10 per cent or more the concentration in the receiving

waters of any substance which is of importance for the quality of the water and the well-being of its flora and fauna, e.g. dissolved oxygen, BOD, suspended solids, ammonia, nitrates, phosphates and dissolved metals.[316]

It appears inevitable that these criteria will be the subject of contention in particular instances. For example, a small discharge of a certain pollutant into a receiving water of very high purity may mean an increase of more than 10 per cent in the presence of that substance in the water but no significant effect on the overall water quality. By contrast, an increase of 10 per cent in the presence of certain substances may be regarded as being of major significance.[317]

It has been estimated that approximately 90 per cent of applications for consent have not been publicised in the past in reliance on this rule.

An applicant may apply to the Secretary of State for the Environment for a certificate exempting the application from the publicity provisions or the entry of details regarding the discharge in registers maintained by the NRA, on the grounds that it would be contrary to the public interest or would unreasonably prejudice a private interest by disclosing information about a trade secret.[318] If the Secretary of State is satisfied on either of those grounds, he or she may issue a certificate accordingly.[319]

The NRA must consider any written representations or objections relating to an application which are made within six weeks of the publication of the notice of the application in the London Gazette. It is then under a duty to consider whether to give consent either unconditionally or subject to conditions, or to refuse it.[320] An application is automatically deemed to have been refused if consent is not given within four months from the date of receipt of the application by the NRA, or such longer period as may be agreed in writing between the NRA and the applicant.[321]

The NRA may impose such conditions as it thinks fit in giving a consent. In particular it may include conditions as to the following:

1. The places at which the discharges to which the consent relates may be made and as to the design and construction of any outlets for the discharges.
2. The nature, origin, composition, temperature, volume and rate of the discharges and as to the periods during which the discharges may be made.
3. The steps to be taken, in relation to the discharges or by way of subjecting any substance likely to affect the description of matter

discharged to treatment or any other process, for minimising the polluting effects of the discharge on any controlled waters.[322]

4. The provision of facilities for taking samples of the matter discharged and, in particular, as to the provision, maintenance and use of manholes, inspection chambers, observation wells and boreholes in connection with the discharges.

5. The provision, maintenance and testing of meters for measuring or recording the volume and rate of the discharges and apparatus for determining the nature, composition and temperature of the discharge.

6. The keeping of records of the nature, origin, composition, temperature, volume and rate of the discharges and, in particular, of records of readings of meters and other recording apparatus provided in accordance with any other condition attached to the consent.

7. The making of returns and the giving of other information to the Authority about the nature, origin, composition, temperature, volume and rate of the discharges.[323]

A consent may be given subject to different conditions in respect of different periods and is not limited to discharges made by a particular person but extends to discharges made by any person.[324] Therefore, the right to discharge pursuant to a consent passes to successors in title, or tenants of the original grantee of the consent.

In refusing or granting consents and conditions to consents, the NRA is under a duty to exercise its powers so as to ensure so far as practicable that any statutory water quality objectives set by the Secretary of State[325] are achieved at all times.[326] It is also required, under the direction of the Secretary of State, to achieve compliance with the non-statutory standards set by various European Community Directives.[327]

One problem in particular arises with this system of discharge consents. This is the inadequate coverage given to the discharge of substances introduced into a discharge after the consent has been given and therefore not specified in that consent. Depending on the wording of the consent, there is often no provision made for new pollutants which begin to be discharged after the consent has been given. Under the previous legislation the law seemed to be that, where a holder of a discharge consent began to discharge a substance not named in the consent, that discharge remained generally in compliance with the consent and the discharger was consequently protected from prosecution.[328]

In addition, the discharger's co-operation was generally needed if a consent was revised within a period of two years from the last revision and the discharger appeared to be under no obligation to bring to the attention of the water authority the fact that its discharge contained a new pollutant.

Despite a recommendation by the House of Commons Environment Committee in its 1987 Report that a duty should be imposed on dischargers to notify all pollutants in their effluent to the NRA, and that the NRA should be free to revise the consent without financial penalty, the legal position appears not to have been altered by the Water Act 1989. This, it is suggested, is so despite the contention of the Government[329] that where a discharger adds to his or her discharge a new pollutant not covered by the consent, which materially adds to the noxious quality of the effluent, he or she will be guilty of an offence unless he or she seeks a review of his or her consent. The question is one of degree and subjective assessment of the effects of a new pollutant in a discharge, and the situation remains confusing and unsatisfactory.

In cases where the NRA proposes to give its consent to an application and representations or objections have been made, it must serve notice of its proposal to give consent on every person who made representations or objections.[330] The notice must also state that such persons may within twenty-one days from the date of service of the notice request the Secretary of State to 'call in' the application.

The NRA may not give consent until the end of the twenty-one day period. If during that period a request is made to the Secretary of State to 'call in' the application and notice of the request is served on the NRA it must not give consent unless the Secretary of State serves notice on the NRA stating that he or she does not propose to call in the application.

The Secretary of State has the power to call in an application whether or not representations or objections have been made, and whether or not a request has been made to him or her to call in the application.[331] In relation to applications which are called in, a modified form of publicity procedure is provided for by the Control of Pollution (Consents for Discharges, etc.) (Secretary of State Functions) Regulations 1989.[332]

A person who requests the Secretary of State to call in an application demand (termed a 'transmitted application') must provide him or her with the following:

1. A copy of the notice served by the NRA on the person making the request of its proposal to give consent, and a copy of any published notice of the original application.
2. A written statement containing:
   (a) the name of the applicant for consent;
   (b) the reference number or letter identifying the relevant application;
   (c) an identification of the land from which and the waters into or land onto which the discharge for which consent is sought is to be made;
   (d) a description of the effluent or other matter to which the consent is to relate;
   (e) the date on which the person making the request was served with a notice of his or her right to request a direction;
   (f) a request that the Secretary of State give a direction; and
   (g) a statement of the reasons why the applicant considers that his or her request should be granted.

Copies of these documents must be sent to the Authority at the same time.[333] If the Authority has not publicised the application by the time it is called in by the Secretary of State, it must do so in a prescribed form.[334]

Before determining the application, the Secretary of State may hold a local inquiry or afford the applicant and the NRA, and those who have made representations and objections, an opportunity of appearing before, and being heard by, a person appointed by the Secretary of State for that purpose. The Secretary of State must exercise these powers if requested to do so by an applicant or the NRA (but not by objectors or people who have made representations) in writing within twenty-eight days of receipt by the applicant of the notice that his or her application has been called in.[335] The Secretary of State must then determine the application by directing the NRA to refuse consent or to give consent either unconditionally or subject to specified conditions.

Where contraventions of section 107[336] have occurred and the NRA considers that similar contraventions are likely, it may serve on the person responsible a written instrument giving consent, subject to any conditions, for such discharges as are specified. The consent must be publicised in the same manner as other applications for consent and the NRA must consider written representations or objections made within the usual six-week period.[337] The consent does not, however, have retrospective effect, in that it is not to relate to any discharge which occurred before the instrument containing the consent was served on · the recipient.[338]

The Authority has a duty to review consents from time to time and may by notice revoke a consent, make modifications to conditions, or in the case of an unconditional consent, provide that it shall be subject to specified conditions.[339] If on review it appears to the NRA that no discharge has been made pursuant to a consent at any time during the preceding twelve months it may by notice revoke the consent.

The Secretary of State for the Environment may direct the NRA to revoke a consent, modify conditions or add conditions if he or she considers it appropriate to do so to give effect to any European Community obligations or international agreements or for the protection of public health or of flora or fauna dependent upon an aquatic environment, or in consequence of any representations or objections made to him or her or otherwise.[340]

In order to prevent the over-use of the review procedure by the NRA, thereby frustrating the reasonable expectations of a discharger, any consent given by the NRA and any notice modifying or adding conditions must specify a period (not less than two years from the date on which the consent takes effect or the variation notice is served) within which no such modifying notice may be served.[341] In the case of consents given without an application, the restriction does not prevent a notice being given revoking, modifying or adding conditons provided that it is served not more than three months after the beginning of the period for making objections and representions and the NRA or the Secretary of State considers, in consequence of any representations or objections received by it or him or her within that period, that it is appropriate for the notice to be served.[342]

The restrictions on serving a notice which revokes, modifies or adds to conditions do not apply to directions by the Secretary of State to the NRA for the purpose of: (a) giving effect to European Community obligations or to international agreements; or (b) protecting public health or flora or fauna dependent on an aquatic environment. However, in the case of (b), the NRA is liable to pay compensation for any loss or damage sustained by a person as a result of the notice if the alterations to or revocations of the consent occur during the otherwise restricted period, unless the Secretary of State's direction is given as a result of a change of circumstances that was not reasonably foreseeable or material information[343] on which he or she acted was not reasonably available to the NRA.

5.6.3.2 *Appeals*

Any person who applied for the consent in question, or any person whose deposits, discharges or other conduct is or would be authorised by the consent, may appeal in writing to the Secretary of State against an adverse decision of the NRA within three months of the notification (or deemed refusal)[344] to the appellant.[345] The decisions of the NRA which can be appealed to the Secretary of State are as follows:[346]

1. The refusal of a consent for a discharge.
2. The making of a consent for any discharges or description of discharge subject to conditions.
3. The modification or revocation of a consent or making an unconditional consent subject to conditions.
4. Specifying a period of less than two years in respect of which a modification or a revocation may be made.
5. The refusal of a consent to deposit the solid refuse of a mine or quarry onto land.[347]
6. The refusal of a consent to undertake works in a river bed or to deposit vegetation in rivers, or the making of such consent subject to conditions.[348]

The Secretary of State may require an appellant to send him or her further information and must send the NRA a copy of the notice of appeal and grounds of appeal. Where the appeal is against a refusal to grant consent, the NRA is required to serve notice in writing within fourteen days of the receipt of the notice of appeal on any person who initially made representations or objections. This notice by the NRA is to state that further representations may be made to the Secretary of State within twenty-one days from the date of service of the notice. The Secretary of State must then send to the appellant and the NRA copies of any such representations and may, if he or she thinks fit, require further evidence from them.

The Secretary of State may determine the appeal on the basis of written representations, but if he or she intends to do so, he or she must give notice to the appellant and the NRA, and either of them may, within fourteen days, request him or her not to determine the appeal without further investigation. The Secretary of State must then either hold a local inquiry or give the appellant and the NRA an opportunity of appearing before, and being heard by, a person appointed by him or her for that purpose.[349]

5.6.3.3 *Charges*

The NRA is empowered to draw up a scheme for the payment of charges for applications and consents.[350] Such a scheme requires the approval of the Secretary of State (with Treasury consent). The proposed scheme must be publicised and an opportunity given for persons likely to be affected by it to make representations or objections to the Secretary of State. In deciding whether or not to approve the scheme, the Secretary of State must consider any representations or objections made. He or she must also have regard to the desirability of ensuring that the charges do not exceed the amount necessary to enable the NRA to recover its expenses and the need to ensure that there is no undue discrimination in fixing charges under the scheme. However, the scheme may make different provisions for different cases, including different persons, circumstances or localities.

5.6.3.4 *Discharges by the NRA*

Where the NRA proposes to discharge matter or effluent that is subject to the consent procedure, the consent is to be given by the Secretary of State. The procedure for obtaining a consent is specified in the Control of Pollution (Discharges by the National Rivers Authority) Regulations 1989[351] and is essentially the same as for other applications for consent. Notice must be published in local newspapers and the London Gazette of an application and copies sent to local authorities and water undertakers within whose areas the proposed discharge is to occur. The notice must state that representations and objections may be made in writing to the Secretary of State, who may give the consent applied for either unconditionally or subject to conditions, or refuse it.

Where, however, the Secretary of State has received objections or representations, he or she must, if a request to be heard is made by the NRA within ten weeks after publication of the notice, either hold a local inquiry or give the NRA and any persons who made objections and representations an opportunity of appearing before, and being heard by, a person appointed by him or her for that purpose.

The Secretary of State must review consents from time to time and may revoke, modify or impose conditions on those consents. Neither this nor his or her initial decision whether to give a consent or not can be the subject of an appeal by the NRA.

5.6.3.5 *Monitoring compliance with consents*

In section 145, the NRA is given power to do anything which, in its opinion, is calculated to facilitate, or is conducive, or incidental to, the carrying out of its functions.[352] More particularly, any person designated in writing for the purpose by the Secretary of State, the Minister of Agriculture or the NRA has power to do the following:

1. Enter any premises or vessel for the purpose of:
    (a) ascertaining whether any provision or byelaw is being or has been contravened;
    (b) determining whether and if so, in what manner, any power or duty conferred or imposed on the Secretary of State, the Minister or the Authority should be exercised or performed; or
    (c) exercising or performing any such power or duty.
2. Carrying out such inspections, measurements and tests on any premises or vessel and take away such samples of water or effluent or of any land or articles as they consider appropriate.[353]

Subject to obtaining a warrant from a justice of the peace,[354] no person may enter premises or vessels except in an emergency or at a reasonable time and, if the premises or vessel is used for domestic purposes or the entry is to be with heavy equipment, after seven days' notice of the intended entry has been given to the occupier of the premises or vessel.[355]

5.6.3.6 *Application of EC Directives*

In granting discharge consents and in setting emission limits in conditions attached to such consents, the NRA and the Secretary of State must take into account their obligations with respect to various European Community Directives on water quality.

In England and Wales the general practice of the Government in respect of the implementation of EC Directives on water quality is to issue Department of the Environment and Welsh Office circulars detailing the measures to be taken to ensure compliance with the Directives. In the past, they have been addressed to water authorities, but now their application is mainly to the NRA as the 'competent authority' in terms of the EC Directives.

(a) *Dangerous Substances Directive*[356]

In respect of discharges to water by industry, agriculture, etc., the most important Directive is the 1976 Directive on pollution caused by certain dangerous substances discharged into the aquatic environment of the Community, and those Directives made under it.

The Annex to the Directive contains two lists of substances harmful to the aquatic environment. List I (the 'black list') comprises groups of substances selected primarily on the basis of their toxicity, persistence and bio-accumulation, while List II (the 'grey list') consists of substances which can also have a harmful effect on the aquatic environment, but which may 'be confined to a given area and which depend on the characteristics and location of the water into which they are discharged'.

Member states are required to take steps to eliminate pollution by List I substances and reduce pollution by List II substances. 'Pollution' is defined by the Directive as:

> the discharge by man, directly or indirectly, of substances or energy into the aquatic environment, the results of which are such as to cause hazards to human health, harm to living resources and aquatic ecosystems, damage to amenities or interference with other legitimate uses of water.[357]

Different methods for the control of List I and List II substances are provided for, but in the UK the requirements of both are met by the system of consents granted by the NRA.

For all water affected by discharges of the specified substances, the NRA is to select the appropriate water quality standards[358] having regard to the intended use of the water concerned. In addition, where a water quality objective is set for any water by the Secretary of State[359] it is the duty of the NRA in exercising its powers to ensure that those objectives are met at all times.[360]

(i) List I substances

The list contains certain individual substances which belong to the following families and groups of substances:

1. Organohalogen compounds and substances which may form such compounds in the aquatic environment.
2. Organophosphorus compounds.
3. Organotin compounds.
4. Substances which have been proved to possess carcinogenic properties in or via the aquatic environment.
5. Mercury and its compounds.
6. Cadmium and its compounds.

7. Persistent mineral oils and hydrocarbons of petroleum origin.
8. Persistent synthetic substances which may float, remain in suspension or sink and which may interfere with any use of the waters.

However, a particular substance is not confirmed as warranting List I method of control until a 'daughter' Directive has been agreed setting limit values for its discharge. The following 'daughter' Directives have been made:

82/176/EEC (mercury from the chloralkalis industry)
83/513/EEC (cadmium)
84/156/EEC (mercury from other sources)
84/491/EEC (hexachlorocyclohexane) (HCH)
86/280 (carbon tetrachloride, DDT, PCP)
88/347 (HCB, HCBD, chloroform)

Directive 86/280 specifies new procedures with respect to the adoption of List I substances. Its aim is to accelerate the process of formulating and adopting daughter Directives and it specifies general provisions for the control of List I substances.

All substances that belong to the groups and families included in List I, but for which a 'daughter' Directive has not been agreed, are for the time being to be treated as List II substances.

Control of discharges containing List I substances is by discharge consents granted under the Water Act 1989, in relation to inland surface waters, territorial waters and internal coastal waters.[361]

Conditions attached to any consent to discharge List I substances must determine both the maximum concentration and the maximum quantity of a period of time that are permissible in the discharge. They should, where appropriate, provide a basis of calculating the ratio (with reference to the weight) of the amount of the substance discharged to the amount handled by the plant in question.

The NRA must identify those industrial plants liable to handle and discharge List I substances and attach appropriate conditions to any consent, except where: (a) the substance concerned is liable to be present in concentrations which, taking into account the limits of detection specified in the directives, could not readily be determined; or (b) the substance concerned is already present in water taken for use in the industrial process (either from public supply or from the body of water to which the effluent was discharged) and to which no additional amounts of the substance have been added by the process.

Generally, the standards to which individual discharges are required to conform are such as to ensure that a prescribed level of water quality (the 'water quality standard' in the UK terminology) is achieved and maintained in the waters affected. However, in cases where the appropriate water quality standard cannot initially be met, the NRA may apply the limit value approach setting down limit values for each industrial sector listed in the daughter Directives. Use of limit values will normally involve a requirement for twenty-four hour sampling and flow measurement of discharges.

In relation to discharges of List I substances to sewers, the Secretary of State is the competent authority for granting consents.[362]

Each Directive[363] specifies that discharges from 'new plant' may be authorised only if the plant employs the best technical means available (btma), where this is necessary to eliminate pollution or prevent distortion of competition. A 'new plant' is defined[364] as any new industrial plant which has become operational or had its handling capacity substantially increased more than twelve months after the date of notification of the specific measure relating to the substance concerned. The Government has interpreted the term 'substantially increased' to mean an overall increase of 20 per cent or more in the handling capacity of the particular substance.[365]

The Directives give no guidance on the interpretation of btma (with the exception of 82/176/EEC on the chlor-alkali industry) but it is generally accepted that the concept should take into account the economic availability of those means. Consultation with the NRA and with HMIP about the availability of relevant pollution control technology should be entered into.

The NRA is required to monitor background concentrations of List I substances, discharges and receiving waters in compliance with the Directives, and to make reports to the Department of the Environment, which in turn provides information to the European Commission.

(ii) List II substances
The List II substances are as follows:

1. | | | | |
    |---|---|---|---|
    | zinc | selenium | tin | vanadium |
    | copper | arsenic | barium | cobalt |
    | nickel | antimony | beryllium | thallium |
    | chromium | molybdenum | boron | tellurium |
    | lead | titanium | uranium | silver |

2. Biocides and their derivatives not appearing in List I.

3. Substances which have a deleterious effect on the taste and/or smell of the products for human consumption derived from the aquatic environment and compounds liable to give rise to such substances in water.

4. Toxic or persistent organic compounds of silicon, and substances which may give rise to such compounds in water, excluding those which are biologically harmless or are rapidly converted in water into harmless substance.

5. Inorganic compounds of phosphorus and elemental phosphorus.

6. Non-persistent mineral oils and hydrocarbons of petroleum origin.

7. Cyanides and fluorides.

8. Substances which have an adverse effect on the oxygen balance, particularly ammonia and nitrates.

9. Substances belonging to the families and groups of substances in List I for which the limit values have not been determined.

The Dangerous Substances Directive requires member states to establish programmes, with deadlines for implementation, in order to reduce pollution by these substances.

For discharges containing these substances, emission standards (conditions of consent) must be specified in accordance with national quality standards. The Department of the Environment has established national quality standards for a number of List II substances based on work carried out by the Water Research Centre.[366] Following consultation procedures, the NRA must select and apply the appropriate quality standards with regard to the use or intended use of the water. Where a particular stretch of water has more than one water quality objective (e.g. drinking water and the protection of sensitive aquatic life), the most stringent standards must be used.

The Department of the Environment also advises[367] that discharges containing significant quantities of iron or which are liable significantly to affect the pH of receiving water, should be treated in the same way as discharges containing a List II substance.

In some waters the NRA may consider that the quality standards listed may be unattainable in the immediate future. In these cases the NRA must apply a strict standstill. That is, there should be no decline in quality over a number of years taking into account recognised statistical variation, and it must seek to ensure that pollution by these substances is reduced.

(b) Other EC Directives

A number of other Directives are relevant in the setting of water quality objectives for particular waters or stretches of water, and these in turn determine the emission standards from industry as reflected in the conditions attached to a discharge consent.

(i) Groundwater Directive[368]

The purpose of the Groundwater Directive is to prevent pollution of groundwater by the substances listed in the Annex. Member states are required to prevent the substances in List I from entering groundwater, while the introduction of List II substances must be limited so as to avoid pollution. The lists contained in the Annex are substantially similar, although not identical, to those in the Dangerous Substances Directive.

'Groundwater' is defined as meaning all water which is below the surface of the ground in the saturation zone and in direct contact with the ground or subsoil.

Pollution means the discharge by man, directly or indirectly, of substances or energy into groundwater, the results of which are such as to endanger human health or water supplies, harm living resources or the aquatic ecosystem or interfere with other legitimate uses of water.

All discharges or disposal activities which might contain listed substances, whether the discharge is made directly into groundwater or indirectly through percolation into the ground, must be authorised by a consent. This requirement does not apply to: (a) discharges of domestic effluent from isolated dwellings not connected to a sewerage system and outside areas protected for the abstraction of water for human consumption; (b) discharges found to contain listed substances in a quantity and concentration so small as to obviate any future danger of deterioration in the quality of the receiving water; or (c) discharges of matter containing radioactive substances.

(ii) Directive on Water Standards for Freshwater Fish[369]

The Directive provides for the voluntary designation of rivers and still waters[370] as being suitable for stated freshwater fish life. For those, the Directive sets both imperative and guide values with respect to various physical and chemical parameters and provides for sampling to ensure that water quality is maintained at the required standards.[371] Having designated waters pursuant to the Directive, Member States must establish programmes to reduce pollution and attain compliance within a period of five years.

Within the designated waters the aim of the Directive is to protect or improve water quality and consequently the capacity of the water to support either indigenous species, or species the presence of which is judged desirable for water management purposes.[372]

The Directive draws a distinction between salmonoid waters (i.e. those suitable for species such as salmon or trout) and cyprinid waters (i.e. those suitable for cyprinid species such as eel, pike and perch),[373] with differing imperative and guide parameters in respect of each class of water.

Compliance with the specified values is achieved when 95 per cent of samples of most parameters meet the requirements, except in the case of temperature, dissolved oxygen and suspended solids where differing criteria apply.[374]

The designation of waters under the Directive and the water quality standards applicable will be factors taken into account by the NRA when setting conditions to individual discharge consents.[375]

(iii) Directive on Quality Required for Shellfish Waters[376]

The Shellfish Water Directive is expressed in similar terms to the Freshwater Fish Directive. The Directive applies to coastal and brackish waters designated as needing protection or improvement in order to support shellfish life and growth and so to contribute to the high quality of edible shellfish products.[377] 'Shellfish' means bivalve and gastropod molluscs. Where shellfish waters are designated, the Member State is required to reduce pollution to ensure that the water conforms with the Directive's specified water quality parameters in respect of a range of 'imperative' and 'guide' values.[378]

Compliance with the Directive is achieved when samples show conformity of 100 per cent in the case of substances controlled by the Dangerous Substances Directive, 95 per cent in respect of the values for salinity and dissolved oxygen, and 75 per cent in respect of the other parameters listed in the Annex.[379]

There is no obligation to designate waters, but in the twenty-nine waters designated to date by the United Kingdom, the Directive specifies the manner and frequency of sampling to measure compliance. As with the other Directives, information must be forwarded to the European Commission on revisions to designations, derogations from the Directive, and results of monitoring.

In exercising its powers to set limits and values in discharge consents, the NRA, where appropriate, will take into account the water quality parameters specified in the Shellfish Directive.

(iv) Asbestos Directive[380]

The Directive applies to discharges from plants and processes where over 100 kg. per year of raw asbestos is used.[381]

Member states are required to ensure that, so far as reasonably practicable, discharges of asbestos into the aquatic environment are reduced at source and prevented. Plants and processes covered by the Directive are required to use the best technology available not entailing excessive cost, including, where appropriate, recycling or treatment.[382]

5.6.4   REGISTERS

One of the new features introduced into the law on water pollution by Part II of the Control of Pollution Act 1974 was the requirement that Water Authorities maintain registers which were open to the public, containing certain particulars relating to consents, exemptions from publicity, and samples of waste or effluent taken. These requirements have been substantially re-enacted by section 117 of the Water Act 1989.

The NRA must maintain registers containing prescribed[383] particulars of the following:

1.   Notices of water quality objectives.[384]
2.   Applications for consents.
3.   Consents given and any conditions to which they are subject.
4.   Certificates by the Secretary of State exempting applicants for consents from the publicity requirements.
5.   Samples of water or effluent taken by the NRA or another person on its behalf or under an arrangement with it for the purpose of the legislation, and information produced by analysis of those samples and the steps taken in consequence.

The register must be so indexed as to enable information relating to a particular discharge or to a particular place to be traced, and entries must be kept for a period of five years or for such longer time as is necessary for the exercise of the NRA's functions in respect of the control of pollution.[385]

Entries in respect of water quality objectives are to state: (a) the date of the notice; (b) the waters to which it relates; (c) the applicable classification; and (d) the date specified in relation to that classification This will enable interested parties to check, in respect of any particular waters, whether the stated objectives are being met, by examining the entries of water samples and their analyses.[386]

The particulars relating to applications for consent must contain the names of the applicant, the proposal to which the application relates, the date on which it was received or transmitted to the Secretary of State and a copy of the accompanying information.

Entries with respect to consents and conditions must include: (a) the name of the person to whom the consent is given; (b) the date of the consent and, if different from the date of consent, the date on which it and any condition to which it is subject came into or comes into force; (c) the date at which the discharge is being made, or the activity is taking place;[387](d) particulars of any conditions to which the consent is subject; (e) the period during which no modification or revocation may be made; (f) the enactment under which the consent is given; and (g) particulars of any notice served in relation to the consent.[388]

The registers must also contain the place, date and time of day when a sample was taken, the results of any analysis of the sample and whether they are admissible in any proceedings,[389] and any steps taken in consequence of the results of any such analysis.[390]

Normally, entries in the register must be made within twenty-eight days of the relevant event, but for an analysis of a sample the time limit for entering the results is two months from the day on which the sample was taken, or, if the analysis was not taken by or on behalf of the NRA, twenty-eight days after the results are notified to the NRA.

Where legal proceedings are initiated in consequence of the taking of a sample, the relevant entry must be made within fourteen days of the determination of the proceedings.

If an applicant for consent does not wish any of the above details to appear on the registers, he or she may apply to the Secretary of State for a certificate stating that the requirements of section 117 shall not apply.[391] As a prerequisite, he or she must satisfy the Secretary of State that it would be contrary to the public interest or would unreasonably prejudice a private interest by disclosing a trade secret if a certificate were not issued. If he or she is so satisfied, the Secretary of State may issue a certificate to the applicant stating that particulars of any of the above matters which are specified in the certificate shall not be entered on the registers. However, with respect to every such certificate, the registers are to contain the name of the person to whom it is issued and the date of the certificate, the place to which the relevant application, consent, sample or information relates, and a statement of what type of information the certificate covers.[392]

5.6.5   PROVISION AND ACQUISITION OF INFORMATION

The NRA is under a duty to provide all such advice and assistance requested by the Secretary of State and the Minister of Agriculture as appears to it to be appropriate for facilitating the carrying out of their functions in respect of the control of pollution.[393]

The Secretary of State, the Minister of Agriculture and the NRA may serve a notice on any person requiring him or her to furnish specified information[394] reasonably required for the purpose of carrying out their functions with respect to the control of pollution.[395] Regulations may be made which make provision for restructuring the information which may be required under this section and for determining the forms in which the information is to be required.[396] It is an offence to fail without reasonable excuse to comply with the requirement of a notice and a person found guilty is liable to a fine not exceeding level 5 on the standard scale.[397]

For the purposes connected with the carrying out of their functions, the NRA and water undertaker must provide each other with any information requested by them about the quality of any waters or about any incident in which any poisonous, noxious or polluting matter or any solid waste matter has entered any water.[398] The reciprocal duty under this section may cause problems in practice. For example, is a water undertaker required to provide information to the NRA which is to be used for the prosecution of an alleged offence by the water undertaker? Conversely, where a prosecution of a water undertaker is being considered by the NRA, must the NRA provide such information relating to the incident as is requested by that undertaker?

In the final analysis the duty of a water undertaker is enforceable by the Secretary of State under section 20,[399] while he or she may issue specific directions to the NRA under section 146.[400]

If the Secretary of State considers it appropriate to do so, he or she may cause a local inquiry to be held to establish or review a water quality objective,[401] with a view to preventing or dealing with pollution of any controlled waters, or in relation to any other matter relevant to the quality of such waters.[403] The procedure for local inquiries is determined by the Local Government Act 1972.[403]

5.6.6   CONFIDENTIALITY

The release of information which is not required to be placed on the register is inhibited by section 174, which prohibits the disclosure of information with respect to any business which has been obtained by virtue of the provisions of the Water Act 1989 and relates to the affairs of any individual or to any particular business, unless the consent of that individual or person carrying on the business has been obtained. The prohibition does not apply to the disclosure of information which is made for the purpose of carrying on certain governmental business, facilitating the performance of various duties imposed by the Water Act, for purposes of criminal or certain civil proceedings, or in pursuance of a European Community obligation.

It is an offence to contravene the prohibition on disclosing information, the penalties on summary conviction being a fine not exceeding the statutory maximum (at present £2,000) and on conviction on indictment a term of imprisonment for a maximum of two years or an unlimited fine, or both.[404]

5.7   Discharges from agricultural activities

In recent years there has been evidence of an upward trend in pollution from agricultural sources along with the improvements in agricultural productivity and increasing specialisation within the industry.[405]

The most important polluting by-products of intensive animal husbandry are animal slurry and silage effluent. Slurry can be up to 100 times and silage 200 times as polluting as untreated domestic sewage.[406] Slurry and silage account for some 80 per cent of pollution incidents occurring as a result of agricultural practice. Indeed, this was a key factor in the net decline of river quality between 1980 and 1985.

Generally, it appears that the basic cause of most slurry and silage pollution incidents is the inadequate structure and maintenance of storage facilities ranging from slurry pits to lagoons and silage stores.[407] A further problem is the safe disposal of slurry and silage liquors and other farm wastes such as sheep dip which are generally spread onto land and may eventually seep into water. This is similar to the problem of leaking of nitrates into surface and groundwaters which has resulted from the increased use of nitrogen fertilisers. Enrichment of rivers and estuaries caused by the introduction of nutrients such as nitrogen and phosphate can result in excessive plant growth leading to the depletion of oxygen supplies in the water, with its sometimes drastic effects on aquatic life.[408] The difficulties associated with nitrates stem from the time which elapses between the application of fertiliser and its presence in deep aquifers. In some areas the effects of nitrates spread on land a decade ago are only just being seen today. The areas particularly at risk from nitrate pollution are areas of intensive agriculture sustained by heavy applications of nitrate fertilisers and where the soil is highly porous.

Control of incidents of agricultural pollution is primarily under-taken by the NRA through prosecution of offences and other enforcement measures, but both the Ministry of Agriculture, Fisheries and Food and the Welsh Office Agricultural Department play a major role in offering advice and educating farmers on the avoidance of pollution.

Under the Control of Pollution Act 1974, it was an offence for a farmer to cause pollution unless the activity in question was considered as being consistent with good agricultural practice. This was defined in a series of publications approved by the Ministry of Agriculture, Fisheries and Food as a code of good agricultural practice.

Compliance with the code of good agricultural practice is no longer a defence to a prosecution under section 107 of the Water Act 1989. Nor does contravention of the code give rise to criminal or civil liability. However, it remains an authoritative guide for persons engaged in agriculture with respect to activities that may affect controlled waters and for promoting desirable practices for avoiding or minimising the pollution of any such waters. The NRA is required to take any contraventions or likely contraventions into account in deciding whether to exercise its powers to impose a relevant prohibition,[409] or any powers conferred on it by regulations[410] relating to taking precautions against pollution.[411] The Government is expected shortly to make regulations on the location, construction and maintenance of stores to be used for hazardous substances, either adjacent to water or likely to drain into the sewerage system. They have issued draft regulations covering the construction of new and extended silage and slurry facilities, as well as their management and maintenance. In relation to existing facilities, the NRA will be empowered to serve notice on particular sites, bringing the facilities immediately within the scope of the regulations, wherever they see reasonable cause to believe that pollution may otherwise occur.[412]

In certain circumstances capital grants are available to farmers who invest in new waste storage or treatment facilities, subject to a limitation on the grant-aidable investment of £35,000 per labour unit, with a ceiling of £50,000 per business. The present rates of grant are 30 per cent in the lowlands and 60 per cent in the less favoured areas. To be eligible for grant aid, facilities must comply with certain standards.

They must be properly designed for their purpose in accordance with British Standards specifications, and must have a design life of at least ten years. In addition, farmers must consult the NRA before any application for grant on facilities involving potential pollution risks will be accepted by the Ministry of Agriculture, Fisheries and Food. Under the new regulations, the statutory requirements will have to be met before a project will be accepted for grant assistance.[413] In response to the problem of the leaking of nitrate into surface and groundwaters, the Minister of Agriculture is empowered to designate nitrate-sensitive areas and control agricultural activities within those areas.[414]

Recent changes in the EC Common Agricultural Policy are likely to affect agricultural land use, particularly where marginal agricultural land is converted to coniferous afforestation, which in turn has implications for water quality through increased acidification, leaching of water and toxins, release of nutrients and discoloration.[415] Control over potential pollution is currently exercised by the Forestry Commission through a process of consultation prior to the approval of planting grants. The Commission seeks advice from local authorities and where appropriate, the NRA, in considering whether to grant approval or not.[416]

5.8   Discharges of radioactive matter

Except as otherwise provided for in regulations made by the Secretary of State, nothing in Chapter I of Part III of the Act (Control of Pollution) applies to radioactive waste within the meaning of the Radioactive Substances Act 1960.[417] Regulations may provide for the provisions of the Chapter to have effect, subject to such modifications as the Secretary of State considers appropriate for the purposes of dealing with radioactive waste. He or she may also make regulations modifying the Radioactive Substances Act 1960, or any other Act, in consequence of the provisions of Chapter I and any regulations made for dealing with radioactive waste.[418]

The Control of Pollution (Radioactive Waste) Regulations 1976[419] and the Control of Pollution (Radioactive Waste) Regulations 1984[420] together provide that Chapter I of Part III to the Water Act 1989 applies to radioactive substances in the same manner as to other polluting substances, but in such a way as not to take into account their radioactive properties, which remain subject to control under the Radioactive Substances Act 1960.[421]

5.9   Discharges of trade effluent into sewers

A different regime operates for the control of discharge of trade effluent into sewers than for the control of discharges into water. Since the Water Act 1989 came into force there are in fact two regimes governing the discharge of trade effluent into sewers. The first deals with 'ordinary' trade effluent and is covered by the Public Health (Drainage of Trade Premises) Act 1937 (as amended). The second regime, which is a modified version of the first, governs those trade effluents which contain prescribed substances[422] in excess of a background concentration or which result from prescribed processes if either asbestos or chloroform is present in a concentration greater than the background concentration. Jurisdiction for the control of the discharge of trade effluent into sewers lies with sewerage undertakers.

5.9.1   'ORDINARY' TRADE EFFLUENT

The occupier of any trade premises within the area of a sewerage undertaker may, with the consent of that undertaker, discharge any trade effluent from the premises into the public sewers.[423] 'Trade premises' means any premises used or intended to be used for carrying on any trade or industry. 'Trade effluent' means any liquid, either with or without particles of matter in suspension therein, which is wholly or in part produced in the course of any trade or industry carried on at trade premises, but does not include domestic sewage.[424]

An application to a sewerage undertaker for consent to discharge trade effluent from any trade premises into the public sewer must be by written notice known as a 'trade effluent notice' from the owner or occupier[425] of the premises stating: (a) the nature or composition of the trade effluent; (b) the maximum quantity of the trade effluent which it is proposed to discharge on any one day; and (c) the highest rate at which it is proposed to discharge the trade effluent.[426]

No trade effluent may be discharged for a period of two months ('the initial period') from the date of service of notice on the undertaker.[427]

A sewerage undertaker may give consent either unconditionally or subject to such conditions as it thinks fit with respect to the following:

1. The sewer or sewers into which any trade effluent may be discharged.
2. The nature or composition of the trade effluent which may be so discharged.

3. The maximum quantity of any trade effluent which may be discharged on any one day, either generally or into a particular sewer.

4. The highest rate at which any trade effluent may be discharged, either generally or into a particular sewer.

5. The period or periods of the day during which trade effluent may be discharged.

6. The exclusion from the trade effluent of condensing water.

7. The elimination or diminution of any specified constituent of the trade effluent, before it enters the sewer, where the constituent would, either alone or in combination with any other matter with which it is likely to come into contact while passing through any sewer:

    (a) injure or obstruct those sewers, or make especially difficult or expensive the treatment or disposal of the sewage; or

    (b) (where the trade effluent is to be, or is, discharged into a sewer having an outfall in any harbour or tidal water, or into a sewer which connects either directly or indirectly with a sewer or a sewage disposal works having such an outfall), cause or tend to cause injury or obstruction to the navigation on, or the use of, the harbour or tidal water.

8. The temperature of the trade effluent when it is discharged into the sewer, and its acidity or alkalinity at that time.

9. The payment by the occupier of the trade premises to the sewerage undertaker of charges for the reception of the trade effluent into the sewer, and for the disposal thereof.

10. The provision and maintenance of an inspection chamber or manhole which will enable a person to take samples of what is passing into the sewer from trade premises.

11. The provision and maintenance of meters to measure the volume and rate of discharge of any trade effluent and for the testing of such meters.

12. The provision and maintenance of apparatus for determining the nature and composition of any trade effluent being discharged, and for the testing of the apparatus.

13. The keeping of records of the volume, rate of discharge, nature and composition of any trade effluent being discharged, and in particular of records of readings of meters and other recording apparatus provided in compliance with any other condition attached to the consent.

14. The making of returns and giving of other information to the

sewerage undertaker concerning the volume, rate of discharge, nature and composition of any trade effluent discharged.[428]

No express power is given to a sewerage undertaker to refuse consent. However, such a power must be implied for two reasons. First, the sewerage undertaker has a power and not a duty to give consent under section 2 of the 1937 Act. The power to give consent necessarily has a concomitant power to withhold or refuse consent. Secondly, the appeal provisions contemplate a refusal as well as a failure to give consent.

If trade effluent is discharged without a consent or in contravention of a condition, the occupier of the premises is guilty of an offence and liable on summary conviction (i.e. in the Magistrates' Court) to a fine not exceeding the statutory maximum,[429] and on conviction on indictment (i.e. in the Crown Court) to an unlimited fine.[430]

The amendments to the 1937 Act by the Water Act 1989 have changed the basis of the consent system. Previously, trade effluent could be discharged after the expiry of a two-month period from the service of the trade effluent notice if the Water Authority had not either given consent within that period or made a direction that no trade effluent should be discharged until a later specified date. Now, the consent system for the discharge of trade effluent into sewers has been brought into line with the system operating in respect of the discharge of trade effluent into rivers, etc. Failure to give consent within the two-month period does not operate as a deemed consent: an actual consent is required.

Any 'person aggrieved'[431] by a refusal or failure to give consent within two months from the date of service of the notice, or by any condition attached to a consent may appeal to the Director General of Water Services.[432]

In determining an appeal against a refusal to give consent, the Director General may give consent unconditionally, or subject to any conditions which the sewerage undertaker could have imposed. Where the appeal is against a condition, the Director General may review all the conditions attached to the consent, whether appealed against or not, and may substitute another set of conditions, whether more or less favourable to the appellant, or he or she may annul any of the conditions. On any appeal, the Director General may give a direction that no trade effluent shall be discharged pursuant to the trade effluent notice until a specified date.[433]

An appeal relating to conditions providing for the payment of charges to a sewerage undertaker may only be considered by the Director if the sewerage undertaker has no charging scheme in force under section 76 of the Act. In determining such an appeal, the Director must have regard to the desirability of the undertaker recovering the expenses of complying with its obligations in consequence of the consent or agreement to which the conditions relate and of securing a reasonable return on its capital.[434]

Sewerage undertakers have power to charge for carrying out their functions under the 1937 Act and such charges may be by agreement with the persons to be charged, in accordance with a charges scheme[435] or attached as a separate condition to a consent. Where payment is required as a condition to a consent, the undertaker must have regard to the nature and composition and to the volume and rate of discharge of the trade effluent discharged, to any additional expenses incurred or likely to be incurred by a sewerage undertaker in connection with the reception or disposal of the trade effluent, and to any revenue likely to be derived by a sewerage undertaker from the trade effluent.[436] In all other instances they may fix charges by reference to such matters, and may adopt such methods and principles for the calculation and imposition of the charges as appear to them to be appropriate[437] and as are consistent with the terms of the Instruments of Appointment.[438]

A charges scheme may impose a single charge in respect of the whole period for which the consent is in force, or separate charges in respect of different parts of that period and may make different provision for different cases, including different provision in relation to different circumstances or localities.[439]

Under section 7 of the 1937 Act, a sewerage undertaker may enter into an agreement with the owner or occupier of any trade premises for the reception and disposal of any trade effluent produced on those premises. Such an agreement may provide for the construction by the sewerage undertaker of any works for the reception and disposal of trade effluent (subject to repayment by the owner or occupier), and for the removal and disposal of substances produced in the course of treating any trade effluent on or in connection with those premises. An agreement under this section is an alternative to the procedure of applying for and giving consent.

After giving consent, a sewerage undertaker may give a direction varying conditions attached to it or adding or annulling conditions.[440] It must give notice of the direction to the owner or occupier of the trade premises affected. The notice must state the date on which it is to take effect, being not less than two months after it is given. Subject to one exception,[441] no direction may be given within two years from the date of the consent or notice of a previous direction without the written consent of the owner and occupier. The notice must contain information about the right of appeal.

The owner or occupier may appeal against the direction to the Director General within two months after notice of it has been given to him or her (or later, with the written permission of the Director General). Provided that the appeal is brought before the date on which the direction takes effect, it does not take effect until the appeal is withdrawn or finally disposed of. However, insofar as the direction relates to charges payable by the owner or occupier, it may take effect on any date after the giving of the notice. In determining the appeal, the Director General may annul the direction or substitute another direction whether more or less favourable to the appellant.

The exception to the rule against giving directions within the two-year period relates to the situation where the sewerage undertaker considers it necessary to give a direction within that period in order to provide proper protection for persons likely to be affected by discharges which could lawfully be made apart from the direction. Under those circumstances, the sewerage undertaker must pay compensation to the owner or occupier of the premises, unless it believes that the direction is required as a result of an unforeseeable change in circumstances occurring since the beginning of the two-year period. In that case, it must give notice of its reasons to the owner and occupier who may appeal against it to the Director General.

5.9.2   PRESCRIBED SUBSTANCES AND PROCESSES

The provision relating to the discharge of trade effluent into sewers apply in modified form in certain circumstances where prescribed substances are present in the effluent or the effluent derives from a prescribed process.[442]

The Trade Effluent (Prescribed Processes and Substances) Regulations 1989 list twenty-three so-called 'red list'[443] substances which are some of the more dangerous substances if allowed to enter the aquatic environment. The Regulations enable the United Kingdom to begin implementing the 1987 and 1990 Ministerial Agreements on the North Sea which require a reduction of some 50 per cent in inputs of dangerous substances to the North Sea via rivers and estuaries between 1985 and 1995.

The prescribed substances are:[444]

Mercury and its compounds
Cadmium and its compounds
gamma-Hexachlorocyclohexane
DDT
Pentachlorophenol
Hexachlorobenzene
Hexachlorobutadene
Aldrin
Dieldrin
Endrin
Carbon Tetrachloride
Dichlorvos
1, 2-Dichloroethane
Trichlorobenzene
Atrazine
Simazine
Tributyltin compounds
Triphenyltin compounds
Trifluralin
Fenitrothion
Azinphos-methyl
Malathion
Endosulfan

The modified rules apply to trade effluent in which any of the prescribed substances is present in a concentration greater than the background concentration.[445] 'Background concentration' means such concentration of the substance as would, but for anything done on the premises in question, be present in the effluent discharged from those premises, and includes such concentrations of the substance as are present:

(a) in water supplied to the premises;
(b) in water abstracted for use on the premises; and
(c) in precipitation onto the site within which the premises are situated.[446]

The prescribed processes are as follows:[447]

any process for the production of chlorinated organic chemicals
any process for the manufacture of paper pulp

any industrial process in which cooling waters or effluents are
 chlorinated
any process for the manufacture of asbestos cement
any process for the manufacture of asbestos paper or board.

The modified rules also apply to trade effluent deriving from a
prescribed process if either asbestos[448] or chloroform is present in a
concentration greater than the background concentration.[449]

The modifications to the rules are set out in Schedule 9 to the Water
Act 1989. Where the modified rules apply and a trade effluent notice is
served on the sewerage undertaker or an agreement under section 7 of
the 1937 Act is planned, the sewerage undertaker must refer to the
Secretary of State for the Environment the question whether the
proposed operations should be prohibited and if not, whether any
conditions should be imposed. Where a sewerage undertaker proposes
to vary conditions in circumstances where the modified rules apply, it
must also refer the matter to the Secretary of State.[450] In the case of a
trade effluent notice, the reference to the Secretary of State must be
made within two months from the day after its service. However, no
reference need be made if the sewerage undertaker refuses its consent
before the end of that period.

If, on appeal under section 3 of the 1937 Act, it appears to the
Director General that the case is one in which a reference must be made
to the Secretary of State, he or she cannot determine the appeal except
by upholding a refusal, unless he or she has him- or herself referred the
questions to the Secretary of State and obtained a copy of the notice of
the Secretary of State's determination.[451]

A sewerage undertaker may not give any consent or enter into any
agreement with respect to the proposed operations until the Secretary
of State has determined the reference. Where a reference is made, a
copy must be served on the owner or occupier of the premises in
question and on the sewerage undertaker.

For the purposes of appealing against a failure to grant consent within
the initial two-month period, that period does not begin to run until
the beginning of the day after the Secretary of State serves notice of
his or her determination of the reference on the sewerage undertaker.

The Secretary of State may review (independently of a reference to
him or her) consents and agreements which are covered by the
modified provisions to see whether or not authorised operations
should be prohibited, or if not, whether conditions should be modified
or imposed.[452]

Unless there has been a contravention of a provision of a consent or agreement, the Secretary of State generally may not carry out a review within two years from the service of notice of determination of the previous review. This limitation does not apply if the review is carried out to give effect to a European Community obligation or international agreement or for the protection of public health or flora and fauna dependent on an aquatic environment.[453]

Compensation is payable to an owner or occupier in respect of any loss or damage resulting from a review carried out for the protection of public health or flora and fauna dependent on an aquatic environment within the two-year period, unless the review has resulted from a change in circumstances which could not reasonably have been foreseen at the time of the last review or from a consideration by the Secretary of State of material information which was not reasonably available to him or her at that time.[454]

Before determining the questions which are the subject of a reference or review, the Secretary of State must give an opportunity to the sewerage undertaker and the owner or occupier to make representations or objections. He or she is then under a duty to consider any such representations or obligations which are not withdrawn.

On determining any question on a reference or review, the Secretary of State must serve notice on the sewerage undertaker and the owner or occupier (and forward a copy to the Director) stating any operations which are to be prohibited, or any conditions which are to be imposed,[455] or that he or she has no objection to the operations being carried out and does not intend to require conditions to be imposed.[456] In addition, he or she may vary or revoke the provisions of a previous notice, consent or agreement.

Where the Secretary of State has served a notice of determination it is the duty of a sewerage undertaker to ensure compliance with the provisions of the notice in relation to its powers to grant consents, impose or vary conditions or to enter into any agreements under section 7 of the 1937 Act. It is also the duty of the Director General in the case of an appeal to exercise his or her powers to ensure compliance with the Secretary of State's determination.[457]

Any duties imposed on sewerage undertakers by the regulations or schedule 9 are enforceable by the Secretary of State under section 20 of the Act, but where an application is made to him in respect of a failure by an undertaker to make a reference, the Secretary of State may proceed with the matter as if the application were a reference.[458]

It is the duty of every sewerage undertaker to secure that copies of:

(a) every consent given;
(b) every agreement entered into under section 7;
(c) every direction varying consent given under section 60 of the Public Health Act 1961;
(d) every direction given under section 43(3) of the Control of Pollution Act 1974; and
(e) every notice served on an undertaker under paragraph 3 of Schedule 9 of the Water Act 1989 for a determination of a reference or review by the Secretary of State with regard to prescribed processes and substances

are kept available at all reasonable times for inspection by the public free of charge at the office of the undertaker. Sewerage undertakers must also supply copies on request to any person on payment of a reasonable sum.[459]

The information available to the public under this section is not as wide as that which must be kept in the public registers under section 117 of the Water Act in relation to discharges into rivers, etc.[460] In particular, there is no provision for information to be made public about the results of tests carried out on effluent to monitor compliance with conditions.

The owner or occupier of any trade premises used or intended to be used for discharging trade effluent must, when requested to do so by a sewerage undertaker, produce any plans of the sewer, drain, pipe, channel or outlet that they may have, and furnish all information they may reasonably have with regard to the sewer, drain, pipe, channel or outlet. A person who fails to comply with such a request is guilty of an offence and liable to a fine not exceeding level 3 on the standard scale.[461]

It is a criminal offence for any person to disclose information furnished to him or her under the 1937 Act or Part V of the Public Health Act 1961, unless he or she has the consent of the person who furnished it or the disclosure is made in connection with the execution of duties under the Acts, or for the purpose of Court proceedings or a report of such proceedings.[462] However, this prohibition does not appear to extend to information obtained by sewerage undertakers from tests carried out by their own officials. That information has not been 'furnished to' them and so is not covered by the prohibition.

5.10   Precautions against pollution

5.10.1   WATER PROTECTION ZONES

Where the Secretary of State, on application of the NRA and after consultation with the Minister of Agriculture (if the area is within England), considers that it is appropriate in order to prevent or control the entry of any poisonous, noxious or polluting matter[463] into controlled waters, to prohibit or restrict certain activities in a particular area, he or she may designate that area as a water protection zone.[464]

Water protection zones are relevant to the protection of both surface water and groundwater which may be vulnerable to pollution from diffuse sources, including run-off and spillages.[465] Certain rivers are particularly vulnerable in that they combine major chemical stores and industrial processes upstream with abstractions for water supply.

An order designating an area as a water protection zone may confer on the NRA power to determine which activities are to be controlled and when such controls are to be exercised, or may apply a prohibition or restriction on certain activities subject to the consent of the NRA. The Secretary of State may make regulations providing for the procedure for applications for consent, the conditions of such consent and the procedure on such matters as revocations, variations, appeals and charges,[466] may provide for criminal sanctions in respect of contraventions of the order and may make different provision for different cases, including different provision in relation to different persons, circumstances or localities. For example, in areas close to water abstraction intakes the NRA may prohibit the storage or use of hazardous substances which could in the event of an accident result in concentrations of substances in water that would be hazardous to health. In the whole of the river catchment upstream from the lowest intake, the NRA could require that prescribed activities involving the storage or use of hazardous substances be subject to a consent procedure. Prior to consent being given, the undertaker of the activity in question would have to show that it has carried out a hazard identification and risk assessment and that sufficient measures have been taken to minimise the risk and consequences of accidents.

The procedure for making an order is laid down in Schedule 7 to the Act. Where the NRA applies to the Secretary of State for an order, it must submit to him a draft of the order applied for, publish notices with respect to the application in local newspapers and in the London Gazette, and serve a copy of the notice on every local authority and water undertaker in whose area the proposed zone is situated.[467] The notice must state the general effect of the order applied for, specify a place where a copy of the draft order may be inspected free of charge within twenty-eight days of the first publication of the notice, and state that any person may, within that period, object to the making of the order to the Secretary of State.

The Secretary of State may hold a public inquiry if he or she considers it appropriate or determine the matter on the basis of the application and any written objections.[468] He or she may make the order in the terms of the draft order submitted to him or her, or with such modifications[469] as he or she thinks fit. However, he or she may not make a modification which he or she considers likely adversely to affect any person unless he or she is satisfied that the NRA has given and published such additional notices as he or she may have required.[470]

5.10.2 NITRATE SENSITIVE AREAS

A new feature of the Water Act is the provision for nitrate sensitive areas. A report of the Nitrate Co-ordination Group published in December 1986 highlighted the problem of nitrate concentrations in drinking water as a result of the agricultural use of land. Discussions since then have centred on the appropriate means of control and the House of Commons Environment Committee in the Third Report 1987[471] recommended that trial zones be set up in selected sensitive catchments in which the use of nitrogen fertilisers is regulated or prohibited.

On application of the NRA, the Minister of Agriculture (or the Secretary of State for Wales) may with the consent of Treasury, designate nitrate sensitive areas for the purpose of preventing or controlling the entry of nitrate into controlled waters as a result of the agricultural use of land.[472] The Act allows for three types of nitrate sensitive areas. The first relates to areas within which management agreements are entered into voluntarily between farmers and the Ministry of Agriculture in return for compensation. The second type allows for the composition of mandatory requirements, again with compensation to the affected farmers. The third covers areas in which mandatory requirements are imposed, with no compensation, backed up by a system of consents and with contraventions sanctioned by criminal offences.

Where a nitrate sensitive area has been designated, the Minister may enter into an agreement with the freehold owner[473] of agricultural land within the area, under which in consideration of payments to be made by the Minister, the owner accepts certain obligations with respect to the management of land. Such an agreement binds all persons deriving title from or under the person who enters into it to the extent that the agreement is expressed to bind the land in relation to those persons.[474] Such an agreement bears the hallmarks of a property right, being apparently assignable with the land, and binding successors in title. However, no link is made between the provision and the various property statutes which deal with the protection of third party interests in land and it appears, therefore, that nitrate sensitive area agreements should not be regarded as property interests, but merely as contracts which breach the normal rule that contracts do not bind third parties.[475]

Where it appears to the Minister to be appropriate, he or she may, either in the order designating the nitrate sensitive area, or in a subsequent order, require, prohibit or restrict the carrying on of specified activities in relation to agricultural land, and provide for compensation to be paid to those affected by the obligations.[476] Such an order may confer on the Minister or the Secretary of State power to determine those activities which are to be prohibited or restricted, when such prohibitions and restrictions are to be exercised, and the granting of consent by the Minister or Secretary of State to carry out otherwise prohibited or restricted activities. Regulations have been made specifying the procedure for applications for consent and for their subsequent modification or revocation.[477] The order may impose criminal liability for any contravention of the order, and may make different provision for different cases, including different provision in relation to different persons, circumstances or localities.

The procedures for an application by the NRA for an order designating a nitrate sensitive area and for an order containing mandatory provisions in respect of that area are specified in Schedule 11 to the Act. The NRA may not apply to the Minister for an order unless it believes that pollution is or is likely to be caused by the entry of nitrate into waters and that any controls in force in relation to those waters are not sufficient to deal with the problem. There is no provision for public notification or consultation.[478]

However, before making an order which restricts or prohibits any activities within a designated zone or a modification order which further restricts certain activities, the Minister must publish notices with respect to the proposed order in local newspapers and the London Gazette, and serve copies on the NRA, relevant local authorities and water undertakers.[479]

The notice must state the general effect of the proposed order, specify a place where a copy of it may be inspected free of charge within a period of forty-two days from the first publication of the notice, and state that any person may, within that period, object to the making of the order to the Minister.[480]

The Minister may hold a public inquiry before making a determination,[481] or may make it on the basis of any objections received. However, the Minister may not make a modification[482] which he or she considers is likely adversely to affect any person, unless he or she has given such notice as he or she considers appropriate for enabling that person to object to the modification.[483]

5.10.3 RELEVANT PROHIBITIONS

It is an offence to discharge matter other than trade or sewage effluent from a drain or sewer or to discharge trade or sewage effluent onto land in contravention of any relevant prohibition.[484]

A relevant prohibition is made by the NRA serving notice on a person prohibiting him or her from making or continuing a discharge, either absolutely or unless specified conditions are met.[485] It is also made by regulations which prohibit a discharge of effluent or matter containing a prescribed substance or a prescribed concentration of such a substance or which derives from a prescribed process or from a process involving the use of prescribed substances.[486]

5.10.4 OTHER POWERS

Under section 110 the Secretary of State may make regulations for prohibiting a person from having custody or control of any poisonous, noxious or polluting matter unless prescribed steps have been taken to prevent or control the entry of the matter into any controlled waters. A person who already has custody or control of such substances may be required to take prescribed steps for that purpose.

The Government has issued draft regulations on the location, construction and maintenance of stores to be used for hazardous substances either adjacent to water or likely to drain into the sewerage system. The draft regulations concentrate on the control of spillages of oil, silage and slurry, and apply only to new structures or plants. The NRA would have power to serve enforcement notices on existing installations where pollution risks are deemed to exist and bring them within the scope of the regulations. Similar controls may subsequently be extended to other types of installation.[487]

In respect of major industrial plants, particularly chemical and petrochemical industries, the Control of Major Industrial Accident Hazards (CIMAH) Regulations, enforced by the Health and Safety Executive, require necessary precautions against major accidents to be taken.

The NRA is given power to make byelaws for prohibiting or regulating the washing or clearing in any controlled waters of specific things, and for prohibiting or regulating the keeping or use of vessels which are provided with sanitary appliances on any controlled waters.[488]

Where it appears to the NRA that any poisonous, noxious or polluting matter or any solid waste matter is likely to enter or to be or to have been present in any controlled waters, it is given power to carry out anti-pollution works and operations. In particular, it may either carry out works to prevent the matter entering water, remove and dispose of such matter, mitigate any pollution caused by its presence, and, so far as is reasonably practicable, restore the waters and any flora and fauna dependent on the water, to their original state.[489] Powers of entry onto premises to exercise these powers are conferred on the NRA[490] with provision to obtain a Justice's warrant in certain circumstances.[491]

Where the NRA carries out such works or operations it is entitled to recover the expenses reasonably incurred in so doing from any person who caused or knowingly permitted the matter in question to be present in controlled waters or in a place where it was likely to enter any controlled waters.[492]

It is unclear whether the term 'entitled to recover the expenses reasonably incurred' in carrying out any works and operations empowered by this section extends to the costs of, for example, the giving of advice or providing supervisory and analytical services.[493]

Where a person has been convicted of an offence under this or any other Act, the Court, instead of or in addition to imposing another sentence, may make an order requiring him or her to pay compensation for any loss or damage resulting from that offence.[494]

Compensation orders are to be of such amount as the Court considers appropriate, having regard to the evidence and to any representations made,[495] although in the Magistrates' Court the maximum amount that may be ordered by way of compensation is £2,000 for each offence of which the offender is convicted.[496] An important instance where this power may be used is where a water pollution offence has resulted in fish mortality in a particular water. Compensation may now be awarded to the NRA,[497] or the owner or manager of the fisheries, for costs incurred in restocking the fishery.

Section 18 of the Water Act 1945 empowers statutory water undertakers to make byelaws, if it appears to them to be necessary for the purpose of protecting surface or underground water belonging to them or which they are for the time being authorised to take.[498] Such byelaws may define the area necessary for exercising control, and prohibit or regulate the doing within the area of any specified act, and may contain different provisions in respect of different parts of the defined area.[499] When an area has been defined, the undertaker may by notice to the owner or occupier of premises require him or her to execute and keep in good repair such works as it considers necessary for preventing pollution of water.

An appeal procedure is provided for and the water undertaker may, in the event of a failure to comply with a requirement, undertake any required works itself and recover the expenses reasonably incurred in so doing.[500] Byelaws may also prohibit certain inland waters within its area from being used for boating, swimming or other recreational purposes, or regulate the way in which these waters may be used for those purposes.[501] Any person who contravenes or fails to comply with such a byelaw commits an offence and is liable on summary conviction to a fine not exceeding level 1 on the standard scale.[502] In the event of a contravention or failure to comply, the water authority may take such action as it considers necessary and recover any expenses reasonably incurred from the person in default.[503]

Although both section 18 of the Water Act 1945 and section 79 of the Water Resources Act 1963 are currently in force, they are repealed from a date to be appointed by the Secretary of State.[504] The Water Act 1989 contains transitional provisions with respect to byelaws made under section 18 of the Water Act 1945.[505] Any such byelaws in force immediately before the transfer date[506] have effect as if the power to make byelaws under section 158 of the Water Act 1989[507] included a power to make such byelaws.[508]

Without prejudicing his or her powers to bring the repeal of section 18 of the 1945 Act into force, the Secretary of State may, in the exercise of his or her powers in relation to water protection zones, modify the effect of these transitional provisions or revoke or amend such byelaws.[509]

The NRA and water undertakers have, on any land belonging to them or land over or in which they have acquired the necessary easements or rights, powers to deal with foul water and pollution. In particular they may construct and maintain drains, sewers, water-courses, catchpits and other works[510] for the following purposes:

1. Intercepting, treating or disposing of any foul water arising or flowing upon that land.
2. Otherwise preventing the pollution:
   (a) of any surface or underground water which belong to them or from which they are authorised to take water;
   (b) of any reservoir owned or operated by them or which they propose to acquire or construct;
   (c) of any underground strata from which they are for the time being authorised to abstract water in pursuance of a licence under the Water Resources Act 1963.[511]

A water undertaker must consult with the NRA before carrying out any works which will affect any watercourse,[512] and nothing in this section can be taken to authorise the NRA or a water authority to intercept or take any water which a navigation authority is authorised to take or use, without the consent of that authority.[513]

5.10.5 BYELAWS

Byelaws made by the NRA or by any water or sewerage undertaker under section 158 of the Water Act 1989 must be confirmed by the Secretary of State for the Environment[514] and made in accordance with the procedure specified in Schedule 24 to the Act.

At least one month before the application for confirmation of a byelaw the NRA or undertaker (the 'relevant body') must cause a notice of its intention to make the application to be published in the London Gazette and in such other manner as it considers appropriate for informing persons likely to be affected, and cause copies of the notice to be served on any public bodies who appear to it to be concerned.[515] During this period, a copy of the proposed byelaw must be deposited at the offices of the relevant body, where reasonable facilities are to be provided for public inspection free of charge, and any person may be furnished on application with a copy of the byelaw.[516]

The Secretary of State may, with or without a local inquiry, refuse to confirm either the byelaw submitted to him or her, or may confirm the byelaw either without, or if the relevant body consents, with modifications, and the relevant body must, if so directed by the Secretary of State, cause notice of any proposed modifications to be given in accordance with his or her directions.[517]

A byelaw made by the NRA under section 114[518] may only be confirmed without a local inquiry if no written objection to its confirmation has been received by the Secretary of State, any objections received have been withdrawn, or the Secretary of State considers that the person making the objection has no material interest in the controlled waters to which the byelaw relates.[519] The Secretary of State may fix the date on which any byelaw confirmed by him or her is to come into force, but if no such date is fixed, the byelaw comes into force one month from the date of confirmation.[520] Once the byelaw has been confirmed it must be printed and deposited at the offices of the relevant body, where copies are to be made available for inspection by the public free of charge. Any person is entitled, on application to the relevant body, to be furnished with a copy of the byelaw on payment of such reasonable sum as the relevant body may determine.[521] Where it appears to the Secretary of State that the revocation of a byelaw is necessary or expedient, he or she may, after giving notice to the relevant body and considering any representations or objections made by it, and if required by that body after holding a local inquiry, revoke that byelaw.[522]

Notes

1. *John Young & Co.* v. *Bankier Distillery Co.* [1891–4], All E. Rep. 439.
2. See below, sections 5.6.3.6 and 5.5.1.
3. See, generally, J. C. Lawls, *Water Quality and its Control* (New York: John Wiley & Sons, 1985).
4. For 'controlled water', see below, section 5.6.1.1.
5. S.105.
6. See 'Observations by the Government on the Third Report of the House of Commons Environment Committee in Session: 1986–87' (22 June 1988), panel 19.
7. S.104(2).
8. S.I.1989, No. 1148.
9. See Appendix E.
10. S.105(4) and (5).

11. S.105(3).
12. S.105(2).
13. See generally, W. Howarth, *Water Pollution Law* (London: Shaw & Sons, 1988), Ch.10.
14. Particularly Arts. 100 and 235.
15. Bull, EC. Supp.2/86.
16. Arts.13OR–13OT.
17. Art.13OR(1).
18. Art.14OR(2).
19. Art.189.
20. Power to make Regulations to implement Directives is given in s.2(3) of the European Communities Act 1957.
21. For example, the DoE circular 'Water and the environment'; see below, section 5.6.3.6.
22. Re the EEC Directive concerning the quality of bathing water: *EC Commission* v. *Kingdom of Netherlands*, case 96/81 [1982] ECR 1791.
23. See above, sections 5.2 and 5.4.
24. 28/76 *Molkerei–Zentrale Westfalen/Lippe GmbH* v. *Hauptzoellamt* [1968] ECR 143.
25. See Howarth, *op.cit.*, para.10.07.
26. For example, the 'Dangerous Substances Directives' and Directives concerning mercury, cadmium, etc.; see below, section 5.6.3.6.
27. For example, the 'Bathing Water Directive' and 'Shellfish Waters Directive'; see 5.5.1.2.
28. S.52(1)(a).
29. S.189(2).
30. S.189(3).
31. S.52(1)(b).
32. S.52(2); see the discussion on water supply.
33. S.52(3); see the discussion of Regulation 24 of the Water Supply (Water Quality) Regulations 1989 in section 5.4.4.2, below.
34. Under s.20; see below, section 5.4.8.
35. For example, *McColl* v. *Strathclyde Regional Council* [1984] J.P.L. 350, where wholesome water was considered to be water that was safe and pleasant to drink.
36. S.I.1989 No.1147, as amended by the Water Supply (Water Quality) (Amendment) Regulations 1989 (S.I.1989 No.1384).
37. Effect is given in Part II of the Regulations to Art.7 of Council Directive 80/778/EEC (OJ No. L229 30.8.80, p.11) relating to the quality of water intended for human consumption (the 'Drinking Water Directive'). Part IV gives effect to para.1 to 4 of Art.12 (monitoring of the quality of water intended for human consumption) of that Directive. Part VI of the Regulations gives effect, in part, to Art.2 of Council Directive 75/440/EEC (quality required of surface water intended for the abstraction of drinking water) and to para.3 of Art.4 of that Directive. It is a matter of debate whether the provisions of these Regulations satisfy the requirements of the two EC Directives, and indeed whether their complete implementation can be effected by administrative procedures pursuant to the Water Act 1989. For a discussion of the implementation of EC Directives, see Howarth, *op.cit.*, Ch.10.
38. The most notable are the requirements relating to lead.
39. It may be noted that the regulations do not state in general that, if the concentration or values do not comply with those specified, water is to be regarded as unwholesome. The wording of the regulations thus leaves open the possibility that water failing to comply could nevertheless be regarded as wholesome for the purposes of the Act.
40. Reg.3(3)(a) and (b).
41. Tables A, B and C of Schedule 2 to the Regulations; see Appendix A.
42. Item 9, Table A.
43. Reg.3(5).
44. Item 1, Table C.
45. Reg.3(6), as amended by the Water Supply (Water Quality) (Amendment) Regulations 1989.
46. Table D, Schedule 2; see Appendix A.
47. Reg.3(3)(e) contains a further requirement, viz. that samples taken have established that

the average concentrations over the three preceding months of trihalomethanes (being the aggregate of the concentrations of trichloromethane, dichlorobromomethane, dibromochloromethane and tribromomethane), did not exceed 100 u/e, or where less than four samples are taken in any year, no sample contained a concentration of trihalomethanes in excess of 100 u/e.

48. Table E, Schedule 2; see Appendix A.
49. Listed in Table C, Schedule 2.
50. Reg.3(7).
51. The circumstances in which such relaxations are permissible are consistent with those specified in paras.1 and 3 of Art.9 and para.1 of Art.10 of Council Directive 80/778 EEC.
52. Reg.4(1). In the circumstances mentioned in para.1(c), the Secretary of State may authorise a relaxation of the requirements without an application by a water undertaker. Reg.4(2).
53. Reg.4(3).
54. Reg.5.
55. In relation to authorisations granted under Reg.4(1)(b) or (c) (meteorological conditions or nature and structure of the ground), the parameters in Tables B and C and Item 7 of Table D listed in Sch.2 to the Regulations.
56. Reg.5(2).
57. Reg. 5(3). This is optional for authorisations granted in relation to the nature and structure of the ground.
58. Reg.6.
59. Reg.7.
60. Reg.7(4).
61. The general duties in s.52 only apply to water undertakers. Ss.57–9 relate to private supplies of water for domestic purposes. Those sections make it clear that private supplies must also be only of wholesome water; see below, section 5.4.6.2.
62. Reg.4(4).
63. Reg.8(1).
64. Reg.8(4).
65. An area designated by a water undertaker (whether by reference to a source of supply, the number of persons supplied from any source, or otherwise) in which, in the undertaker's estimation, not more than 50,000 people reside; Reg.2.
66. In respect of the parameters listed in Tables A to E of Sch.2.
67. Reg.11.
68. Reg.12.
69. Reg.1. Sch.3 contains six such Tables, the standard numbers for samples of which are not less than those specified in Annex II to Council Directive 80/778/EEC. In relation to pH values, total hardness or alkalinity, and where a concentration is less than 50 per cent of a prescribed concentration or value over a period of three consecutive years (with appropriate modifications for the years 1990 to 1992), the number of samples to be taken in that year in respect of these parameters may be reduced; Reg.13(3)–(6).
70. Reg.13(7) and (8).
71. Reg.13(9).
72. Table 7 of Sch.3.
73. Regs.17–19.
74. Reg.20.
75. Reg.21.
76. Normally after twenty-four hours' notice, s.64(5)(a), unless the case is one of emergency or a warrant has been obtained from a justice of the peace, s.64(4).
77. S.64.
78. So as to satisfy the requirements in respect of the parameters listed in Table C of Schedule 2, Reg.2 (as amended). The Regulation contains a proviso that the Secretary of State may give an authorisation whereby a water undertaker is not required to disinfect specified ground water.
79. Which does not include water from a spring, Reg.22.
80. 75/440/EEC, No.L194 25.7.1975, p.26.

81. That is, as falling within categories A1, A2 or A3 set out in Annex I to the Directive.
82. S.I.1989 No.1148.
83. See Appendix B. The twenty-one parameters specified are those listed as mandatory in the Directive. There is no mention, however, of the remaining twenty-five 'guide' values set in the Directive. In the Directive, limits are set to which in general only 95 per cent of surface water samples must comply, but in the Regulations the limits are expressed as absolute maxima.
84. That is, of pipes which are subject to water pressure from a water main, or which would be so subject but for the closing of some valve.
85. Reg.24.
86. *ibid.*
87. Reg.25. The Secretary of State is able to make charges in respect of such applications, Reg.27.
88. Issued in March 1989 by the DoE. Even in these circumstances, the Secretary of State may by notice in writing prohibit the application to, or introduction into, water of such substances or products, Reg.25(4).
89. Reg.26.
90. Regs.25(8) and 26(4).
91. Reg.28(1).
92. Reg.28(2).
93. Reg.29.
94. Reg.29(2)(b).
95. Reg.29(3) and (4).
96. Reg.30(1).
97. Reg.30(2).
98. Sch.4.
99. Reg.30(4).
100. Reg.30(5).
101. Reg.31; Schedule 5.
102. S.56(1).
103. Reg.33(1)(b) of the Water Supply (Water Quality) Regulations 1989.
104. Reg.33(2).
105. S.56(2).
106. S.55(1).
107. S.56(2). This duty will also apply where the failure of a private water supply to provide either sufficient or wholesome water leads to a public health danger in a location where it would be uneconomical for a water undertaker to provide a supply by means of pipes.
108. S.55(2).
109. S.55(3).
110. S.55(4).
111. See 5.4.9.
112. 'Private supply' means a supply of water provided otherwise than by a water undertaker (including a supply provided for the purposes of the bottling of water), s.66(1), and also includes water which is abstracted for the purpose of being used or consumed on those premises, from a source situated on the premises themselves, s.66(2).
113. The general duty in s.52 to supply only wholesome water does not apply to private supplies, but this section enables local authorities to require that private supplies meet these standards of wholesomeness laid down in the Water Supply (Water Quality) Regulations 1989.
114. S.57(1). 'Relevant persons' are the owners and occupiers of premises receiving water from a private supply, and (whether or not the source of private supply is in the local authority's area), the owners and occupiers of premises where that source is situated and any other person who exercises powers of management and control in relation to that source, s.57(7).
115. S.57(2).
116. S.57(3).

117. S.57(6).
118. S.58(1); at least twenty-eight days.
119. S.58(2) and (3).
120. S.58(5) and (6).
121. S.58(7).
122. S.58(8).
123. S.58(9) and (10).
124. S.59(1).
125. S.59(5).
126. S.59(2).
127. S.59(3).
128. S.178.
129. S.164.
130. Under s.162.
131. S.52(1)(a).
132. S.52(1)(b).
133. S.55(1).
134. Part IV, Water Supply (Water Quality) Regulations 1989.
135. Part V *ibid.*
136. Part VI *ibid.*
137. S.20.
138. S.20(3).
139. S.20(10).
140. S.22(4) and (5).
141. Under s.52(1); s.22(6).
142. S.22(7).
143. Under s.60.
144. S.60(2); these powers include the power to make regulations.
145. S.60(3) and (6).
146. Except in cases of emergency or where the inspector has obtained a warrant from a justice of the peace to exercise his or her powers under ss.178 and 60(5).
147. S.60(4).
148. S.60.
149. S.60(4).
150. S.52; see above, section 5.4.1.
151. S.54(1).
152. S.54(4).
153. 'Waterworks' includes any spring, well, adit, borehole, service reservoir or tank, and any main or other pipe or conduit of a water undertaker, s.21(4), Water Act 1945.
154. S.21, Water Act 1954.
155. 'Water fittings' includes pipes (other than water mains), taps, cocks, valves, ferrules, meters, cisterns, baths, water closets, soil pans and other similar apparatus used in connection with the supply and use of water, s.66(1).
156. S.61(10).
157. S.62.
158. S.63(1).
159. A 'service pipe' means so much of a pipe which is, or is to be, connected with a water main for supplying water from that main to any premises as is or is to be subject to water pressure from that main or as would be so subject but for the closing of some valve, s.189(1).
160. S.63(2)(a).
161. A 'consumer' means a person who is for the time being the person on whom liability to pay charges to an undertaker in respect of a supply of water would fall, s.66(1).
162. S.63(3).
163. S.63(4).
164. S.63(2)(b) and (5).
165. S.63(6).

166. S.63(7). Where it can be shown that any steps required by the undertaker to be taken were not necessary in the circumstances, the undertaker cannot recover those expenses incurred and must pay to any other person who took those specified steps their expenses, s.63(8).
167. S.62(4).
168. Under s.178.
169. S.62(5).
170. S.64(5).
171. See above, section 5.4.10.
172. 'Sewage effluent' includes any effluent from the sewerage works of a sewerage undertaker, but does not include surface water, s.124(1).
173. 'Third Report of the House of Commons Environment Committee 1987–8', para.24.
174. See below, section 5.6.3.
175. See Third Report, para.27.
176. The annual rate of spending on improved sewage treatment facilities in England and Wales, in current prices, has increased from £164.6 million in 1980/81 to £259.8 million in 1988/89 – a 57.8 per cent increase. By the time of the introduction of the Water Act it accounted for one fifth of the total capital programme of water authorities.
177. Third Report, op.cit., para.29.
178. House of Commons Water Bill Second Reading, Hansard, Vol.143, 7 December 1988, p.336; DoE News Release, 1988/688.
179. The 'Directive Concerning the Quality of Certain Bathing Waters', 76/160/EEC.
180. Art.1.
181. Art.2(a).
182. DoE Pollution Paper No.22, 'Controlling pollution: principles and prospects' (1984), para.33.
183. Coliforms are discharged from the large intestines of warm-blooded animals, including humans, and their presence in water is an indication of the degree of sewage contamination in that particular water and has been found to bear a close association with the probability that pathogenic organisms are also present in the water.
184. Art.5(1).
185. Art.6.
186. A list can be found in Appendix D.
187. DoE News Release, 1988/688.
188. Third Report, op.cit., para.53.
189. See below, section 5.6.3.
190. See below, section 5.9.
191. DoE Circular 7/89, para.21.
192. See below, section 5.6.3.6.
193. On about 1 per cent of the land area.
194. Fifteen per cent of sewage (i.e. liquid effluent with untreated solids) is disposed of directly into the sea by sea outfall, ranging from short outfalls with little pre-treatment to satisfactory long outfalls with full preliminary treatment of grit removal and screening, Third Report, op.cit., para.53. At the Third North Sea Conference the United Kingdom announced that, in future, all significant discharges of sewage would be treated, although the degree of treatment was not specified.
195. Declaration reference.
196. Cmmd 4984.
197. See note 195, above.
198. Com (89) 518 final.
199. See below, section 5.6.3.6.
200. S.107(1)(c) and (6); see below, section 5.6.1.8.
201. See below, section 5.6.1.11.
202. See Howarth, op.cit., para.4.30.
203. The relevant provisions of which have now been replaced by the Water Act 1989.
204. Third Report, op.cit., para.47.
205. Third Report, op.cit., para.25.

206. Para.26.
207. Aylesbury Magistrates Court, 14 May 1987; see note: *Environmental Law*, 1988, Vol.2, No.1, p.3, and S. Jackson, 'Private prosecutions under the Control of Pollution Act 1974' (1988), 2, *Environmental Law*, 3.
208. See below, section 5.6.4.
209. See also below, section 5.6.1.10.
210. See 'Third Report of the House of Commons Environment Committee 1987–88', para.96.
211. *ibid.*, para.89.
212. 'Observations by the Government', *op.cit.*, para.4.7.
213. S.I.1984 No.1902.
214. Pursuant to s.110 of the Water Act 1989; DoE Green Paper: Observations by the Government, *op.cit.*, para.4.13.
215. Observations by the Government, *op.cit.*, para.4.17.
216. See below, section 5.6.3.
217. A 'person' includes a company.
218. As to 'trade effluent', see below, section 5.10. 'Sewage effluent' includes any effluent from the sewage disposal or sewerage works of a sewerage undertaker but does not include surface water, s.124(1).
219. S.107(1).
220. S.107(6).
221. 'Mile' means an international nautical mile of 1,852 metres, s.103(4).
222. S.105(1)(a); unless the Secretary of State has by order declared an area not to be so treated, s.103(5)(a).
223. S.103(1)(b). The destruction between coastal and inland waters is of little practical relevance, except in the case of an offence under s.109 which only applies to inland waters, because the offences apply with respect to controlled waters, which cover both coastal and inland waters.
224. As specified by the Secretary of State on maps deposited with the NRA and available for free public inspection, s.103(2) and (3).
225. S.103(1)(c). The definition of 'relevant lake or pond' has been extended by the Controlled Waters (Lakes and Ponds) Order 1989 S.I.1149 to include a reservoir which does not discharge into a relevant river, watercourse, lake or pond and which does not contain water treated under the Water Supply (Water Quality) Regulations 1989. A reference to the waters of any lake or pond or of any river or watercourse includes a reference to the bottom, channel or bed of any lake, pond, river or watercourse which is for the time being dry, s.124(2)(a).
226. Ss.103(1)(d) and 124(2)(b).
227. [1940] 2 A11 ER 179 per Lord Wright at 187.
228. [1972] 2 A11 ER 475.
229. In most cases, a criminal offence consists of two aspects. The actual forbidden act or omission itself (the *res integra*) and an intention, recklessness or negligence on the part of the person who so acts or fails to act (*mens rea*, or 'guilty mind'). In offences of strict liability this second aspect does not need to be proved by the prosecution.
230. [1984] Crim. L.R. 43.
231. *Times* Law Reports, 1 March 1989.
232. Three Law Lords in *Alphacell Ltd* v. *Woodward* suggested that the defence of Act of God may be applicable: Lord Pearson [1972] 2 A11 ER 475 at 488, Lord Cross *ibid.* at 489, Lord Salmon *ibid.* at 490.
233. [1971] 2 A11 ER 357.
234. [1975] 2 A11 ER 113.
235. Lord Widgery CJ at p.118.
236. See *Alphacell Ltd* v. *Woodward* per Lord Wilberforce.
237. 1975 2 A11 ER 113 at 119.
238. See J. F. Garner, *Control of Pollution Encyclopaedia*, (London: Butterworths, 1976).
239. In relation to s.2(1)(a) of the Rivers (Prevention of Pollution) Act 1951 (the predecessor to s.31 of the Control of Pollution Act 1989) it was suggested that 'poisonous' implies

destruction of life, human or animal; 'noxious' is lower in degree and signifies some injury, but not of necessity immediately dangerous to life; 'polluting' will include both the other qualities and also what is foul and offensive to the senses, except innocuous discoloration: Simes, E., and Scholfield, C. E., *Lumley's Public Health Law*, The Public Health Acts Annotated 12th ed., vol. V (Butterworths) 1954, p.5158, note (e).

240. See R. Macrory, *Water Law, Principles and Practice* (Harlow, Middx.: Longman Professional, 1985), pp.21–22.

241. A notice may not be given by the NRA in respect of discharges from a vessel; see also s.104.

242. S.107(4).

243. S.124(3).

244. S.124(1).

245. S.107(5).

246. S.107(6).

247. Divisional Court (1989) 153 J.P. 126, concerning an offence under s.32 of the Control of Pollution Act 1974.

248. A consent by the NRA may be made subject to such conditions as it considers appropriate, s.109(5).

249. Or any coastal waters as prescribed by the Secretary of State, s.109(6).

250. S.109(1).

251. S.109(2). Both offences carry a penalty of a fine not exceeding level 4 on the standard scale (currently £1,000), s.109(3).

252. S.109(4).

253. Jackson, 'Private prosecutions', *op.cit.*

254. G. Turner, *Environmental Law* (1988), Vol.2, No.2.

255. Power to the instutute criminal proceedings is given to the NRA in s.145.

256. See the figure on p.xxi of the 1987 Third Report, *op.cit.*

257. Dicussed in Macrory, *Water Law, op.cit.*, p.37–38.

258. Para.46.

259. Para.45.

260. See para.5.35, Observations by the Government, *op.cit.*

261. S.106.

262. Para.5.35, Observations by the Government, *op.cit.*

263. S.148.

264. 'Analyse', in relation to any sample of land, water or effluent, includes subjecting the sample to a test of any description, s.189(1).

265. Under s.117; see below, section 5.6.4.

266. The register must show whether the samples taken were routine monitoring or whether the statutory sampling procedure has been followed, Control of Pollution (Registers) Regulations 1989, S.I.1989 No.1160.

267. S.10(1), Rivers (Prevention of Pollution) Act 1961.

268. *ibid.*, s.10(2). The general powers of the NRA to enter premises and take samples are contained in ss.145 and 147 of the Water Act 1989.

269. S.10(3).

270. S.10(4). He or she is then required to review if necessary and vary any such decision from time to time.

271. S.10(5).

272. The NRA is required to furnish to the Secretary of State such information as he or she may reasonably require under s.149(1) and to prepare an annual report under s.150.

273. See Observations by the Government, *op.cit.*, para.5.32.

274. Similar information is currently found in 'Water facts', Water Authorities Association; DoE's *Annual Digest of Environmental Protection and Water Statistics*; 'Water pollution of farm waste', England and Wales' Water Authorities Association and ADAS.

275. S.107(6)(a).

276. S.107(6)(b).

277. S.109; see above, section 5.6.1.9.

278. Currently £1,000.
279. S.127, Magistrates' Court Act 1980.
280. S.121(2).
281. S.121(1).
282. See below, section 5.6.4.
283. 14 May 1987, Aylesbury Magistrates' Court; see above, section 5.5.3, for details.
284. See S. Jackson, 'Private prosecutions', *op.cit.*
285. *R. v. West Metropolitan Stipendiary Magistrate ex parte Klahn* [1979] 1 WLR 933.
286. See below, section 5.6.3.
287. S.108(1)(a). It appears that a discharge consent may also serve as a defence to a prosecution for a discharge even where that discharge contains a polluting substance not provided for under the consent.
288. Ss. 5 and 6.
289. S.108(1)(b) and (c). 'Controlled waste' means household, industrial and commercial waste, s.30(1) COPA. Generally, it is an offence to deposit such waste on land or cause or knowingly permit it to be deposited on any land, without having obtained a licence to do so from the appropriate disposal authority, *ibid.* s.5. A disposal licence only provides a defence in respect of offences under s.107(1)(a) and (e). Before granting a licence, the disposal authority must consult the NRA, *ibid.* s.5(4).
290. A 'local statutory provision' means: (a) a provision of a Local Act; (b) a provision of so much of any public general Act as has effect with respect to a particular area, particular persons or works; (c) a provision of an instrument made under any provision falling within (a) or (b); and (d) a provision of any other instrument which is in the nature of a local enactment, s.189(1).
291. S.108(1)(d) and (e). A 'statutory order' means an order made by the Minister of Agriculture conferring compulsory powers for carrying out works (under s.155), or any order by law, scheme or award made under any other enactment, s.108(9).
292. S.108(2).
293. Howarth, *Water Pollution Law, op.cit.*, para.4.09.
294. S.108(3) – 'vessel' includes a hovercraft.
295. S.I.1989 No.1378.
296. Byelaws made before 1 April 1974 continue to apply after that date by virtue of para.11 of Sch.6 to the Water Act 1973.
297. 'Mine' is defined to mean an excavation or system of excavations made for the purpose of, or in connection with, the getting, wholly or substantially by means involving the employment of persons below ground, of minerals (whether in their natural state or in solution or in suspension) or products of minerals, s.180(1) Mines and Quarries Act 1954; s.189(1) Water Act.
298. S.108(4).
299. S.108(5).
300. *Edwards v. National Coal Board* [1949] 1 KB 704 at 712; Garner, *Control of Pollution Encyclopaedia, op.cit.*, Ch.III, para.60.
301. S.108(6).
302. S.108(7).
303. S.108(8).
304. Pollution of waters containing fish.
305. Offences of causing pollution of waters by gas.
306. S.113(4).
307. The procedures for obtaining consent are contained in Schedule 12 of the Act.
308. S.122(b). A discussion of the Common Law on Water Pollution is beyond the scope of this work. See generally, Howarth, *op.cit.*, Ch.3.
309. Formerly, pursuant to regulations made under section 34 of COPA, an application for consent was to state: (a) the place at which it was proposed to make the discharges to which the application relates; (b) the nature and composition of the matter proposed to be discharged and the maximum temperature of it at the time when it was proposed to be discharged; (c) the maximum quantity of the matter which it was proposed to

discharge on any one day and the highest rate at which it was proposed to discharge it. It is expected that the NRA will require equivalent information in most instances.

310. Currently £2,000.
311. S.175(2).
312. Control of Pollution (Consents for Discharges) (Notices) Regulations 1984, S.I.1984 No. 864.
313. Sch.12, para.1(6).
314. Sch.12, para.1(4).
315. No.17/84, 'Water and the environment'.
316. *ibid.*, Annex 3, para.3.
317. See Howarth, *Water Pollution Law, op.cit.*, 4.17.
318. An application for a certificate may be made at any time before the application for consent is submitted or not later than seven days after it is submitted. Control of Pollution (Consent for Discharge) (Secretary of State Functions) Regulations 1989, S.I.1989 No.1151, Reg.6.
319. Sch.12, para.1(7). It has been stated that it would be wrong for these provisions to be used to exempt publication of information 'merely because it might cause embarrassment', Royal Commission on Environmental Pollution, Tenth Report (1984), para.2.68. It appears therefore that a certificate will only be given in exceptional circumstances.
320. Sch.12, para.2(1).
321. Sch.12, para.2(2).
322. This condition did not appear in the former section 34 of the Control of Pollution Act 1974.
323. Sch.12, para.2.
324. Para.2(4).
325. Under s.105; see above, section 5.2.
326. S.106(1).
327. See below, sections 5.6.3.6 and 5.6.3.7.
328. Third Report, *op.cit.*, para.102.
329. Observations by the Government, *op.cit.*, para.4.4.
330. Sch.12, para.3.
331. Sch.12, para.4.
332. S.I.1989 No.1151.
333. Reg.3.
334. As set out in the Schedule to the Regulations, reg.4(1)(a).
335. Reg.5.
336. That is, s.107(1)(b), (c) or (d).
337. Sch.12, para.5.
338. Sch.12, para.5(2).
339. Sch.12, para.6.
340. Sch.12, para.6(4).
341. Sch.12, para.7. In *Trent River Authority* v. *Drabble & Sons Ltd* [1970] 1 A11 ER 22 (in respect of offences under the Rivers (Prevention of Pollution) Act 1961), the defendant company was granted a consent on 13 October 1966 subject to certain conditions which were stated to operate as from 1 April 1968. It was also provided in the consent that the consent would not be altered before the expiration of two years from its grant without the written permission of the company. In September 1968, the company was prosecuted for failing to comply with the conditions of the consent. In its defence, the defendant company pleaded that the conditions stated to operate from 1 April 1968 were invalid as the consent in reality amounted to two consents, the latter consent contravening the stated term that no alteration would be made within a two-year period. The court found that the Act did not prevent a consent containing conditions which varied the discharge limits from time to time and the fact that those variations took place within the two-year period did not invalidate those conditions; see Sch.12, para.2(3).
342. Para.7(4).

343. Information is material if it relates to any discharge made or to be made by virtue of the consent, to the interaction of any such discharge with any other discharge or to the combined effect of the matter discharged and any other matter, Sch.12, para.6(6).
344. If the NRA fails to give consent within four months of an application, Sch.12, para.2(2).
345. Reg.7.
346. Sch.12, para.8.
347. S.108(5)(a).
348. S.109.
349. Reg.7.
350. Sch.12, para.9. For powers to charge generally, see s.145(1)(c).
351. S.I.1989 No.1157.
352. S.145(1)(a).
353. S.147(1).
354. Under s.178.
355. S.147(3).
356. 76/464/EEC OJ, 'Directive on Pollution Caused by Certain Dangerous Substances Discharged into the Aquatic Environment of the Community'. Advice on the implementation of this and associated Directives is found in DoE 7/89 (Welsh Office 16/89). See also N. Haigh, *EEC Environmental Policy and Britain*, 2nd ed. (London: Longman, 1987).
357. Art.1.
358. See 5.2.
359. Under s.105.
360. S.106.
361. Groundwater is excluded by virtue of Directive 80/68/EEC.
362. See below, section 5.9.2.
363. Except 82/176/EEC on mercury.
364. In Directive 86/280/EEC.
365. DoE Circular 7/89, para.22.
366. See Appendix C. The standards are subject to review in the light of experience or fresh scientific evidence.
367. 7/89, para.47.
368. 80/68/EEC OJ. Advice on the application and implementation of the Directive by the Department of the Environment and the Welsh Office is given in DoE Circular 4/82 (Welsh Office 7/820), 'EC Directive on the Protection of Groundwater Against Pollution caused by Certain Dangerous Substances' (1982).
369. 'Council Directive on the Quality of Fresh Waters Needing Protection or Improvement in Order to Support Fish Life', 78/659/EEC OJ.
370. Not including water in natural or artificial fish ponds used for intensive fish farming, Art.1(1) and (2).
371. Sampling may be dispensed with as unnecessary where there is no pollution and no risk of deterioration in the quality of water, Art.7(2).
372. Art.1(3).
373. Art.1(4).
374. Art.6(1).
375. In addition, the NRA is empowered to institute proceedings against persons who cause or permit liquid or solid matter to flow to such an extent as to cause the waters to be poisonous or injurious to fish, s.4(1) Salmon and Freshwater Fisheries Act 1975.
376. 79/923/EEC. See P. Wathern, S. Young, I. Brown, and D. Roberts, 'UK interpretation and implementation of the EEC Shellfish Directive' (1987), 11, *Environmental Management*, 7.
377. Art.1.
378. Art.5; Annex.
379. Art.6.
380. Council Directive of 19 March 1987 on the prevention and reduction of environmental pollution by asbestos 87/217/EEC. Advice on this Directive from the Department of the

Environment is given in DoE Circular 7/89 (W.O. 16/89). It covers discharges to air, land and water.

381. 'Asbestos' means crocodilite (blue asbestos), actinolite, anthophyllite, chrysotile (white asbestos), amosite (brown asbestos) and tremolite. 'Raw asbestos' means the product resulting from the primary crushing of asbestos ore. 'Use of asbestos' means the production of raw asbestos (excluding mining) and the manufacturing and finishing of specified products using raw asbestos.

382. Plant built or authorised before 31 December 1988 have until 30 June 1991 to comply with the Directive.

383. In the Control of Pollution (Registers) Regulations 1989, S.I.1989 No. 1160.

384. S.105.

385. Reg.3.

386. Reg.4.

387. In respect of a consent to remove a deposit from a river or lake bed, s.109(1).

388. Reg.6.

389. In accordance with s.148.

390. Reg.7.

391. Sch.12, para.1(7).

392. Reg.8.

393. S.118(1).

394. Which includes anything contained in records, accounts, estimates or returns, s.189(1).

395. S.118(2).

396. S.118(3).

397. Currently £2,000, s.118(4).

398. S.119.

399. S.118(3).

400. See above, section 2.5.

401. Under s.105; see above, section 5.2.

402. S.120.

403. S.181.

404. S.174(5). A similar provision contained in section 12 of the Rivers (Prevention of Pollution) Act 1961, applies to information which has been furnished under the 1961 Act. Although not repealed, this section is now practically obsolete in light of the disclosure of information provisions in the Water Act 1989 and in relation to trade effluent, the Public Health Act 1961; see below, section 5.9.3, and DoE/Pollution Paper No.23, 'Public access to environmental information' (1986), para.4.3.

405. See, generally, the Third Report, *op.cit.*, and the Government Response Part III.

406. *ibid.* para.65.

407. *ibid.* para.68.

408. *ibid.* para.81.

409. S.107(2)(a) and (b); see above, section 5.4.1.4 and below, section 5.10.3.

410. Made under s.110; see below, section 5.10.4.

411. S.116.

412. Draft Control of Pollution (Silage, Slurry and Agricultural Fuel Oil) Regulations 1990.

413. *ibid.* paras.3.14 and 3.15. It is not expected that grant aid will be available for maintenance work.

414. See below, section 5.10.2.

415. Third Report. *op.cit.*, para.86.

416. Management of afforestation projects is discussed in *The Management of Forest Streams* (1980), Forestry Commission, and *Forestry and Woodland Code* (1985), Timber Growers United Kingdom. It is also necessary in certain circumstances to undertake and complete environmental impact assessment prior to the approval of afforestation projects, including the potential impact on water quality (Environmental Assessment (Afforestation) Regulations 1988, S.I.1988 No.1207).

417. S.123(1).

418. S.123(2).

419. S.I.1976/959.

420. S.I.1984/863.
421. For a complete discussion of the Radioactive Substances Act 1960 and the radioactive pollution of water, see Howarth, *op.cit.*, Ch.6.
422. As prescribed in the Trade Effluents (Prescribed Processes and Substances) Regulations 1989, S.I.1989 No.1156.
423. S.1. Public Health (Drainage of Trade Premises) Act 1937. 'Public sewer' is defined in s.20 of the Public Health Act 1936.
424. S.14(1). In *Thames Water Authority* v. *Blue and White Launderettes Ltd* (1980], 1 WLR 700, effluent discharged from washing machines in a launderette was held to be trade effluent even though it was indistinguishable from effluent from domestic washing machines. The definition of 'trade effluent' relates to the purpose of the activity rather than the nature of the discharge.
425. In order for a person to be an occupier, it is not necessary for him or her to have complete control over the premies, but it is sufficient if he or she shares that control with other persons (*Wheat* v. *Lacon & Co. Ltd* [1966] A11 ER 582 (HL)).
426. S.2(1).
427. S.2(3).
428. Conditions (5) to (14) were added by s.59 of the Public Health Act 1961.
429. Currently £2,000.
430. S.2(5) and (5A) Public Health (Drainage of Trade Premises) Act 1937.
431. The Act does not define the classes of persons falling within this category. In any dispute or proceedings the court will have to consider the purpose for which the right of appeal has been given.
432. S.3(1) as amended by the Water Act 1989.
433. S.61, Public Health Act 1961.
434. Sch.8, para.3(4).
435. Under s.76.
436. S.59, Public Health Act 1961.
437. S.76(3).
438. Particularly Condition B.
439. S.76(2) and (3).
440. S.60, Public Health Act 1961; s.45, Control of Pollution Act 1974.
441. See below, this section.
442. S.74, Water Act 1989. Trade Effluent (Prescribed Processes and Substances) Regulations 1989, S.I.1989 No.1156.
443. This list has been drawn up by the Government to provide a focus for priority action within the United Kingdom. The Department of the Environment has developed a screening system to identify those priority substances based upon a combination of a substance's toxicity, persistence and capacity for bio-accumulation. See, generally, 'Inputs of dangerous substances to water: proposals for a unified system of control', Consultation Paper, DoE, July 1988.
444. Sch.1.
445. Reg.3.
446. Reg.2.
447. Sch.2.
448. Which means any of the fibrous silicates, namely crocidolite, actinolite, anthophyllite, chrysotile, amosite and tremolite.
449. Reg.4. The prescribed processes rules enable the Government to comply with the EC Directive on asbestos pollution (87/217/EEC) and the 1988 'black list' Directive (88/347/EEC, amending 86/280/EEC) in the case of discharges to sewers.
450. Reg.5.
451. There is no need for the Director General to make a reference in cases where the sewerage undertaker has already made one.
452. Sch.9, para.2.
453. Sch.9, para.2(3).
454. Sch.9, para.6.
455. His or her power to impose conditions is not restricted to those matters set out in s.59, Public Health Act 1961 (para.4(3)).

456. Sch.9, para.3.
457. Sch.9, para.4.
458. Sch.9, para.5.
459. S.7A, Public Health (Drainage of Trade Premises) Act 1937, as inserted by para.3(5) of Sch.8, Water Act 1989. These duties imposed on sewerage undertakers are enforceable by the Director General.
460. See above, sections 5.6.4 and 5.6.6.
461. Presently £400, s.9 1937 Act.
462. S.68, Public Health Act 1961.
463. But not including the entry of nitrate into water; see below, section 5.10.2.
464. S.111.
465. Observations of the Government, op.cit., para.4.15.
466. S.111(4).
467. Sch.7, para.2(1).
468. Sch.7, para.5.
469. Including the area designated, para.4(3).
470. Para.4(2).
471. Paras. 83 and 84.
472. S.112. See, generally, Nitrate Sensitive Areas (Designation) Order 1990, S.I. 1990 No.1013.
473. Or with a person having another interest in the land with the written consent of the freehold owner.
474. S.112(2) and (3). But voluntary agreements entered into by agricultural tenants are not binding on subsequent tenants since they derive their title from the freehold owner and not the previous tenant.
475. See para.27, 'Nitrate sensitive areas', Consultation Document by the Agriculture Departments of England and Wales, May 1989.
476. S.112(4).
477. S.112(8); S.I. 1990 No.1013 (see note 472, above).
478. Sch.11, para.2.
479. Sch.11, para.3(2).
480. Para.3(3).
481. Para.6.
482. Including a modification of the designated area, para.5(3).
483. Para.5(2).
484. S.107(1)(b) and (d); see above, section 5.6.1.4.
485. S.107(2).
486. See the Trade Effluents (Prescribed Processes and Substances) Regulations 1989, section 5.9.2. above. This has implications for the application of sewage sludge as 'soil conditioning' containing prescribed substances, etc.; see above, section 5.5.2.
487. Draft Control of Pollution (Silage, Slurry and Agricultural Fuel Oil) Regulations 1990: See [1990] 2 LMELR 8 (M. Forster); see also DoE Green Paper and Observations by the Government, op.cit.
488. S.114. A 'sanitary appliance' is an appliance which is designed to permit polluting matter to pass into the water where the vessel is situated but does not include a sink, bath or shower bath.
489. S.115(1). None of these powers permit the NRA to impede or prevent the making of a discharge in pursuance of a consent, s.115(2).
490. S.147.
491. S.178.
492. S.115(3); see above, section 5.6.1.2. No expenses are recoverable in respect of works or operations in respect of water from an abandoned mine, s.225(4).
493. See J. Roberts, 'River pollution' (1987), 43, The Magistrate, 150.
494. S.35(1), Powers of the Criminal Courts Act 1973, as amended by s.67 of the Criminal Justice Act 1982.
495. S.35 (1A).
496. S.40, Magistrates' Courts Act 1980.
497. In exercise of its powers under s.141.

498. The term 'statutory water undertaker' means, under that Act, water authorities, statutory water companies, joint water boards, and joint water committees and no other bodies, s. 11(6), Water Act 1945. Currently the reference to a statutory water authority is to be construed as a reference to a water authority as established in accordance with s.2 of the Water Act 1973 (s.79(1), Water Resources Act 1963, as amended by s.9(a) of the Water Act 1973) whose functions have been taken over by water undertakers under the Water Act 1989.

499. S.18(1), Water Act, 1945.

500. S.18(4).

501. S.79(3) and (4), Water Resources Act 1963. No byelaw may conflict or interfere with the operation of any byelaw made by a navigation authority, harbour authority or conservancy authority, s.79(7).

502. Currently £50.

503. S.79(9).

504. Under s.108 and Sch.4 of the Control of Pollution Act 1974. It appears that although these two sections have not yet been repealed they now have no prospective operation. The Water Act 1989 has repealed Part II to Schedule 7 of the Water Act 1973, which provided a procedure for the making and confirmation of byelaws, and the Water Act 1989 does not amend those sections so as to give the NRA powers to make such byelaws. Therefore, Schedule 24 to the Water Act 1989 (which specifies a procedure relating to byelaws) does not apply to byelaws made under those sections, as the NRA has no power conferred on it with respect to those sections, see s.186, Water Act 1989.

505. And also to byelaws made under para.(c) of section 22(b) of the Countryside Act 1968 for preventing sewage, etc., from entering a waterway (now repealed), Sch.26, para.57(2).

506. I.E., 1 Sept 1989.

507. See below, section 5.10.5.

508. Sch.26, para.57(2). Despite any repeals by the Water Act 1989, byelaws made under section 18 of the Water Act 1945 are to have effect as if no such repeals had been made and the obligation imposed on water undertakers by the 1945 Act are enforceable by the Secretary of State under section 20 of the Water Act 1989; see Sch.26, para.57(3).

509. Sch.26, para.57(4). In so doing he or she is not required to hold a local inquiry as provided for in Sch.24, para.5 (Sch.26, para.57(5)). Nothing in the Water Act 1989 shall operate so as to alter the area in relation to which the byelaws have effect, para.57(6).

510. Paragraphs 2 and 3 of Sch.19 (street works) are to have effect if the reference in those paragraphs to the laying of a relevant pipe included a reference to the laying of a drain or sewer and the construction of a watercourse for the purposes of this section, s.154(5).

511. S.154(1).

512. S.154(2).

513. S.154(3). Any dispute as to whether any such consent is being unreasonably withheld is to be referred to a single arbitrator, s.154(4).

514. Except in the case of byelaws made by the NRA in respect of their flood defence functions, ss.136–140, where the confirming authority is the Minister of Agriculture, and byelaws made by the NRA in respect of their fisheries functions, s.141, where the confirming authority is either the Secretary of State or the Minister of Agriculture, Sch.24, para.7(1). References in the following discussion to the Secretary of State also refer to the Minister of Agriculture where appropriate.

515. Sch.24, para.2.

516. Para.1(3)–(5).

517. Para.2(1).

518. For preventing pollution of controlled waters; see above, section 5.10.4.

519. Para.2(2). In such a case, the Secretary of State in order to make a modification need only consult the relevant body rather than obtain its consent.

520. Para.2(3).

521. Para.2(4).

522. Para.5.

CHAPTER 6

Land, conservation and recreation

6.1   General duties

The Act imposes certain general duties in relation to environmental and recreational considerations on the National Rivers Authority, water and sewerage undertakers[1] and internal drainage boards (the 'relevant bodies'), as well as the Secretary of State and the Director General of Water Services.

In formulating or considering any proposals relating to the functions of the relevant bodies there is a statutory duty:

(a)   so far as is consistent with other obligations and duties to further the conservation and enhancement of natural beauty and the conservation of flora, fauna and geological or physiographical features of special interest;

(b)   to have regard to the desirability of protecting and conserving buildings, sites and objects of archaeological, architectural or historic interest;

(c)   to take into account any effect which the proposals would have on the beauty or amenity of any rural or urban area or on any such flora, fauna, features, buildings sites or objects.[2]

Subject to these duties, there is also an obligation:

(a)   to have regard to the desirability of preserving for the public any freedom of access to areas of woodland, mountains, moor, heath, down, cliff, or foreshore and other places of natural beauty;

(b)   to have regard to the desirability of maintaining the availability to the public of any facility for visiting or respecting any building (which includes a structure), site or object of archaeological, architectural or historical interest;

(c) to take into account any effect which the proposals would have on any such freedom of access or on the availability of any such facility.[3]

Subject to obtaining the consent of the relevant authority before doing anything which interferes with, or obstructs, navigation, every relevant body is required to ensure that water and land associated with water to which it has rights is made available for recreational purposes and in the best manner.[4]

In complying with this duty, the relevant bodies must, in particular, take into account the needs of chronically sick or disabled persons.[5]

The NRA is required, to such extent as it considers desirable, generally to promote the following:

1. The conservation and enhancement of the natural beauty and amenity of inland and coastal waters and of land associated with such waters.
2. The conservation of flora and fauna which are dependent on an aquatic environment.
3. The use of such waters and land for recreational purposes, taking into account the needs of persons who are chronically sick or disabled.[6]

Nothing in the Act requires a relevant body to make recreational facilities available free of charge.[7]

Special considerations arise in the case of Sites of Special Scientific Interest (SSSIs) and National Parks, and section 9 imposes special notification and consultation procedures in respect of these areas.

The Nature Conservancy Council (NCC) has a duty to notify relevant bodies of land which is of special interest by reason of its flora, fauna or geological or physiographical features, and which might be affected by their works, schemes, operations or activities.[8]

If any relevant body proposes to carry out works or operations which it considers may be likely to damage an SSSI, it is obliged to consult the NCC.[9] However, to avoid any irreversible mistakes, relevant bodies are advised to consult in respect of all works or operations affecting SSSIs, at least until they are confident that reliable assessment procedures have been developed.[10]

In addition, the NRA is required to consult the NCC before authorising any operation which is likely to damage an SSSI. This involves consents for land drainage, discharge consents and abstraction licences. It is a matter for the NRA and the NCC to agree procedures for consultation and for identifying those applications which are most likely to affect SSSIs.

Where relevant bodies own or lease land within an SSSI, the NCC must also notify them pursuant to the Wildlife and Countryside Act 1981. The notification is accompanied by a list of operations likely to damage the SSSI. Owners or occupiers are required to give the NCC four months' written notice if they propose to carry out or authorise within the SSSI any of the listed operations. This requirement does not apply if the operation has been authorised by a specific grant of planning permission.

The general requirements of notification do not apply in the case of an emergency, when details are notified to the NCC as soon as practicable after the commencement of the operation.[11]

In most cases the NCC will follow up the formal notification procedures by explaining to the relevant body the special interest of the site and the likely effect of various types of operations. The aim is to agree an operational plan for individual SSSIs and land holdings.

Water and sewerage undertakers are among the most important landowners within the ten National Parks in England and Wales, and within designated Areas of Outstanding Natural Beauty (AONB), particularly in the Lake District and Peak District, with extensive ownership of land for water gathering purposes.

The planning framework secured by the National Parks and Access to the Countryside Act 1949 applies as fully to the relevant bodies as to other landowners within a National Park.

In addition to their responsibilities for planning, National Park Committees or a joint or special planning board for a National Park promote conservation and provide information services. In sensitive areas, they are concerned with drainage, the protection of wetlands and maintenance of existing ditches, and with agricultural practices including regimes for grazing, ploughing and the use of fertilisers, and with the management and use of woodlands.

Relevant bodies are expected to maintain close liaison with National Parks Authorities (and the Broads Authority) and the local authorities in AONBs, take into account their plans and policies, and consult them on all relevant matters.[12] To ensure that they do so, section 9 also provides for the National Park and Broads Authorities to notify relevant bodies of areas of land within the Parks or Broads which are of significance in terms of their duties under section 8[13] and places a duty on the relevant bodies to consult the Authorities on operations which may affect them.[14] Again, notification need not be made in an emergency, if the Authority in question is notified as soon as practicable after the operation has commenced.[15]

The existence of duties under section 9 does not absolve the relevant bodies from the need for suitable consultation on matters which have not been notified.

These general environmental and recreational duties are enforceable by the Secretary of State under section 20.[16]

Where the Secretary of State makes an order authorising or conferring compulsory powers on the NRA or a water undertaker to construct or operate a reservoir,[17] and it appears to him or her that the works may permanently affect the area in which they are situated and are not primarily intended to benefit the inhabitants of that area, he or she may include in the order provision with respect to facilities for recreation or other leisure-time occupation for the benefit of those inhabitants.[18]

Where any works relating to the construction or maintenance of a reservoir are carried out in Wales permanently affecting one or more communities and which are not primarily intended to benefit inhabitants of those communities, the NRA or water undertaker must provide recreational facilities or assist others to make such facilities available.[19] In so doing, the NRA or water undertaker must consult the community or district councils in question.[20] The duties under this section are enforceable by the Secretary of State under section 20.[21]

The relevant bodies may make a charge for the use of recreational facilities owned by them,[22] but it appears that access to land and water may only be charged for where facilities are provided specially.

6.2   Code of Practice on Conservation, Access and Recreation[23]

Section 10 of the Act enables the relevant Minister[24] to approve codes of practice for the purpose of giving practical guidance to, and promoting desirable practices by, the NRA and undertakers, with respect to the general environmental and recreational duties.[25]

The Code was prepared after consultation with the NRA, the Countryside Commission, the Nature Conservancy Council, the Historic Buildings and Monuments Commission for England, the Sports Council, the Sports Council for Wales and a number of other bodies as required by the Act.[26] The Code of Practice only covers the activities of the NRA and undertakers.

Accordingly, references to the 'relevant bodies' only refer to those bodies and not to internal drainage boards as in sections 8 and 9 of the Act. Internal drainage boards and functions in respect of flood defence are covered in another Code: Conservation Guidelines for Drainage Authorities.

Failure to comply with any provision of the Code does not of itself constitute a breach of the general duties or give rise to any civil or criminal liability. However, the Secretary of State and the Minister of Agriculture are required to take into account whether there has been or is likely to be any such contravention in determining when and how they should exercise their general enforcement powers.[27]

6.2.1. ESTABLISHING A FRAMEWORK FOR PLANNING AND MANAGING THE USE OF WATER AND ASSOCIATED LAND

The relevant bodies are required to discharge their environmental and recreational duties having proper regard to the performance of their statutory functions in respect of the abstraction, use and protection of water resources. It is important for them to have complete and up-to-date information on conservation, recreation and related matters.

In discharging its responsibilities for the protection and management of rivers and other waters, the NRA, advised by regional rivers advisory committees, is required to develop a general framework of policies and procedures for all aspects of river basin management, including conservation and recreation. Undertakers must take account of this framework in exercising their functions, but need to supplement it with the following:[28]

1. Established channels for consultation and liaison with all relevant organisations, including the NRA, and with individuals or groups of individuals who own land, or live or work in the locality in question.
2. Integrated land-use and management plans for sites of particular significance for conservation, recreation and access.
3. Programmes for the training of their employees and for research.
4. Appropriate arrangements for the dissemination of information about their plans.

6.2.2 CONSERVATION AND ENHANCEMENT OF THE ENVIRONMENT

The Code lists a number of sites of particular importance for conservation:[29]

1. National Parks.
2. Areas of Outstanding Natural Beauty.
3. Sites of Special Scientific Interest.
4. Environmentally Sensitive Areas.[30]
5. Nature reserves.
6. Areas of special protection for birds.[31]
7. Special protection areas.[32]
8. Ramsar sites (designated under the Convention on Wetlands of International Importance, especially as Waterfowl Habitat).
9. Conservation areas designated by a local planning authority.
10. Heritage coasts.
11. Listed buildings of historical or architectural interest.
12. Ancient monuments.
13. Sites in respect of which the relevant bodies consider that their proposed operations would have a major environmental impact.

It is in these areas especially that relevant bodies need to consider carefully the effect of works on land-use changes.

The natural beauty and man-made features of the landscape can best be conserved and enhanced if projects are designed to do the following:[33]

1. Maintain and reinforce the existing natural character and ecology of the area.
2. Avoid disturbance of, or intrusion on, archaeological and historic features.
3. Make use of local materials and buildings forms whenever possible.
4. Retain existing ground-cover plants, shrubs and trees where this is the best option and protect these during construction.
5. Restrict new planting to species which are well adapted to local site conditions.

Proposals for tree planting should accord with management guidelines published by the Forestry Commission.[34]

Certain practices helpful to nature conservation may be relevant to all aspects of management and use of the water environment and these include the following:[35]

1. Avoidance of canalisation of channels; design of asymmetric channels of varying width; re-profiling, where needed, carried out in short sections over several years.
2. Retention in rivers of pools, riffle sections, navel bars, shingle banks, cliffs, meanders and braided channels.

3. Retention of landscape features and habitats including brack lagoons, marsh, fen, bog, scrub and marginal trees.
4. Minimum clearance of trees and bushes in strict accordance with project requirements.
5. Pollarding of mature trees in preference to removal during general maintenance; replacement of trees removed with species appropriate to the site.
6. Retention, wherever possible, of overhanging trees, and fallen trees lying adjacent to rivers.
7. Use of natural materials wherever possible.
8. Retention of trees at intervals where general scrub clearance is necessary in the interest of nature conservation.

Generally, it is an offence to fell trees without first having obtained a felling licence from the Forestry Commission. In cases where a tree is protected by a tree preservation order, it is necessary to obtain the prior consent of the local authority before any lopping, topping or felling is carried out.

Archaeological remains and sites, historic buildings, and industrial structures can be damaged or threatened by works which, by creating lower water levels, cause drying out and decay of waterlogged material such as timber or biological environmental remains. Relevant bodies should be aware of the need to protect buildings, monuments, and other historical features from damage caused by misuse or neglect, and they should maintain such features whether or not they are in current use.

Where sites have been identified by conservation bodies as significant for nature or archaeological conservation, the relevant bodies should consider whether establishing a nature heritage reserve is a practicable option. It may be that the best arrangement for securing the protection, management and public interpretation of such sites and features is to lease or licence them to appropriate conservation bodies, with an agreed management plan.

So far as consistent with their obligations to ensure the safety of employees, there should be arrangements to ensure that the conservation duties are taken into account in maintenance works programmes. Relevant conservation considerations should be fully explained to those carrying out the work. Maintenance policies should be reviewed periodically and where there is any doubt as to their appropriateness, appropriate planning and conservation bodies should be consulted.

The Code also contains specific advice on the management of water resources, water supply schemes, sewage disposal and pollution control, pipe-laying, fisheries, bankside activities and navigation.[36]

6.2.3   PRESERVATION OF PUBLIC ACCESS

In the light of the public access duty and having regard to the duty in respect of the recreational use of water and land, public access should normally be allowed to the following:[37]

1. Land of natural beauty or of amenity or recreational value by way of either marked concessionary footpaths and bridleways or open access wherever practicable and having regard to the use and occupation of the land and the interests of third parties.
2. Reservoirs and other water areas of amenity or recreational value provided that appropriate measures can be taken to minimise the risk of pollution and that no public health risk is involved.
3. Archaeological monuments, buildings of historic and architectural interest and other historic features and records, wherever this is reasonably practicable.

Relevant bodies should have arrangements, including appropriate consultation procedures, to inform themselves about the provision of access and its importance to particular interest groups or the public at large. Where any proposals require the termination or modification of any existing freedom of access, the relevant bodies should consult appropriate recreation bodies at the earliest practicable stage, and have regard to their views in seeking to minimise, where possible, the degree of interference with such access.

6.2.4   USE OF WATER AND ASSOCIATED LAND FOR
RECREATION

Certain general considerations should underlie the policies of the relevant bodies towards provision for recreation.[38]

1. Recognition of the social importance of sport and recreation and the particular contributions which they are in a position to make in this field.
2. Contribution, as circumstances allow, to the wider provision of opportunities for sport and recreation and to secure the best use of suitable existing and new resources.
3. Consultation on a regular basis with the regional councils for sport

and recreation and with appropriate representatives of users of their sporting and recreational facilities.

4.   The need to cater fairly and equitably for as broad a range of interest groups as practicable.

5.   The need to ensure that the recreational needs of the surrounding area are taken fully into account, and not unreasonably prejudiced by proposals designed to meet more specialised demands.

The relevant bodies are expected to ensure that the arrangements made by water authorities as to access are not disturbed, so far as is reasonable and practicable.

In the establishment and operation of specific facilities, the principal considerations which should be taken into account are the following:[39]

1.   Subject to suitable terms and conditions, public use of sporting and recreational facilities, once established, should be maintained by the grant or renewal of leases of licences.

2.   Facilities which become available should be offered for recognised recreational pursuits on terms which take account of those applying to similar facilities elsewhere.

3.   Existing users of sporting and recreational facilities on land or water belonging to the relevant bodies, together with appropriate conservation bodies, should be consulted prior to the introduction on those lands or waters of any new sporting or recreational activity.

4.   In considering what steps to take in performance of their recreational duty, provision should be made, where possible, for the needs of chronically sick or disabled people.

5.   Reasonable account should be taken of the need for public car parks, toilets and picnic sites; and facilities upon reasonable conditions for groups to study nature, geology or archaeology on otherwise restricted sites.

Specific advice is given on the management of water resources, sewerage, sewage disposal and pollution control, fisheries, navigation and flood defence.[40]

The Code also contains advice relevant to the performance of general environmental duties with respect to environmentally sensitive areas,[41] scheduled ancient monuments and listed buildings.[42]

6.3   Disposals of land

One condition of the Instrument of Appointment of water undertakers and sewerage undertakers is intended to ensure that the best price is received from disposals of land so as to secure benefits to customers through the application of the proceeds of such disposals to reduce charges.[43]

Section 152 of the Act provides for restrictions on disposals of land by providing that companies holding appointments under the Act may only dispose of land and interests in that land[44] with the consent of the Secretary of State or the Minister of Agriculture or in accordance with a general authorisation given by him or her.[45] A consent must also be given where the NRA disposes of any of its compulsorily acquired land.[46] Compulsorily acquired land is defined as land which was acquired compulsorily under sections 151 or 155; or was acquired at a time when the NRA was authorised under those provisions to acquire it compulsorily; or land which was transferred to the NRA which was compulsorily acquired or acquired at a time when it may have been compulsorily acquired.[47]

A consent or authorisation is given by serving a notice on the person who proposes to dispose of land, and may be given on such conditions as the Secretary of State or the Minister considers appropriate.[48] However, the conditions of a consent or authorisation may include the following:[49]

1. A requirement that, before there is any disposal, an opportunity of acquiring the land in question or an interest in or right over the land, is to be made available to such person as may be so specified or determined.
2. A requirement that a company has complied with the conditions of its appointment in relation to the disposal of land.
3. A requirement that a company, before making a disposal of land situated in a National Park, the Broads, or an area of outstanding natural beauty or special scientific interest,[50] should consult with the Countryside Commission, and, in the case of an area of special scientific interest, the Nature Conservancy Council, and enter into such management agreements[51] or convenants as may be appropriate.[52]

A condition under 1. above may not be made unless the Secretary of State or the Minister is satisfied that the condition will have effect only in relation to land acquired or acquired compulsorily by the NRA or an undertaker, or to land which is situated in a National Park, the Broads or an area of outstanding natural beauty or special scientific interest.[53]

In relation to land situated in an area specified in 3. above, the company proposing to dispose of such land may enter into a covenant with the Secretary of State by virtue of which it accepts obligations with respect to the freedom of access to the land or the use or management of the land. Such a covenant binds all persons deriving title from or under that company and is enforceable by the Secretary of State accordingly.[54]

In proposing a disposal of land in a National Park, the Broads, an area of outstanding natural beauty or special scientific interest, a company must have regard to its general environmental and recreational duties specified in section 8.[55]

6.4   Planning requirements

Nothing in the Water Act 1989 or in any other enactment which relates to the functions of the NRA or any water or sewerage undertaker authorises the carrying out of development[56] without the granting of such planning permission as may be required by the Town and Country Planning Act 1971.[57]

Water and sewerage undertakers and the NRA are deemed to be statutory undertakers for the purposes of the Town and Country Planning Act 1971 and certain development activities, such as the laying of pipes on certain land are deemed to be granted consent under the General Development Order.

6.5   Flood defence/drainage

The NRA has a duty to exercise general supervision over all matters relating to flood defence[58] in England and Wales, and is required to carry out surveys from time to time of the areas in relation to which it carries out those functions.[59] The functions of water authorities relating to flood defence have been transferred to the NRA by the Act[60] by the making of amendments to the Land Drainage Act 1976.

The NRA is obliged to carry out its responsibilities under the 1976 Act through regional flood defence committees set up under section 137 of the Act,[61] and to arrange for any other body or committee to issue levies (within the meaning of the Local Government Finance Act 1988) and make drainage charges under the 1976 Act.[62] The regional flood defence committees exercise their functions in each of the areas for which there was a regional land drainage committee immediately before the transfer date,[63] subject to Schedule 16, which makes provision for the alteration of the boundaries of and the amalgamation of the areas of regional flood defence committees. Their composition is determined by section 138.

The NRA may give a regional flood defence committee general or specific directions as to the carrying out of any function relating to flood defence, other than one of its internal drainage functions,[64] so far as the carrying out of that function appears to be NRA materially to affect its management of waters for purposes other than flood defence.[65]

There is a provision for local flood defence schemes and local flood defence committees to be created or continued under the Land Drainage Act 1976.[66]

Internal drainage districts which existed within the areas of the water authorities have continued, in accordance with section 6 of the 1976 Act, as internal drainage districts within the areas of the regional flood defence committees; and for each such district the authority responsible continues to be an internal drainage board which is a body corporate.[67]

6.6   Salmon and freshwater fisheries

The NRA is required to maintain, improve and develop salmon, trout, freshwater and all fisheries and to establish and maintain advisory committees which it is to consult as to the manner in which it is to perform its duty.[68] The NRA is to establish regional advisory committees and such local advisory committees as it considers necessary for the whole of England and Wales together with the territorial sea extending for six nautical miles from the baselines from which the territorial sea is measured and so much of the River Esk with its banks and tributary streams up to their source as is situated in Scotland.[69]

Schedule 17 to the Act transfers the functions of water authorities relating to fisheries to the NRA by making amendments to various enactments, principally the Salmon and Freshwater Fisheries Act 1975.

6.7   Navigation, conservancy and harbour authority functions

Section 142 has the effect of transferring to the NRA any functions of a water authority immediately before the transfer date which included, by virtue of any local statutory provision, any functions of a navigation, conservancy or harbour authority.

Notes

1. References to a water or sewerage undertaker or to the functions of such an undertaker are to be construed as if those functions included the management, by that company, or any land being held by it for any purpose whatever (whether connected with the carrying out of the functions of a water undertaker or sewerage undertaker or not), s.8(7).
2. S.8(1).
3. S.8(2).
4. S.8(3).
5. S.8(5).
6. S.8(4).
7. S.8(6).
8. S.9(i)
9. S.9(3).
10. Code of Practice, Part IV.
11. S.9(4).
12. Code of Practice, Part V.
13. S.9(2).
14. S.9(3).
15. S.9(4).
16. S.20(8)(c).
17. Under s.155.
18. S.157(1).
19. S.157(2).
20. S.157(3).
21. S.157(4).
22. S.8(6).
23. Joint publication of DoE, MAFF and Welsh Office, July 1989.
24. The Secretary of State or, in the case of the Authority, the Secretary of State or the Minister of Agriculture, Fisheries and Food, s.10(5).
25. S.10(1). The Code of Practice was approved by the Water and Sewerage (Conservation, Access and Recreation) (Code of Practice) Order 1989, S.I.1989/1152; see also 1 LMELR 8 (M. Forster).
26. S.10(4).
27. S.10(2).
28. Code of Practice on Conservation, Access and Recreation, DoE, MAFF and Welsh Office, July 1989, p.4.
29. Annex B.
30. Designated under s.18 of the Agriculture Act 1986.
31. Designated under the Wildlife and Countryside Act 1981.
32. Designated under the EC Directive on Conservation of Wild Birds, 79/409/EEC.
33. Code, *op.cit.*, pp.9–10.
34. For example, *Forests and Water Guidelines* (1988).
35. Code, *op.cit.*, p.11.
36. Code, *op.cit.*, pp.13–19.
37. Code, *op.cit.*, pp.20–21; see also s.8.
38. Code, *op.cit.*, pp.23–25.
39. Code, *op.cit.*, p.25.
40. Code, *op.cit.*, pp.25–29.
41. As designated under s.18 of the Agriculture Act 1986.
42. Code, *op.cit.*, pp.33–35.
43. Condition K.
44. That is, 'protected land' which is defined as any land which, or any interest in or right over land which: (a) was transferred to the company under an initial scheme; (b) is or has at any time on or after the transfer date been held by the company for purposes connected with its functions as an undertaker; or (c) has been transferred to it in accordance with a scheme relating to a special administration order, s.189(a).

45. S.152(2).
46. S.152(1).
47. S.152(9).
48. S.152(3) and (4).
49. S.152(5).
50. Defined as an area which: (a) is for the time being designated as an area of outstanding natural beauty for the purposes of the National Parks and Access to the Countryside Act 1949; or (b) is an area in relation to which a notification given, or having effect as if given, under s.28 of the Wildlife and Countryside Act 1981 (areas of special scientific interest) for the time being has effect, s.152(10).
51. Under s.39 of the Wildlife and Countryside Act 1981.
52. Under s.152(4), as the Secretary of State may determine, s.152(5).
53. S.152(6).
54. S.152(7).
55. S.152(8).
56. As defined by the Town and Country Planning Act 1971.
57. S.163.
58. Meaning the drainage of land (within the meaning of the Land Drainage Act 1976) and the provision of flood warning systems, s.136(9).
59. S.136(1).
60. S.136(2), Sch.15.
61. S.136(3).
62. S.136(4). See National River Authority (Levies) Regulations 1990, S.I.1990 No.118.
63. S.137(2).
64. Under ss.5 10–16, 68(1)–(4) and (7)–(9), 69(2), (3) and (6), 84 and 86(1) of the 1976 Act.
65. S.136(5).
66. S.139.
67. S.140.
68. S.141(1).
69. S.141(2) and (4).

Index

abstraction licences, 79, 80
access to land
  Code of Practice, 214
  duties and obligations, 2, 5, 207–8, 210
accidental industrial discharges, 146–7
accounts/accounting information, 20–1
adjustment factor (K), 13, 14, 15, 16, 17
administration orders, special, 38, 40–1, 50
afforestation, 175, 203
agricultural activities, discharges from,
  173–5
airports, 66
Anglers' Co-operative Association, 140, 151
appointments of sewerage and water
  undertakers
  conditions of see conditions of
    appointment
  making, 12
  replacement, 30–1
archaeological remains/sites, 213
areas of outstanding natural beauty
  (AONB), 209, 212, 216–17
asbestos, 170, 202–3
auctions, 27
Aylesbury Sewage Treatment Works, 140,
  151

background concentration, 181
bathing waters, 135–7
biological oxygen demand (BOD) test, 115
British Coal Corporation, 66
British Railways Board, 66, 97
Broads, the, 209, 216–17
building operations, 71–2, 99
buildings, historic, 212, 213
bulk supplies of water, transfer of, 53
byelaws, 72–3
  precautions against pollution, 190–2, 206

causing pollution, 142–4

Central Electricity Generating Board, 66,
  101
charges, 2
  conditions of appointment, 13–17;
    customer protection, 19–20;
    infrastructure, 17–18
  metering, 86–9
  NRA: abstraction licences, 79–80;
    consents, 162
  for services, 84–6
  trade effluent, 179
charges schemes, 18–19, 57, 84–5, 179
chemical groups, concentrations of, 114
cisterns with float-operated valves, 56, 57,
  58, 95
Civil Aviation Authority, 66
classifications of water, 115–16
coastal waters, 142, 198
Code of Practice on Conservation, Access
  and Recreation, 210–15, 219
  access, 214
  conservation, 211–14
  planning/management framework, 211
  recreation, 214–15
codes of practice, undertakers'
  customer services, 21
  disconnection, 22
  leakage, 22
coliforms, 115, 119, 136, 197
commercial customers, charging, 14
Committee on Chemicals and Materials of
  Construction for Use in Public Water
  Supply and Swimming Pools, 124
Compendium of the Instruments of
  Appointment, 13, 46
  see also conditions of appointment
compensation
  compulsory acquisition, 64–5, 72
  drought orders, 83–4
  mineral owners, 74

compensation *continued*
    pollution offences, 189–90
    powers of entry, 77, 101
    street works, 65–6
    works on private land, 68, 98
compensation water, 83, 102
complaints procedure (customers), 21
compulsory acquisition
    disposals of land, 216–17
    powers, 2, 5, 64–5, 71, 72
conditions of appointment, 12–31
    accounts/accounting information, 20–1,
        47
    charges, 13–17, 46, 48
    charges schemes, 18–19, 46
    customer protection and charges, 19–20,
        46
    customer services, 21, 47
    disconnection, 22, 47
    fees, 29–30, 48
    infrastructure charges, 17–18, 46
    land disposal and change of use, 25–7,
        47–8
    leakage, 22, 47
    modifications to, 31–2, 48
    provision of information to Director, 29,
        48
    quality of service, 22–5, 47
    replacement appointments, 30–1, 48
    underground asset management plans,
        28–9, 48
confidentiality, 172–3
connections
    charges, 17–18, 85
    conditions of appointment, 17–18, 18–19
    sewerage services, 107, 108–9
    to water mains, 55–6
consents *see* discharge consents
conservancy authorities, 66, 218
conservation
    Code of Practice, 211–14
    duties and obligations, 2, 5, 207–10
    Conservation Guidelines for Drainage
        Authorities, 211
constancy of water supply, 58, 59, 60
consumer protection, 89–93, 111
    charges, 19–20
    code of practice, 21
    quality of service, 22, 25
    see also customer service committees
contamination of water
    from pipes, 123
    powers to prevent, 131–2
    see also pollution
controlled waters, 142
Convention on Wetlands of International
    Importance, 212

copper, 123
Countryside Commission, 210, 216
customer service committees, 21, 22, 91–2,
    97
cut offs
    consumer protection, 93
    powers to, 62–3, 96
    prevention of contamination, 131, 132
    see also disconnection

dangerous substances, 163–7
    List I, 164–6
    List II, 164, 165, 166–7
    stores for, 188–9
Department of the Environment (DoE), 7–8,
    135
    breaches of discharge consents, 139
    European Community Directives, 117
    River Quality Survey, 9, 133
deposits in rivers, 147
development sites, 106, 108
'direct effect' doctrine, 117
Director General of Fair Trading, 32, 33
Director General of Water Services, 6, 104
    charges, 85–6
    complaints about works on private land,
        68–9
    consumer protection, 89–90, 93;
        customer service committees,
        91–2
    enforcement, 36
    functions of, 32–4, 49
    modifications to conditions of
        appointment, 31–2
    provision of information to, 29, 44–5
    register, 33–4, 49
    trade effluent discharge consents, 178–9,
        182, 204
    underground asset management plans, 59
discharge consents, 4, 7, 70–1
    industrial discharges, 154–70; accidental,
        146–7; appeals, 161; application of
        EC Directives, 163–70; application
        procedure, 154–60, 200–1; charges,
        162; contravention of conditions,
        147; discharges by NRA, 162;
        monitoring compliance, 163;
        prosecutions, 148; registers, 171
    sewage effluent, 134–5, 136, 137;
        breaches, 138–40
    trade effluents, 176–80
discharge pipes, 59, 95
disconnection
    code of practice, 22
    powers of, 63–3, 96
    prevention of water contamination, 131,
        132

Disposal Certificates, 26, 27, 47–8
disposals of land, 2–3, 5, 25–7, 215–17
domestic customers, charging, 14
domestic purposes
    sewerage services, 106–7
    water supply, 55, 56–7, 61, 118, 126
drains, 105
Drinking Water Inspectorate (DWI), 7, 77,
    126, 130
drought, 80–4

emergency
    defence to prosecution under s.107, 152
    powers to discharge water, 71
    powers of entry, 100
    prevention of water contamination, 131
emergency drought orders, 82, 83
emission standards, 137
enforcement, 34–9
engineering operations, 71–2, 99
entry, powers of, 75–7
    Drinking Water Inspectorate, 130
    local authorities, 77, 128
    metering, 87
    monitoring compliance with consents,
        163
    prevention of contamination, 132
Environment Committee, House of
    Commons
    nitrate sensitive areas, 186
    notification of pollutants, 158
    pollution prosecutions, 139, 148–9
environment quality managers, 4
European Community (EC), 7, 44
    bathing water directive, 135–7
    Common Agricultural Policy, 175
    directives and industrial discharges,
        163–70; asbestos, 170; dangerous
        substances, 163–7; freshwater fish
        water standards, 168–9;
        groundwater, 168; shellfish water
        quality, 169
    law's role in water quality, 116–18

fees, 29–30
final orders, 35–9, 129
fire-fighting, 58, 59, 60, 85
fish mortality, 190
flood defences, 210–11, 217–18, 220
flotation of water authorities, 41–2
fluoridation, 132–3
Forestry Commission, 175, 212, 213
freshwater fish water quality, 168–9
freshwater fisheries, 218

gas suppliers, 66
general drought orders, 80–2, 83–4

grants, agricultural, 174–5
'green dowry' policy, 51
ground waters, 142
    EC Directive, 168

harbour authorities, 66, 218
Her Majesty's Inspectorate of Pollution
    (HMIP), 7, 130, 134, 135
highway authorities, 66, 153
Historic Buildings and Monuments
    Commission for England, 210

impounding works, 80, 101
indicator organisms, 114–15
    see also coliforms
industrial customers, charging, 14
industry, discharges to water by, 140–73
    confidentiality, 172–3
    consent system see discharge consents
    offences, 141–2; accidental discharges,
        146–7; causes/knowingly permits,
        142–5; contravention of consent
        conditions, 147–8; defences to
        prosecutions, 152–4; poisonous,
        noxious, polluting, 145; private
        prosecutions, 151–2; prosecutions,
        148–51; relevant prohibition, 145
    provision/acquisition of information, 172
    registers, 170–1
information
    provision and acquisition: NRA, 172;
        water and sewerage undertakers,
        44–5
    trade effluent discharges, 183–4
    water supply, 124–5
infrastructure accounting, 28–9
infrastructure charges, 17–18
inland waters, 101, 142, 198
    byelaws, 72–3
    deposits and vegetation in, 147–8
    NRA and flow, 78, 101
    waste from mines and quarries, 153
interference
    with meters, 89
    with works, 74–5
internal drainage boards, 210–11, 218
    conservation and recreation duties,
        207–10
    undertakings of, 66, 98

joint water boards, 52
judicial reviews, 37–8

'knowingly permitting' pollution, 144–5

land
    change of use, 27

land *continued*
  Code of Practice on Conservation, Access
      and Recreation, 210–15
  compulsory acquisition, 2, 5, 64–5, 71, 72
  disposals of, 2–3, 5, 25–7, 215–17
  flood defence/drainage, 217–18
  general duties of relevant bodies, 207–10
  navigation, conservancy and harbour
      authority functions, 218
  planning requirements, 217
  powers in relation to, 71–4
  salmon and freshwater fisheries, 218
  works on private, 67–9
Land and Environmental Affairs Group, 8
landfill sites, 137, 138
Lands Tribunal, 65, 68, 84, 98
lead, 123
leakage, 22
legal requirements, imposition of new,
      16–17
levels of service information, 22–5
local authorities, 8, 44, 52
  disconnections and cut off supplies, 63
  powers of entry, 77, 128
  sewerage services, 110
  undertakings, 67
  water supply functions, 125–7, 195
local flood defence schemes, 218
local inquiries, 172
London Regional Transport, 66, 97

Magistrates' Association, 149
maintenance works programmes, 213
mergers, 33
meters, 19, 56, 76, 94
  charging, 86–9
minerals, 73–4, 99, 100
mines, 73–4, 100, 153, 200
Minister of Agriculture, Fisheries and Food,
      7, 8, 44
  nitrate sensitive areas, 186–8
Ministry of Agriculture, Fisheries and Food,
      8, 174
misuse of water, powers to prevent, 63
monitoring of water supplies, 121–2
Monopolies and Mergers Commission, 6,
      13, 17, 18, 21, 33, 34
  fees to cover costs of referrals to,
      29
  mergers, 33
  modifications of conditions of
      appointment, 31–2, 48, 49

National Parks, 208, 209, 212, 216–17
National Rivers Authority (NRA), 3–6, 9
  Code of Practice on Conservation, Access
      and Recreation, 210, 211

conservation and recreation duties,
      207–10
discharges to water by industry: consents
      see discharge consents; prohibition
      notices, 145, 188; prosecutions,
      148–50, 199
drought orders, 80–1, 101
flood defence/drainage, 217–18
functions, 45
navigation, conservancy and harbour
      authority functions, 218
powers to prevent pollution, 189
provision/acquisition of information, 172
registers, 150, 170–1
river quality surveys, 4, 9
salmon and freshwater fisheries, 218
sewage effluent discharges, 135, 136, 137;
      enforcement, 139
transfers to, 11
undertakings, 66
water protection zones, 185–6
water resources, 53, 77–80
Nature Conservancy Council (NCC),
      208–9, 210, 216
nature heritage reserves, 213
navigation authorities, 66, 70, 218
necessary works, 62, 96
Netherlands, 117
Nitrate Co-ordination Group, 186
nitrate sensitive areas, 186–8
nitrates, 173–4
non-domestic purposes, water supply for, 57
North Sea Agreements, 137–8, 180
noxious matter, 145, 147, 199

Office of Water Services, 46
'ordinary' trade effluent, 176–80
Oslo Convention for the Prevention of
      Marine Pollution by Dumping from
      Ships and Aircraft, 138

pensions, 3
pipes
  contamination from, 123
  ownership/responsibility, 60–2
  see also discharge pipes; service pipes
planning
  requirements, 2, 217
  underground asset management, 28–9, 59
PLC status, 3, 43
poisonous matter, 145, 147, 198–9
polluting matter, 145, 147, 199
pollution
  definitions, 113, 164
  precautions against, 185–92; byelaws,
      191–2; nitrate sensitive areas,
      186–8; relevant prohibitions, 188;
      water protection zones, 185–6

pollution *continued*
  see also industry, discharges to water by
Post Office, 66
powers of entry *see* entry, powers of
powers of works *see* works powers
prescribed substances/processes, 180–4
pressure, water supply, 58, 59, 60
private land, works on, 67–9
private prosecutions, 149–50, 151–2
private water supplies
  local authority functions, 126–7, 195
  wholesomeness, 121
processes, control of, 123–4
products, control of, 123–4
prohibition notices, 145, 188
prosecutions of industrial pollution
    offences, 148–51
  defences to, 152–4
  private, 149–50, 151–2
protected land, 25–6, 219
  see also land
provisional orders, 36–9, 129
public sewers, 106
  provision, 106–8
public water supplies
  local authority functions, 125–6
  wholesomeness, 120–1

radioactive discharges, 175
railways, 66, 97
raw water, treatment of, 123
records
  sewerage undertakers, 109
  water undertakers, 124–5
recreation
  Code of Practice, 214–15
  duties and obligations, 2, 5, 207–10
regional fisheries advisory committees, 5
regional flood defence committees, 5,
    217–18
regional rivers advisory committees, 4
registers, 170
  Director General of Water Services, 33–4,
    49
  NRA, 150, 170–1
replacement appointments, 30–1
reservoirs, 210
resource mains, 59, 95
review notices, 15–16
rivers
  deposits and vegetation in, 147–8
  quality surveys, 4, 9, 133
  see also inland waters

salmon fisheries, 218
samples, water
  for monitoring water quality, 121–2, 194

for prosecution of pollution offences,
    149–50, 171
sea outfall, sewage disposal by, 136–7,
    137–8, 197
Secretary of State for the Environment
  consumer protection, 89–90
  discharge consents, 156, 158–9, 162;
    appeals, 161; prescribed processes/
    substances, 182–3
  drought orders, 80–1, 82
  duties and powers, 7–8, 104
  enforcement role, 35, 36, 128–9, 210
  NRA reports, 4
  provision of information to, 29, 34, 44–5
  water quality objectives, 116, 127
  wholesomeness requirements relaxed,
    120–1
  works on private land, 69
security payments, 54, 56, 107, 108, 112
service obligations, 24
service pipes, 54, 56, 96
  disconnection, 62–3
  ownership and responsibility, 60–2
  on private land, 67
service targets, 22–5
services, charging for, 84–6
sewage effluent, 146, 197, 198
  discharges, 133–7, 147
  drought orders, 81, 102
sewage sludge, 133, 134, 137–8
sewer maps, 109
sewerage undertakers, 1, 2–3
  Code of Practice on Conservation, Access
    and Recreation, 210, 211
  conditions of appointment *see* conditions
    of appointment
  conservation and recreation duties,
    207–10
  consumer protection, 111
  discharges by, 133–40; defence to
    prosecution under s.107, 153;
    enforcement, 138–40
  drought restrictions, 81, 101
  enforcement, 34–9
  finances, 41–2
  'functions', 45
  general duties, 105–10
  making appointments, 12
  ownership, 41–2
  provision/acquisition of information,
    44–5
  rights and powers of works, 111
  special administration orders, 40–1
  trade effluent, 110, 176–80, 182, 183–4
sewers, 105–6
shellfish waters, 169
silage effluent, 173

sites of special scientific interest (SSSIs),
    208–9, 212, 216–17
slurry, animal, 173
sodium, 119
special administration orders, 38, 40–1, 50
Sports Council, 210
Sports Council for Wales, 210
statutory water companies, 3, 42–3, 45, 52
statutory water undertakers, 190, 206
stopcocks, 65, 74
street works, 65–6, 97
substances, control of, 123–4
surface water, 123, 194

telecommunications, 66, 98
territorial waters, 142
Thames Water Authority, 140, 151
time-limited discharge consents, 135
trade effluent, 111, 146, 204
    discharges, 176–84; 'ordinary', 176–80;
        prescribed substances and processes,
        180–4
    sewerage undertakers' duties, 105, 110
transfer of bulk water supplies, 53
transfers, unitial, 11–12
transmitted applications, 158–9
trees, 213
trihalomethanes, 194
trunk mains, 57, 95
turbidity, 114

underground asset management plans,
    28–9, 59
underground works, records of, 59

vegetation in rivers, 147–8
vessels, 153, 163, 200

warrants, 77, 100
water authorities, 11, 52
    flotation of, 41–2
water companies, 52
water fittings, 63–4, 97, 131, 196
water mains
    connections to, 55–6
    requisitioning of, 53–5
water protection zones, 185–6
water quality, 113–92
    agricultural discharges, 173–5
    classifications of water, 115–16
    discharges by industry see industry
    discharges by sewerage undertakers see
        sewerage undertakers
    measurement and standards, 113–15
    precautions against pollution see
        pollution
    radioactive discharges, 175

    role of EC law, 116–18
    trade effluent discharges see trade effluent
    water supply see water supply
water quality objectives, 116, 170
Water Research Centre, 167
water resources, 4–5, 53, 77–80
    management schemes, 77–8
water supply
    charging, 84–9
    consumer protection, 89–93
    cut offs see cut offs
    disconnection see disconnection
    drought, 80–4
    general duties of water undertakers see
        water undertakers
    misuse, 63
    offences in relation to, 63–4
    quality, 118–33; Drinking Water
        Inspectorate, 130; enforcement of
        obligations, 128–9; fluoridation,
        132–3; local authorities, 125–8;
        monitoring, 121–2; offences relating
        to, 130–1; prevention of
        contamination, 131–2; records and
        information, 124–5; water
        treatment, 122–4; wholesomeness,
        119–21
    supply pipes ownership and
        responsibilities, 60–2
    water resources, 77–80
water supply zones, 122, 194
water treatment, 122–4
water undertakers, 1–3, 11–45
    Code of Practice on Conservation, Access
        and Recreation, 210, 211
    conditions of appointment see conditions
        of appointment
    conservation and recreation duties,
        207–10
    drought orders, 81–2
    enforcement, 34–9
    finances, 41–2
    'functions', 45
    general duties, 53–9; connections to
        mains, 55–6; constant supply and
        pressure, 58; domestic purposes,
        56–7; enforcement, 59–60, 128–9;
        fire-fighting, 58; non-domestic
        purposes, 57; records of
        underground works, 59;
        requisitioning of water mains, 53–5;
        water supply, 53
    initial transfers, 11–12
    making appointments, 12
    monitoring of supplies, 121–2
    ownership, 41–2
    prevention of contamination, 131

water undertakers *continued*
  provision and acquisition of information,
    44–5
  rights and powers, 64–77
  special administration orders, 40–1
  see also water supply
waterways, 72–3, 99
Weighted Average Charges Increase, 14–15
Welsh Office Agricultural Department, 174
wholesomeness, 118–21, 193

works powers, 2, 5, 111
  local authorities, 128
  sewerage undertakers, 111
  water undertakers, 65–71; discharges,
    69–71; on private land, 67–9;
    in relation to certain undertakings,
    66–7; street works, 65–6

zinc, 123